To: Frank Baranowski,

May the path you travel be filled with the light of direction.

Be Well Frank,

Speaking Wind,
Land of the Pueblos

10 Feb 95

The Message

by
Patrick Edward Quirk

given name
"Speaking Wind"
Land of The Pueblos

Woodland Press, Inc.
P.O. Box 211466
Salt Lake City, UT 84121-8466

Book orders and correspondence addressed to:

Speaking Wind
c/o Red Path
P.O. Box 12612
Huntsville, AL 35815

Woodland Press, Inc.
P.O. Box 211466
Salt Lake City, UT 84121-8466

Copyright © 1994

International Copyright © Secured

ISBN: 0-9644284-0-7

Printed In the United States of America

DEDICATION

To Grandfather and Two Bears, the ones who raised me when there was no one else around. And to my best friend, Cheeway, the one I traveled so many seasons with on my days of living on the lands of the mesa in northern New Mexico.

Thank you for allowing me to share so much with so many. Our time will soon come when we will once again be as one...together... standing in the light of the Great Spirit.

---AND---

To Black Fish, Bristol, Tennessee and Joe Kelly, Chattanooga, Tennessee of the Cherokee People...our people's cousins. Warren Warnick, Salt Lake City, Utah, Jenet Hansen, Lindon, Utah and Janon Alegre, Las Vegas, Nevada. Thank you for your support and assistance that I needed when I was told that it was time for this book to be released. For each of your individual parts, I wish to thank you sincerely. Know that I hold you in a very special place in my heart.

ACKNOWLEDGMENTS

Painting on front cover done by author's mother, Vi Quirk.
Cover layout and design by Patrick Edward Quirk
    (Speaking Wind).
Photo on back cover by Bryan Rohbock.
Edited by Jenet Hansen and Warren Warnick.

PREFACE

My name is Patrick Edward Quirk. My given name is Speaking Wind.

I am the only one left now out of an original Council of Four and the path I have chosen to travel is one that allows me to share teachings given so long ago with you now. This is the time when a great change is coming over all of this domain that is the Earth Mother's, a great change that will not pass any by.

I wrote *The Message* and three other books early in 1993 and was told to set them aside. In July of 1994, I was told that it was time to release *The Message*, but, I have not yet been told when it would be time for the other three to be released.

The Message is an account of a spirit vision that had been given to me of a great change, and is a process of sharing with those who would have the eyes and ears of the spirit to see and hear...a path to follow...a path that will allow them to exit on the other side of this great event that is about to take place...in one piece...and with their sanity.

I was raised by Grandfather and Two Bears. These are two of whom our people call Spirit Callers. They would reach within one and call out to their spirit for those things that needed to be taught, learned, and understood.

I had one best friend whose name was Cheeway. We shared many seasons of being raised by Grandfather and Two Bears, seasons that shared with us our people's teachings that had been handed down by the old ones-- The Anasazi.

This is the "Season of The Long Shadow" for the Earth Mother now. She is ending this time of her current circle of life and is about to enter into her new one.

It is during this time when the great earth changes take place. A time for her to cleanse herself to make way for the new. It is the time when much is destroyed in this domain in order to make way for the new world she is about to travel into.

It is also the time when all of the old ones of our people have returned in bodies that are not covered only with the red skin. They have entered this domain that is the Earth Mother's in skins that are white, yellow, and black. All this has been done for a reason. They are called The Rainbow Children during this time of their earth walk. The great earth changes began in July of 1992. All of these earth changes and the beginning of the awakening time for all of our ancestors who have entered, is now.

For our ancestors, this awakening is taking place at a very rapid pace...and for the Earth Mother, these earth changes are continuing to accelerate on a daily basis. This is her time of the great cleansing and it is through this process that many will become frightened and feel lost.

Her message to us is that if we cannot come to the place of understanding of how to cleanse ourselves, we will not be allowed to enter this new world she is about to enter. We will not be allowed entry because those things that do not hold the weight of truth on them will have to remain in a time and place that is no longer. And if we cannot separate ourselves from them, then we, too, must be left behind.

It is for this reason that I have been given permission to set my speaking words down in this novel...speaking words that had been given to me many seasons before. All will see many great changes in this domain that we call the Earth Mother's. Many will see these great changes

OTHER WORKS BY AUTHOR:

When Spirits Touch - Book 1 of Red Path Series
ISBN: 1-56901-154-0

and become fearful for what they bring. But there is still a path for them to follow and *The Message* will share it with those who will listen.

I have been given seven steps for those who wish to follow them, who realize that there is more to life than those things they can hold in their hands or see with their eyes.

The speaking words in this novel will allow you to once again find the freedom that you were born to and understand what it is you have come here to do, and to share with many others.

The wisdom within this novel will allow you to understand the difference between being led by others and leading yourself. This is a great offering that is being shared with you--the ones who will listen, the ones who once knew their way but forgot to remember.

Speaking Wind

Speaking Wind

AUTHOR'S NOTE

This work is titled as fiction. However, this is only because the names and locations of the lands on which these events have taken place have been changed, for these places are not to be known to those who have not been led to them.

All of the events and occurrences have actually taken place. These are presented to you as they have been presented to me.

TABLE OF CONTENTS

TABLE OF CONTENTS

CHAPTER ONE

PREPARING THE MESSENGER

THE CALLING OF VOICES

It was almost spring of 1964 on the lands of the mesa. Many of the people were celebrating the promise of another growing season for the Earth Mother. This was a time of many dances and good faces worn on the ones who had learned to listen to the calling of not only the Earth Mother, but of those spirits of the land who held guardianship over the lands we had been given to live in harmony with for many generations.

There were many of the younger ones who were showing off their new found abilities over the last sleeping season (winter) by doing many fancy dance steps, showing off all of those things that had come to them. They would dance to impress all of the ones who had gathered around them; but most importantly, they were trying to impress the parents of the girls they had an interest in.

It would be during these times when the parents of all the girls would look over the faces of these young men to see what they had come to learn. They would look over all of the sign painted on them...and they would look at the dance movements to see how much of their sign these dancers had come to understand.

During these dances, it would be the parents who would know if these young men would be ready to be seen by the grandparents of the girls they were keeping covered until it was the young girl's time of being joined with the one who would one day come for them.

It was the path of the grandparents to make the final determination if both the young man and the young woman were truly ready for the great responsibility they would inherit. This responsibility has been seen through the eyes of our people as one of assisting in the role of the "Message Keeper" for future generations.

This was not the only reason for these kinds of ceremonies of our people. For there were more and deeper reasons for them to be held.

My thoughts were interrupted by the speaking words that were being shared among some of the other members of our village, ones who had not formed a circle of sharing but were standing next to one of the places where food was being prepared.

"Did you notice the one who has come among the circle of the wise?" came the speaking words of the first man.

"Yes, but I did not know that he was, in reality, one who still had a robe to walk in. I had only come to believe that he was one who traveled in spirit," came the response of the next man.

"Who are the both of you speaking of?" came the third man's response.

"It is the one who calls himself Standing Tree," replied the second man. "Have you not heard of him before?"

"Not really," the third man responded. "Is there

$$=\bigoplus=$$

something that is important to his presence here?"

"Yes," came the response of the first man. "When my grandfather was not yet born, Standing Tree came to warn our people of a time when there would be many others who would come to us. Ones who would wear a skin that was much lighter than ours and their ways would be ones that would cause all of us much pain and torture."

"You are referring to the coming of the Spaniards?" questioned the third man.

"Yes...this is what I am speaking of," continued the first man, "and it was during this time of Standing Tree's presence that many of our people had gathered in much the same way we have gathered on this day.

"Standing Tree shared with us that there was a great change about to take place. That before the arrival of these Spaniards, many of the wise ones of our people would leave; they would leave and not return for many generations."

"But we have always had our wise ones among our people. What are you speaking of?" was the response of the second man.

The first man continued on, "Standing Tree told our people that the ones who would remain or continue to return to our people would be very small in number. And those who would remain behind would do so only to keep alive the understanding that would be needed by our people to maintain our path.

"The willingness to understand those sacred teachings of the old ones would not return to life among our people until the time was ready for the great change. This great change would affect all who would be present in this domain that is the Earth Mother's."

"So what has that to do with this one called,

Standing Tree now?" questioned the third man.

"Much," came the response of the second man's speaking words. "I heard him share some of his speaking words to the council of our wise ones when I was passing their circle. And I tell you...what I heard was enough to cause me great fear. This fear came from the knowing that it is once again time for a great change. A change that all of us must be prepared for if we are to survive."

"Are you certain that you are not imagining these things? This is possible you know...especially if you are correct about this one called Standing Tree only coming to our people when there are great changes about to take place. You must be willing to see those things that are here and not only the ones you will imagine," came the speaking words of the second man.

"After all, what more could be done to our people that has not already been done to us?" came the questioning of the third man. "Look around you. We no longer have lands to travel over freely...there are no longer great numbers of game for us to hunt and there is no longer the freedom that we once held with us as a companion.

"I mean really...even our freedom of our religion has almost been taken away from us.

"So I ask you...what additional great change could possibly be waiting to happen to our people? We have been placed in a position of having nothing else left to lose.

"Do you remember how our song legends spoke of Standing Tree's last visit among our people where it was told that many of our wise ones and their levels of understanding would leave?" queried the first man.

"Yes, I recall this," came the immediate response of the second man. "And from what I can see of our wise ones, there are not the great number of wise ones that there once were."

"Well, continued the first man, when I was passing the circle of the wise ones, Standing Tree was talking. Just as I was close enough to hear their words, I could see that what he was sharing with them had caused them to wear their face where their mouths were open with surprise."

"And what was this that you heard?" came the response of the third man. "Can you share it with me so that I, too, will understand why you have become so concerned?"

The first man continued, "When I passed by this circle of the Wise Ones, I heard Standing Tree say, 'THEY HAVE ALL RETURNED NOW AND ARE WAITING TO BE AWAKENED...AND SOON THIS GREAT CHANGE WILL BE FELT BY ALL.'"

"They are all here now?" questioned the third man. "What does this mean?"

"It means that all of the Wise Ones who have ever been as well as all of the Ancient Ones are in this domain now. They are here as earth walkers just like you and me," continued the first man.

"It means their presence here is for a reason and that reason is one of preparing for a great change— the last one that we will have before this domain will disappear as we know it."

"Disappear?" questioned the second man. "How can this be? It does not look like it is in danger to me."

"It means that we are now in the final portion of the 'fourth' world," responded the first man, "and that very soon now, we will have a decision to make...all of us. It will be a decision that will allow us to continue with the Earth Mother into the next age of the world by preparing ourselves in the old ways, or, not to prepare and be dropped behind as if we were an unwanted bundle."

After that, these three men held onto a silence among themselves. It was one that was causing each of them to reflect on these events that had been presented to them on this day.

As for me, I did not hold an understanding of what it was they had been sharing. But I could feel something begin to stir within me. It was like a feeling of new life being formed from within where my spirit resides.

However, without a clear understanding for what it was, I decided to return to my looking at all of the wonderful events that had come over this land, and to replace my thoughts of uncertainty with ones that I could more easily relate to. I thought of the gathering of the ones who would share those many things that had been shared with them over the past seasons on our lands.

Looking to each side of the great circle, many smaller circles had been formed. Ones that also had an abundance of speaking words coming from them.

This was also a time of great sharing and giving thanks to the Great Spirit, the Earth Mother, the Spirits of The Land, as well as all of the children of the Earth Mother within the smaller circles by those who would be in attendance.

During this time of giving thanks to all who had come to assist us, there would be many of the wise ones and elders who would look on the faces of things that were now coming into this domain to see those signs of life that were returning to many of the children of the Earth Mother after another long sleep season.

Those who would come into the center of the large circle would share with all the people those things they had seen. Those things would tell us what the growing season would bring and what kind of children's seed we should plant because of the amount of commitment the water spirit would bring over our lands.

Another meaning to these observations would be given to our people, and this other meaning would come from their speaking words. They would be heard and understood by all who were present.

For in those things that they would share with the people, the blessings that would soon be present, we would know how well as a people we had come to hold those truths that had been given to us in front of all things. We would be shown how well we had learned to carry these teachings of balance from the Earth Mother before all of our actions. This would be evident by the amount of blessings given to our lands during the growing season that was going to be with us soon.

From those speaking words of the wise ones and elders, we would see how well we had preserved the teachings of our ancestors who had known and traveled the good red path. We would know that for a good growing season, many would be greatly blessed by the spirits of the land. When this would come to us...we would know we had followed well the teachings of those who had gone and learned before us. By those who had left their knowledge, teachings, and understandings with us, we would know that we had come to use these great gifts that had been left in a good way. In a way that would give great credit on our people for learning to live in balance with ourselves and the Earth Mother.

In the other parts of the celebration place, other smaller circles had been formed to share those things that had been learned and understood by the ones who had traveled through the sleep season with the Earth Mother in a successful way.

There were circles where those who were the medicine people would gather. They would gather to learn what others who also traveled on their path had come to learn over the times when the Earth Mother had placed her great blanket of sleep over her children.

In these circles, there would be sharing of new applications for healing plants that had been shown to some; and to others they would share what the dream spirit had given to them to work with.

Other circles would be for the ones who were to be members of the dream lodges. During this time of their sharing, there would be many insights exchanged that had been given by the Earth Mother. And, how better to come to the place of understanding on how to use their gifts of nurturing.

Still other circles would be filled by the ones who had been called to travel with the dream spirits and to see and hear the spirits of the lands. Others would be formed by the wise ones to discuss spirit visions that had been given to them. It was in circles such as these that I would most likely find Grandfather and Two Bears sitting in council with other spirit callers and wise ones who had been given many messages to carry with them by the Earth Mother.

It was in the circle of the wise that both Cheeway and I would often find the most comfort. Whether it was because of the presence of Grandfather and Two Bears...or from the great amount of learning that we would be given, I did not yet hold a knowing.

Both Cheeway and I knew that this was where Grandfather and Two Bears were. This was where we both felt strongly that we belonged, as well.

Grandfather and Two Bears were spirit callers and wise ones of our people. There had been many titles given to them over the number of seasons they had traveled on these lands. But, whichever title they would wear...when Cheeway and I looked at them...they would always be Grandfather and Two Bears, the two who had raised us when our parents were not able.

It was through the eyes of great love and respect that we would most often see them. It was through these eyes we learned the value of seeing things for what they were and not for what we would have wished them to be.

As I approached this circle where Grandfather and Two Bears were sitting, I saw that Cheeway had arrived before me.

When he saw me coming, he motioned to me to hurry along and take a sitting place next to him.

I could not tell why he wanted me to hurry, but from a look of urgency that he had placed over his face, I could tell it was for a very important reason.

Seeing this look come over his face, I knew better than to wait for any more time to pass before I would go and sit with him at the outer circle of the gathering of the wise. I knew there had been something shared that had given my best friend a reason for his concern, and he wanted me to hear as well.

Picking up my pace, I arrived very quickly at his sitting place. Without uttering one sound to me, Cheeway reached up and pulled me down to the earth by the sleeve of my shirt so that I could sit quietly with him to observe what was being discussed in this circle.

Making my efforts of tuning out the beating of the drums and the singing of the celebrating people, I was finally able to concentrate on the sharing of the speaking words from the wise ones.

As I centered my listening on what was being shared in this circle of the wise ones, I very quickly placed this same face over me. The face of concern that my best friend Cheeway had been wearing.

As it began to cover me, I was no longer in doubt of the reasons why I had seen what I was shown on Cheeway. For as the speaking words continued to be shared by the wise ones, the ones who were now in the center of this sharing circle, I was being filled with a great feeling of apprehension for those things I held an understanding of, as well as for ones I did not.

As I looked over the faces of the wise ones who were in this center of the circle of sharing, I could see that this same face that was being worn by Cheeway and myself had come over them as well.

However, for them, there was a great difference. They had a great amount of understanding that accompanied this face they were wearing, an understanding that was not present in either Cheeway or myself.

So it was with these things in the front of my thinking mind that I continued to listen to the speaking words they had been willing to share among themselves. These speaking words that they did not mind the two of us hearing.

"...And I tell you all that there will not be the completion of twenty-nine more winters before all who have eyes to see with will know that this time is with them. That this is the time for the ending of those things that have been," came the speaking words of this one called Standing Tree.

Standing Tree was a great friend of both Grandfather and Two Bears, but he was not well known by the others who were sitting in this circle of the wise ones.

He was not well known by them other than by his reputation as one who can see far into the seasons that have not yet been born to us. This reputation that had been given to him was one that had been well earned. For in his many seasons of life in this domain, there had not ever been one vision that had been given to him that had not come true. And not one of them was ever late...or early.

Standing Tree was one of great medicine among the wise ones. Whenever he was given a vision to share, it was one that had been shared with him for a reason. A reason that may not have been known to him at the time...but a reason nonetheless.

And now...now that this sharing time had come to our people, Standing Tree had come to share another vision, but it was not to share this vision with many. His purpose was to receive more of an understanding that he had not yet found from the wise ones of our people.

This was the reason that this one called Standing Tree had come among the ones who had been traveling the path of the wise for many of their seasons.

Looking over the faces of the ones who had been sitting in the center of the circle of sharing of the wise, I could see that many of them were taking this time to not only listen to the speaking words of this one called Standing Tree, but they were using this time to study him, as well. For they did not know much more about him other than what they had heard spoken about him around the council fires of the night.

He had become a powerful legend to many who had heard of him. They were looking at him as one would look at one who had just come among them from a far off place in the star nation as a visitor.

Grandfather and Two Bears had shared with Cheeway and myself that this one called Standing Tree had been given a powerful vision when he was a very young boy.

It was a vision that had told him his place was not to be among any of our people. There had been prepared for him a place among the standing people and the rock people in the mountains.

To be chosen to live among these children of the Earth Mother, the standing people (the trees) and the rock people, was considered to be a great honor because of all the great sharing that would be given. It was an honor because they had chosen him to live among them—not only as a brother to their ways, but as one of them. One who would be a part of their great mystery of life.

For one to be chosen to live among the standing people meant they would be a part of the life and peace they had been given to share with all. But to be a part of this knowing and understanding meant that he would have the understanding of how this part of Great Mystery would work. And, with this knowledge and understanding of them, he could choose to be either a two-legged one or a standing one. It would all depend on what the situation called for.

And, to be invited to live among the rock people also gave a great weight to the meaning of the one who had received this invitation. For it is the rock people who are the holders of all that has ever taken place in this domain...of all things both great and small that have ever been done from the beginning of life...to now. Whether it had been done by one of the two-legs, or one of the children of the Earth Mother...or even by the spirits of the land, the Earth Mother, or the Great Spirit.

Having been invited to live among the rock people meant that Standing Tree could become one of them as well...depending on what was needed.

And, when he would become one of them, he would be given complete freedom to read from all of the extensive libraries that were contained within the Earth Mother. He would be given all knowledge and understanding that had ever come into this domain.

With the knowledge from the rock people and the understanding from the standing people, he would be given the path to understanding all things that had ever been or ever would be.

The standing people have always been the in-between deliverers of all messages, not only from the smaller children of the Earth Mother but for the two-legs, as well. This is true, at least, for the ones who hold the understanding of what it is they are being offered.

The standing people would always be the ones who would hold up all prayers and messages for ones who did not have the ability of doing so themselves.

And for those who would come and sit among the standing people, these giving and loving ones we have come to see as the trees would see our needs.

As the standing people see the ones who wander close to them and perhaps sit next to them, they fill them with the peace that is theirs to share and listen to those things that are on the front of their thinking minds.

The standing people hold the knowing and understanding for the ones who do not yet hold their own understanding of the Great Mystery's purpose for them. They have a great need for understanding those things that come to them that are not seen clearly that keep them trapped not only in their sleep of illusion, but also in a trap that is filled with fear. A fear for all those things they do not understand.

When the standing people see many of the two-legs suffer in this way, they are filled with a great compassion. This assists them in taking all their worries and carrying them into their highest branches to the spirit wind.

And when they give these concerns or prayers that are not yet seen as prayers by the two-legs, they wait patiently for the answer to come back to them. When it does, they allow it to climb down their own bodies and pour into the two-legs that have been so worried.

Even though many of the two-legs do not understand this process, it is one of the many gifts that the standing people and all of their nations continually share.

It is through measures such as these that have given the name of "the truly noble ones of the Earth Mother's children" to the standing people, the ones who will always make time to assist those who need assisting.

This one called Standing Tree had spent all of his seasons in this domain with the standing people and the rock people. It had been they who had shared much of the knowledge and understanding for those things that were needed by all of us to see.

From the time of his very young days with the Earth Mother, Standing Tree had kept himself away from all the other villages. He had not ever taken another to walk beside him. All of the wisdom and understanding he had received from the nations of the standing people and the rock people, he returned and shared with those who were able to understand and who would assist him in furthering those visions Great Mystery had charged him with sharing.

This was the case on this day, for Standing Tree had been given a great vision. That much both Cheeway and I could see from the weight that we had seen come over all of the wise ones who were sitting in this council with him.

This vision that he had come to deliver on this day, a message that held a great weight, was not completely understood by this one called Standing Tree and because of the lack of understanding, he had returned among us to find it; or at least to hold out this offering that he had received from his spirit vision to see what could be added to it. What could be shared with him so that he, too, may see its meaning and direction more clearly.

A silence had gathered around this council of the wise. A silence that had made itself known even to those who were not taking a part in it. But as it was with all things in another's life path, the ones who had come to the within place of this council of the wise were left to work with those things that had come to them so they could come to understand what it was that was now being offered.

Looking around at the faces of our people who had gathered on this day, I could see that they, too, felt the presence of a great weight of truth that had come into this circle of the wise. But even though they were curious about what was being shared in this circle, they did not once ever make their presence or attention to what was taking place in it so much that they would be an intrusion. This had come to them from the learning to respect the path of another, knowing it would be shared with them when it was time to do so.

The spirit vision of Standing Tree was about to be unfolded to those who were within this circle of the wise as well as to Cheeway and myself who had been allowed to listen to these events unfold from our sitting positions that were just to the outside of the circle but still within its awareness of our presence.

"Then there is no mistaking for this time that is soon to be upon all of us?" came the questioning remarks from Grandfather to Standing Tree.

"No, my brother. There is no mistaking for this time that will soon be with all who are left within this domain we now travel in," Standing Tree responded.

"And you have been told that there should not be any sharing of these times you have been shown with any of our people?" came the speaking words of Two Bears to Standing Tree.

"No, my brother. There should not be any relating of this to any who have not been chosen by the spirits of the land to hold this knowing," Standing Tree responded once again.

"Then why have you chosen to share this with us,

my brother? Why with us when none of the others of our people are to know of this vision? This vision that carries a great weight to it," Grandfather asked Standing Tree.

"It is for the ones who have shared their life path with me to know this answer. For it is far beyond my seeing to know their reasons why all of you have been the only ones to know of this. To know of these times that will soon be with us."

Looking around at those who were sharing this circle of the wise with him, Standing Tree placed a warm smile over his face so that all seated could see that his heart was one that was good and not filled with secrecy for any reasons of greed.

Standing Tree continued, "Perhaps it is because when I had been given this vision of the spirit, this vision of the times and events that are soon to enter this domain of the Earth Mother's, perhaps it was because I, too, did not hold a complete understanding of them. Or at least of why I had been the one chosen to see them.

"But, whatever the reason, I know well, as all of you do, that it is one of truth. And with this in the front of your thinking minds, know that I was given a picture of all who are gathered in this circle on this day. Even the two small ones who are seated on the outside of our circle of sharing."

As he finished his speaking words, all of the eyes that were on the inside of the speaking circle turned to see who it was that Standing Tree was making reference to. When they turned to see that it was Cheeway and myself, there was a sound of relief given by all of them.

"These are the two who have come with Grandfather and Two Bears," came the speaking voice of another called Sleeping Bear.

"They are like the ones each of us have been given to teach in the ways of the old ones. Those ways that have been carried by our people from the ones we once knew as the Anasazi."

"And how did this all come about?" came the curious voice from the one called Standing Tree.

"How did each of you come to have one young one to share those things of the spirit of our ancestors with?" Standing Tree asked of those who were in attendance in this circle of sharing.

"It was from the spirit visions that had been given to the old ones in our days, Standing Tree," came the response from Grandfather. "It was a time when many were receiving messages from the dream spirits of our old ones that there would soon be a time in this domain when many of the old ones would return. And this time when they would return would be called *when spirits touch*."

"Yes..., " said Standing Tree.

"Yes, I too have been told of this time that has come into this domain. And I have seen the many great quests that will be performed in this domain by the old ones who have entered to do such things.

"And these two?" Standing Tree continued.

"What will their purpose among this Great Mystery be?"

"They will be callers, Standing Tree," was Grandfather's response. "It will be through ones such as they who will call to awaken the spirits of all the old ones who are now traveling throughout this domain. To wake from their sleep of preparing and discover who and what they are in truth.

=⊕=

"It will be through the speaking words of the ones like these two young ones that many of our old ones will see what it is they have returned to perform. Quests they have come back to do will be shown to them by their wakening spirit. This spirit will be called back to them from what these two little ones will do in those seasons that are yet to be born to them."

With a large smile over his face, Standing Tree was taking time to look deep into our within places. The place where our spirit resides.

From having had this done to us many times by Grandfather and Two Bears, we did not mind...nor did we resist, for we felt no harm would ever come to us when we were near Grandfather or Two Bears. This feeling was not ever to let us down for the many seasons that had been left to us to travel here.

Returning his look to the ones who were in this circle of sharing with him, Standing Tree continued.

"I have seen to their within place and have seen their hearts, their spirits, and their path. They are good...and they are strong.

"Tell me, are all of the ones who have come to you of equal measure?"

"A few are, Standing Tree...but not all," came the response of Two Bears.

"Then it is with this understanding that I now know why I had been shown this spirit picture of all of you. It is through my message that each of you will be better able to prepare those who have come to you in the ways of the spirit's path. The ways that will have to be seen by those who are chosen," spoke Standing Tree.

"Then it is with this wisdom that we will follow

=✴=

these things of the spirit vision you have shared with us, Standing Tree. We will follow this path that has been shared with you and we will follow the wisdom of your speaking words," Grandfather said, still looking deep within each of the members of this council that had gathered on this day.

"But remember...all of you," Standing Tree continued, "that it is not for you to share the speaking words with anyone else. That is, not until they have been chosen by those spirits of the land. Not until they have been chosen by a vision from the Ancient Ones will they know that they are ready to undertake such a great quest that is soon to be unfolded.

"For the knowledge in this vision that I have shared with you, it is too great for understanding at such a time and would cause too much fear to come into the hearts of those who have not been prepared.

"I fear that it will be great even for the ones who will be chosen over the next few suns...I fear for them as well.

"This knowing is a great burden if it is not understood from the spirit. And to try and understand it before one is prepared...it would surely cause them a great fear. One that would not easily be relieved from them by either themselves or another.

"So my brothers, take care in what I have shared with you. Do not let it fall onto ears that are not yet ready. Or at least not until the time is right for this knowing to be seen and heard by all who reside within this domain that is the Earth Mother's."

Finishing with his speaking words, Standing Tree rose from his sitting position and looked over the others who had remained seated.

"Remember well these speaking words of caution,

my brothers. If you would share any of this vision that I have been given to another who is not yet ready, I would fear for the harm that would come over them.

"These are my speaking words of truth. Now I must leave to return to my own kind once again and sleep. I will sleep the sleep of the dreamer until I am needed among you once again.

"Be well...all of you."

Just as the one called Standing Tree was about to leave, we could see that another message had come to him. And, hearing this with the ears of his spirit, he turned once again for his sharing of it.

However, he did not turn to address any of the wise ones who had been gathered within the circle of sharing. He turned to the place where Cheeway and I were sitting.

Raising his right hand to the sky nation above us and his left hand to the direction of where the other council members were sitting....he kept both of his eyes on the two of us and said,

"Remember to stand at the edge of the circle and make your efforts to the center. Do not be fooled by those foolish words of the others, the ones who would try to convince you that yours is to stand at the edge of the circle and make all of your efforts to the outside. For to do such a thing would surely be a waste of your time here...and there is no longer a place for that. There is no longer any time left to be foolish."

With the last of his speaking words finished, Standing Tree left the circle of the wise ones and the village. The direction that he traveled into was his home, the Jemez Mountains. The lands that are considered sacred to our people.

For the number of seasons that had been given to

Cheeway and me, we did not see this one called Standing Tree again. Yet, from those speaking words shared with us from Grandfather and Two Bears, we knew he was still there, standing among the standing people and rock people...waiting for his next calling when he would be in service to our people.

It was not until later that Cheeway and I asked Grandfather and Two Bears if they had also been young boys on these lands with Standing Tree. Looking at us with a knowing smile on their faces, they told us that this one called Standing Tree did not live with them as children. The last time either of them saw him was when there had been a great plague among our people in the time of the first fences being placed around our people.

They told us that when our people would have a great need for something, he would always come to assist them in coming to the place of understanding the events that had fallen over all of our people.

From the song legends that had been written about him, he has come to us from the first memory of our being on these lands of the mesa. He would always come to us and be the same age and same way that we saw him on this day.

I asked Grandfather if he looked the same way when he had seen him when he was in his younger seasons here.

Looking over both Cheeway and myself, Grandfather said that from what he remembered of this one, that there was no change in him at all. He was still as he remembered him in those many seasons of the past.

Two Bears then called our attention to him and shared that we also would see him in this season that we had been born into, this "Season Of The Long Shadow." And when we would see him, there would be nothing changed about him. He would look to both of us the same way he looked to us on this day. And, Two Bears continued, this was only another part of Great Mystery that we were sharing...and learning from.

"Remember his presence well, little ones," Grandfather said.

"Remember to keep in the front of your thinking minds what you were feeling from this one called Standing Tree. For when it is time and our people have need of his assistance once again, this same feeling—this feeling that is his living spirit—will be carried to you on the back of the spirit wind. And this will be the knowing you will receive that he will return again...and soon."

Holding these speaking words in the front of my thinking mind, I turned my head from the place where Grandfather and Two Bears were sitting and looked to the direction where the one called Standing Tree went, where the Jemez Mountains could be seen just over the horizon.

Looking at this sight of the sleeping giants, I wondered where Standing Tree would be, where I could find him...and how I could call on him.

Hearing my thinking thoughts, Grandfather reached over and placed his right hand on my left shoulder and said,

"Remember, little one. Not all things that you will come to know and later to understand mean for you to be able to call on them. Some of them will only call on you...and that will be when the time is right."

Looking over to the place where Grandfather was

=⊕=

sitting, I could see a lightness come to me from his within place. It was a feeling that I placed in a good part of myself. I did not want to ever forget this feeling that Grandfather was now willing to share with me. It was one that allowed me to feel my spirit lighten from its own weight, and I knew that this was another of the many gifts he had presented to me on this day. Another gift and with its own weight of truth that so many of them held for both my best friend Cheeway and myself.

For the next few moments, Grandfather, Two Bears, Cheeway, and I looked deep into the silence that had come over us from what had been shared.

At this time I was feeling the weight of those things I did not hold an understanding of that had been partially shared with me from this one called Standing Tree.

I was looking for answers to these things as I continued my journey into the silence where all questions that are properly formed are answered.

However, from that which was coming over me...I held the knowing that I did not understand those things that were bothering me well enough to form them into the proper questions to ask the spirit of silence about.

So, with that in the front of my thinking mind, my journey into the silence on that day was one that would allow me to send my thanks to this one who had come to us. This one who was called Standing Tree. For both Cheeway and myself, this had begun a great adventure of sharing that would be made clear by both Grandfather and Two Bears when the time was right.

=⊛=

A CALLING FROM THE DOORWAY

Continuing to discuss those events that had been brought into this circle, both Grandfather and Two Bears' attention was taken away from them for a moment by a disturbance from behind.

As they turned their heads, they both saw where the noise was coming from. It was coming from Cheeway and myself.

I was being very busy in trying to chase away a dragonfly that was pestering me. Cheeway was the other one who was helping make this disturbance. He was finding my efforts at trying to chase away this small child quite amusing.

In fact, there were times when he found it so amusing that he broke out into uncontrollable laughter and the sounds were being carried all through the places where our people were holding their ceremony.

"What are the two of you trying to do now?" came the speaking words from Grandfather.

Without turning my eyes to meet with his, I cried out, "I am trying to keep from being bitten by this dragonfly, Grandfather!"

And with a laughing voice, Cheeway added, "Yes, Grandfather, Speaking Wind has become a great delicacy for this small one. Look at the hunger that it holds in its eyes when it sees him."

By now, this small one of a dragonfly was really trying to bomb me. It was charging my head continually, but it was being blessed with the sight of the hunting hawk in its eyes.

I knew this to be true because each time that I would try to hit it with my hands, it would successfully avoid them. Once it was clear of each of my failed attempts, it would position itself on the back of the wind and charge me once again.

I could feel that I had been the one centered out among all who were within the village on this day. And, if I had not been the one who was the center of this little one's attention, then perhaps I, too, would have been laughing as hard as Cheeway was.

By the time I took my third swipe at this small one, and he had made another three dives toward my head, I could hear the laughing increase. This laughing that was being performed by my best friend Cheeway was now being joined in by the other members of our elders who were sitting in the circle of sharing with Grandfather and Two Bears.

Once again, this small dragonfly buzzed into my face and once again I tried to swipe him out of my way. This time, however, I was not successful in hitting the little one who was coming at me. But I did manage to strike myself square in the nose. Besides causing my nose to sting a lot, my actions seemed to bring out a great laugh among all of those who had been gathered in the circle of sharing now, and they seemed to be laughing almost uncontrollably at all of my actions.

It seemed as though I and this small dragonfly were the center of a great amusement, one that I was not being allowed to see.

The harder I would try to shoo the dragonfly away from me, the more intent his actions became. This account went on for what seemed to me as a very long time.

As I took my next swipe at this small one, a swipe that was only being offered in a gesture of keeping him away or at least as a prodding to him to leave me alone. I saw from the corner of my eye that Cheeway was no longer sitting in his position. He had been laughing so hard, that he had fallen down on the earth that was beneath him and was holding his sides with his arms.

Looking over to the center of the circle of the wise ones, I was surprised to see that they, too, had been receiving such a great and wonderful form of entertainment from this small dragonfly and myself. They had been laughing so hard that I could see small tears of laughter coming out of some of their eyes.

As I continued to make my futile attempts at swiping away this small dragonfly, I noticed that many of the others who were in attendance at this great ceremony of giving thanks to the Earth Mother were beginning to gather. Many of the ones who had formed their own circles were now leaving so they could see what it was that was causing so many of our wise ones to laugh in such a deep way.

Looking at almost all of the directions that were around me, I could see them walking to where all of this action was taking place-not with a slow and deliberate pace, but one that was quick.

I knew that from what they had heard out of this circle of the wise one's sharing place, they did not want to miss out on such an event. Especially one that would allow the ones they had come to know as having wisdom, laugh so greatly.

Soon, it seemed to me as if all of the world had gathered close to this place. Everywhere I would look, there were a great number of the people standing and observing this new show of which I was the center of attention.

They had all formed a large circle around the one

Grandfather and Two Bears had been sitting in and where Cheeway was now laying down and where I was making so many attempts at chasing away this small one of a dragonfly.

I did not know what the final outcome of all this would be, but I did hold the knowing that I would not be willing to sit and remain the target for this small one much longer.

Finally, just as I was about to get up from my sitting position and leave this place where I was being the target for this small one and the focus of the attention of so many, I heard the calling voice of Grandfather call to me from the inside of his sitting circle.

"Speaking Wind!" came his calling voice to me as it was still being filled with laughter.

"Speaking Wind...be still, little one. Be still and hear what this messenger is bringing to you."

Hearing the calling voice of Grandfather took me away from the thought of leaving this position and running away from this attacker.

The speaking words of "messenger" came to me as true ones from the one I had learned to trust so well. But because of the echoing of the laughters from all of those who had gathered on this place, I was not sure if I was going to listen...now that I was being the center of not only what I had seen as an attack on me by this small dragonfly, but as one who was now the center of such a great amount of laughter.

However, my thinking mind cleared for a bit, enough to recognize the tone of the speaking words Grandfather was trying to call me with. Hearing this tone allowed me to rerememember that all he would ever share with me would be for a specific reason. And that reason would be to assist me in finding those things that I needed for my spirit to grow.

Coming to rest on this knowing that I should hear and listen to all such things that would be shared with me by Grandfather, I stopped my hands from moving in a futile effort against this small dragonfly and let them fall over the front of my knees that were still raised in front of me.

However, for what would next take place, neither the ones who had gathered around me nor myself were ready for.

Stopping my efforts of trying to swish away this small child of the Earth Mother seemed to make its path to what it wanted much easier so that it remained motionless in the air in front of my face.

It seemed to be looking at me as if it were studying for the right place to deliver this message. And, from the look that had come over its face, I did receive the understanding that this small one could have continued these efforts much longer than I.

For if I had chosen to run away from this place, I knew that this small one would have continued to chase me until it could have done what it had originally been charged to do...and Grandfather's speaking words seemed to make that clear to me. For this small one had been charged with delivering a message, one that I was not going to be allowed to ignore.

For this reason, he had chosen this place to bring it to me where there would be so many eyes on the both of us that its purpose was sure to be recognized by at least one person.

Sitting very still now and with both of my hands on my knees, I looked at the motionless dragonfly who was now hovering in the front of me in a very effortless manner.

I could no longer hear any more of the laughter from those who had come to see what had been causing so much entertainment from the wise ones in the circle. I was only feeling as if all who were present were focusing their attention on this small child of the Earth Mother who was floating on the air currents in front of my face.

I could feel their attention on this small one to see what its next effort would be. And the calling voice that Grandfather had shared with me only added to the anticipation of all who were gathered around me now, knowing that there would not ever be an event that would be presented to any that would not have a great reason behind it.

The introduction of this small child of the Earth Mother was not going to be any different for them. It was this that was being held in the front of their thinking minds that was keeping them as motionless as I was at this time, including those who were still seated within the circle of the wise ones.

I knew there was much more to this event than I could see at present. But from the trusting I continued to hold in Grandfather and Two Bears, I also knew that they would find the right time to explain this event to me in more detail, enough so that I, too, could hold at least a partial understanding of what was now taking place between me and this small dragonfly that Grandfather had called the "messenger."

So I continued to sit in a motionless fashion. Motionless and observing what this small child would do next.

Finally, as if it had seen its path so clearly, it stopped hovering in the front of my face and found a place to land. But this place of landing it had found was not one that gave me any great comfort at all.

It had left its place on the currents of air and found the very end of my nose to land on...the very same spot that I had hit earlier.

As it landed on my nose, our eyes met. And, when they did, there were many messages that were being sent to me from him. Messages that I could feel...but messages I was not understanding.

Seeing this in me, the small one then turned around and was facing me with its behind. With very deliberate and pronounced movements, it struck the middle of my nose with four distinct beats of its back part.

Finishing this, the little one turned around once again to face me. Seeing that I had not taken my attention off him, he then lifted off my nose and positioned himself on the top of my left hand which had remained motionless on the top of my bent knee.

Once this little one had positioned himself on my hand, he turned to make sure I was still looking at him. Seeing that my attention was still with his actions he was willing to share with me, he next turned around and repeated those same movements again.

However, in this case, he did not stop at four distinct movements, but continued on with seven more. This seemed to hold a great deal of importance to the ones who had gathered around me and to the circle of the wise ones.

When he had finished his seventh beating of his back side, there were many sounds of amazement that were coming to me. Those sounds were not only being made by the ones who had lately gathered near my position, but they were also coming to me from

those who had been seated with Grandfather and
Two Bears in the circle of sharing.

Once this small one had finished the seventh beat
of his back side onto my left hand, he turned around
to face me.

We were exchanging glances and there was much
that was being shared. Of this I was sure. But I did not
have an understanding of what it was that was being
shared with me. All I held onto was the speaking
words that Grandfather had shared with me earlier
that this was a messenger for me and I should be still
and listen to what I was being told.

After this final course of events had taken place
between us, the little one rose from my left hand and
followed another path that he seemed to be very
much aware of, but one that I could only follow with
my eyes.

As he left to follow this new path that had been
given to him, all of those eyes that had once been on
me were now on the path of the flight of this small
dragonfly, following him into the blueness of our
skies until they could no longer see him.

Having disappeared from sight, all of the people
returned to those things they had been doing.

Once all of the activity returned to the level it had
been, I was ready to sit and listen to those speaking
words of sharing once again from the wise ones who
had found a place of sitting next to Grandfather and
Two Bears.

However, from what I saw sitting next to me, I was
very tempted to restart this round of laughing once
again. For as I turned my head into the direction of
where Cheeway was sitting, I saw what appeared to
be a soggy mud ball. This had come into existence by

=⊕=

all of the dirt and water from tears gathering on the face of Cheeway.

He looked like an animated clump of earth sitting next to me, and I was very much tempted to break out in laughter. But, just as I was about to begin, Cheeway called my attention to the center of the circle once again with his pointing finger.

So, instead of laughing out loud, I turned my head into the direction of the wise ones' circle, back to the place where they were once again sharing their speaking words with each other.

"Well, Grandfather...," came the speaking words of one who was sitting directly across from him.

"It looks as if the doorway has been opened. This doorway that had been shared with all of us in the speaking words of Standing Tree."

"Yes...," came the return from Grandfather.

"I can see now who this path has chosen."

"Remember the counsel that was given to us by this one who is called Standing Tree," came the speaking words of Two Bears.

"Remember that the one who is chosen must find the path of sharing. The path that will allow them to share those things they are shown by Great Mystery.

"For it will be by this sharing of those things that many will find their way through this time that is soon to be on them. That it will be by the directions that this sharer will offer to them that they may find their way into the next world of the Earth Mother."

"Yes, Two Bears," came the response from Grandfather.

"Yes, there will have to be much in the path of understanding for this messenger to see clearly those things that must be done. Those things that will be needed so much...and by so many."

"Have you been shown the place where this is to take place, Grandfather?" came the question from one called Night Wind.

"Yes...yes I have been shown where we are all to go now. Where this message to the little one will take place."

"And when will you leave then, Grandfather?" Night Wind asked. "And will you be in need of any of our assistance?"

"I will take my brother Two Bears with me....as well as the two little ones who have come to us so that they may see better the path they have chosen to travel," was Grandfather's response.

"This is good then my brother. And when will you leave?" Night Wind asked.

"We will leave on the first light of tomorrow," replied Grandfather.

All who had gathered in the circle of sharing were nodding their heads in an up and down manner. This allowed them to share with those who had also gathered within this circle of sharing that they were in agreement with the speaking words as well as with the vision bearer who had come to all of us on this day. They had heard these things with their hearts and spirit and held the knowing of their weight of importance.

Everyone seemed to hold an understanding for what had taken place on this day. Everyone except me. And I knew that I would have to remain content to hold this not knowing until Grandfather and Two Bears found the right time to share with me.

Rising from their sitting positions, both Grandfather and Two Bears left the circle of the wise ones.

=⊕=

"We have much to prepare, my brothers. Please accept our early departure," came the speaking words from both of them.

Then, turning to the place where both Cheeway and I were sitting, they continued.

"Two Bears and I have much to do, little ones. There is a great deal of preparing that must be done before we all leave in the morning," came the speaking words from Grandfather.

"However, there is none of this preparing that can be assisted with or done by the two of you. So take this time that has been given and enjoy yourselves at this ceremony of giving thanks to the Earth Mother and all of her children.

"Two Bears and I will be by for both of you very early in the morning. Do not be late when we arrive."

When Grandfather finished, Cheeway and I continued to sit in our positions. We looked at each other with the same kinds of faces we would always wear whenever some event such as this would happen to us. We knew this would surely involve the both of us, but we did not have any idea what our parts were.

But, as it was with so many things that would take place among the both of us...and at this age of ours...we did not stay long with these kinds of thoughts.

In a very short time, we were visiting many of the people we knew and getting plenty to eat.

My favorite was the roasted corn and pinion nuts, and for Cheeway, it was the fried bread and the pinion nuts.

These really worked out well for the both of us over the seasons we had to travel together, for whenever we would go on any kind of a camping trip, there was sure to be plenty of these three items among us.

And for this, we would always have our fill.

However, by the end of this day, both of us had really eaten more than we should have. Because of the events that had come to us earlier that had been seen and discussed by all who had gathered around the circle of the wise, we had been given more than our fair share to eat. And, it was from eating so much that both Cheeway and I felt like two of the rock people on our lands. While we could not really move on our own...we were still in a place of observing all that was taking place around us.

"I do not think I will ever eat again, Cheeway," I said, leaning against one of the wood poles in the village.

"I do not think that I will ever think of food again, Speaking Wind," came Cheeway's reply. "How do you think that we will ever get home? I do not believe that we can walk there all alone."

"If we will just take some time to stop eating and perhaps take a little nap, then we will regain some of our strength, Cheeway. Then we could manage our walk home. What do you think?" I replied to his statement.

However, from where my best friend had been standing, I did not receive a reply. When I turned my head to the direction I had last heard from him, I was surprised to find he had already gone to visit with the dream spirit. And soon...I had joined him.

It was not long after I had joined my best friend in finding the dream spirit that I felt a hand jerking me from behind.

Turning my head and trying to halfway open my eyes, I saw that it was one of the women of the village who had been trying to get my attention. As she was shaking me, I could hear her repeating something as well.

With the passing of a few moments, and the recalling of what it was to be awake, I did manage to hear those things she was speaking to me.

"If you do not want to see these things anymore, little one, then you will have to return to this domain of the walking spirit," came her audible speaking words at last.

"What do you mean?" I asked, sitting up and rubbing my eyes with one of my hands.

"Oh good, little one. You are awake now."

"Of course I am awake now. Why did you wake me?" I asked, placing a good tone of respect in the speaking words I was now sharing with her.

"I woke you because you were speaking very loudly with the dream spirit. In fact, you were speaking so loud that most all of the ones gathered in this ceremony place heard you."

Looking over the faces of the ones who had gathered in this place, I could see that she had been right. For almost all of them were still looking at me and wearing a surprised face over themselves.

Returning my gaze to the woman who had taken the time to wake me, I asked her what it was that I had been so involved in saying.

"You were speaking of a terrible time that had come over the face of the Earth Mother. How there was so much destruction that had come to her and all of those who had been within her domain," came the reply from the old woman.

"Then you were speaking of a great and golden doorway. One that was just now beginning to open itself. And from this place, there were many blessings that were behind it...but those blessings would not be allowed to enter this domain until many had left. Left in a way that was not pleasant at all to hear," she continued.

Sitting very straight now and with my best friend Cheeway sitting next to me, I asked the old woman to share more with me in detail those things I had been speaking of so that I, too, could hold onto a better understanding. At least to hear them in my waking place so I could understand why all of those people were looking at me with this great look of surprise on their faces.

"Oh!" came her reply. "If you had not heard it for yourself, it would not be believed, little one. Besides, of those things that you have spoken of from the dreamer's place, I would not want to say any of them again."

"And why would that be?" was my reply.

Looking at me with the concerned look of a caring grandmother, she said,

"You were speaking of a death that I had not heard of before. The kind that is final and I do not want to repeat any of it because it fills me with great fear.

"If you still want to hear about it, then I would suggest you ask some of the others in this village. The ones who also heard you speaking will not be hard to find. All you will have to do is to look for the ones who are wearing a face of fear or concern and you will know them."

As the old woman finished these things with us, both Cheeway and I rose from our positions and began to walk into the direction of our houses. There, at least, would be a place where we would not get into so much trouble.

"What do you think the old woman meant, Cheeway?"

"I am sure that if she had been the only one to hear whatever it was you were speaking of....well, then perhaps I would have thought that she was only dreaming, also. That the dream spirit that had paid her a visit included a picture of you in it, as well.

"But since there were so many of the others in our village who also heard you, then there must be the weight of truth in those speaking words of hers."

"But what do you think all of this could mean, Cheeway?" I replied.

"I do not know, Speaking Wind. I can only say this. And that will be when Grandfather and Two Bears come for us tomorrow morning, we had better be ready. After all, since they seem to be the ones who will assist us in looking through these kinds of events, we would do well not to upset them."

"Yes...yes, I see what you mean. It was becoming very obvious to me that the ones in the village who had heard me speaking of those things the old woman did were not ready to discuss this event with either of us."

"This should not surprise you, my brother," came the reassuring speaking words from Cheeway.

"No, Cheeway, this does not surprise me at all. I realize that each of us has a specific path to travel. And for those things that have come to me and the one I am following, then it is only considered to be polite to allow me to do my own work."

"This is the truth you speak, Speaking Wind.

However, I only hope that Grandfather and Two Bears do not feel the same way...don't you?"

I could only look on the face that Cheeway had decided to show to me and wonder where all of this was taking us.

"Why do you suppose that there has been so much take place in such a short time, Cheeway?" I asked.

"I do not have a knowing for this, Speaking Wind. I can only say that it is my highest hopes that Grandfather and Two Bears will be able to share their thinking over these things."

"Me, too, Cheeway," came my response.

We had reached the split in the road that would lead to my house as well as the one that would lead to Cheeway's. Reaching this place, we could both see that neither of us had any further speaking words to share on this day.

I could see from the look that was over Cheeway's face that he was as tired as I felt and to see our own beds once again would bring both of us great joy.

"See you in the morning, Speaking Wind," came the farewell greeting from Cheeway.

"Sleep well, Cheeway," was my return.

A SECOND CALLING

It did not take me very long to fall asleep on that night. As I was laying there, I could feel that there were many spirit pictures that wanted to come to me. Ones that would carry with them a great message for me to learn from.

However, with the sleep that was flooding into my

eyes, I could not stay with them for long and drifted off to find my time with the dream spirit, later to return to my body part which is the shell that had been gracious enough to carry my spirit in.

We had been told by the speaking words of Grandfather and Two Bears that all of those things that the spirit would encounter and learn from when it would travel with the dream spirit would be the things that would soon be coming to us. It was in this time of the dreaming that our spirit would set them into motion.

It was almost like we were living at the edge of a great pool of still water waiting for the ripples of change to reach the shore we were on. These would come to us to share another way of learning and understanding ourselves. Those same ripples would be started by our own spirit in the dream time.

With this on the front of my thinking mind, I allowed myself to openly embrace the falling of sleep that was coming to me. I could only hope that these ripples that would be begun on this night by my spirit would also bring to me a clear understanding of what I could feel was beginning within me, but without any form of understanding for what it was or would be.

All through these kinds of thoughts, I was feeling a weight come over me of what had taken place on this day. There were many lessons being offered and a beginning to something that was to be of great importance.

As it was with most of the days I had been allowed to spend on the lands of the mesa, sleep came to me so quickly that I did not remember when it had arrived. The sleep of answering that would come to me on this night would mark the beginning of a great adventure. An adventure that would be explained to me on the morning of tomorrow.

I woke quite early the next morning. It was the kind of awakening that was well before the time I had needed to get up. The only reason this happened to me on this morning was that I had spent a great deal of time with the dream spirit and the time that those things needed to be answered was over.

The weight of yesterday as well as of the dream spirits' messages and answers to me were weighing heavy this morning. But as Grandfather had often shared with Cheeway and me, when the dream time was spent in learning those things that were needed, all of this learning and understanding done by the spirit would take time to find its way to the conscious part of the body. This was a way of beginning something on a spirit level that would take time to work its way and lessons of understanding down to the body level. And when this would happen, then the body part of ourselves would often feel the weight of these lessons as something that had been placed on it.

But this was not for a reason of punishing or reminding, it was only a way of preparing itself for the wisdom and understanding that would soon be coming to it. A way of sharing with itself that there was more to the life path it was traveling than those things it could only see.

Morning had come over our lands once again, and I was standing in the driveway in front of my parents' house. I knew that Grandfather and Two Bears had told us they would be by very early. And, if I were to be the one they would have to wait on...I would hear about it for many days after that.

Even though their reminding was always in a very gentle manner, there were many other events that I

=⊕=

would wish to go through before I wanted to repeat something that would cause this to happen. I did not want to risk being unprepared for those things they had to share with me. And meeting them this morning was no different.

So, standing in the almost dark place of the day where the day meets the night, I felt as if I had already achieved a great accomplishment. And that was to not only be out of bed, but to be dressed and waiting for both of them before they arrived.

As this feeling of accomplishment was filling me, I was suddenly interrupted by the calling of my given name. It was not as direct as I had become used to hearing from another. Rather, it was like it was being sounded by the spirit wind that was crossing our lands now. It was reminding all of the children who were growing here that it was time for them to awaken to another day of learning with the Earth Mother.

However, as this calling of my given name seemed to pass by, I decided that perhaps it was only in my imagination that I had heard this in the first place.

I remembered how Grandfather and Two Bears would tell Cheeway and myself that it was in this in-between time when the night would give way to the coming day that so many of the in-between places of the spirit could be found. And this place of their residing was one that allowed them to gain great strength in order to accomplish what it was they were in search of.

Thinking on these things, I decided that perhaps this hearing of my name being called was just from being up too early and not listening correctly.

However, just as I was about to place this out of my thinking mind, I heard it repeat itself to me once again. Looking into the direction it seemed to be coming from, I could see the solitary movement of one of the standing people.

This was the tall pine tree, this child of the Earth Mother who was so willing to share its peace and love with those who would be willing to listen that had been planted in the front of my parents' house. Its movements were coinciding with the calling voice who was repeating my given name.

"Speaking Wind...," came the calling voice over the top of the pine tree.

"Speaking Wind..."

I turned my head away from this pine tree, yet it was the only thing that appeared to be moving on this in-between morning I was standing in.

Even though there was a strong spirit wind that I could hear, it seemed as if it was passing by all things that were near me, for there was no other movement other than this tall standing person of our lands...and it was echoing the calling of my given name.

However, when I turned my head to face another direction, I felt a sudden tugging on my left shoulder. It was a tug that was requesting me to turn back around to the direction I had been looking before.

But, when I turned around to see who or what had pulled my attention, there was no one or no thing in the space where this tug had come from. There was nothing there but me, the spirit wind, and the large standing person...the tall tree that had been growing in the front of my parents' house.

Seeing there was not another person around me, I was beginning to feel a little uneasy with myself because I was now in very unfamiliar territory. This was a territory that was governed by the spirits of the lands here. And in this place, I did not hold a good enough understanding of what was taking place with me.

All I could think of was that Grandfather's truck would break this silence that was around me...this silence that was only interrupted by the spirit wind and the continual calling of my name.

Then, as if out of the voice that was being carried by the spirit wind, there appeared another dragonfly. It was either the same one or one that was closely related to the one that had come to me yesterday and had given messages that were beyond my level of understanding. Yet it was those same messages that had driven Grandfather and Two Bears to make this trip to the Jemez with me and Cheeway.

This small one was not being as pesky as yesterday's occurrence, perhaps due to the fact that I was not trying to shoo it away from me now.

Collecting my thoughts from this mid morning and night place, I was thinking how strange it was for this small child of the Earth Mother's to be awake. Normally, there would not be any activity of these small ones until the sun was well into the morning sky. And even then, there was not a great deal of activity from them.

Looking over to the place where this small one was floating, I could feel that it was looking deep within me. This was a feeling that I had not yet received from one of the children in this domain. Until now, I had only received this feeling from either Grandfather or Two Bears...or one of the wise ones who had grown with them.

As we exchanged looking into the eyes of the other, this small dragonfly did not seem to move. It was floating on a piece of the air that seemed to be his home, or at least this was the feeling I was now receiving.

But, as our exchange of glances became stronger, I was becoming more aware of the sounds the spirit wind was making through all of the tops of the trees. And I was beginning to receive many of the messages that he was willing to carry on his wings.

This was the kind of event that normally would have only come to me after making a great effort of journeying into the spirit of silence, who is the spirit ally of our people where we journey to have many of our questions answered. But now...standing in the in-between time of the day and night and looking into the dark eyes of this dragonfly, I was hearing those same things that before I would only hear when I had worked at journeying very hard. And all of this was coming to me in picture forms.

In the beginning, these pictures of all the messages seemed to be like glances. But with the passing of time, they became stronger and longer in their duration.

As I continued to look into the eyes of this small child, I felt another presence come to me. It was one that was filling me with great expectation of something that was going to happen to me. Something that was very big...but something that would not make sense to me until the time was right. It came to pass with the assistance of this small child of the Earth Mother's guidance to me.

Looking into me from a place in the air that was not moving him, this small child was changing much about itself and all of those things that were around me as well. Soon, as the position of both of us

=⊛=

remained very still, the air that was around both of us began to thicken to an almost very heavy soup consistency.

This was allowing the small child to not beat his wings in such a fast manner, and it was making all movement that was coming to me appear as if it were almost stationary.

During this thickening of the air around both of us...this thickening that is the usual precedent to a spirit vision, I found that my position of standing was being assisted by the thickness of the air that was around me.

I was holding the feeling that even if I had wanted to move, it would have been very difficult. I knew this was a spirit vision that was about to come to me. And in this setting, I did not have a desire to remove myself from it. For to move would mean to ignore this spirit vision of seeing, and this would be one of the greatest insults of all from what I had been prepared with. From those teachings of Grandfather and Two Bears...and our ancestors.

Looking deep into the eyes of this small dragonfly and his looking deep into my within place where my spirit resides, there was an acceptance of each other's presence and those messages that had been given to the small one to share with me.

By now, the moon had almost vanished over the top of the in-between sky over our lands and the promise of the Great Spirit's reflection in the sun was about to unfold another day. And, then...it finally came. The spirit vision came that had been given to this small one...this one that has been called the door-keeper to the other side. This was when the spirit picture flooded my entire body and mind. And from it, I saw what was meant for me to see.

I saw myself standing in the flat part of a great mountain land, looking up to the great star nation and the gathering of some of the cloud people in the night sky.

The reflection of the Earth Mother's face in the full moon was filling all of the land with her sleeping light and with this light, I could tell that there was a small pond of water next to me, and a place next to a great cliff where I had built a ceremonial fire.

From the place I was standing, I held both of my hands up to the star nation asking them to clear this vision for me and to share with me some of their light of direction. Show me the path I was to follow that would assist me in attaining the needed levels of understanding for these feelings and events that had come to me in the last two days.

Once this spirit vision had formed between the place where the small dragonfly was holding itself and where I was standing...it vanished. And, as it vanished, so did the dragonfly and the spirit wind.

I was left alone. But I had been left with a clue of what it was that was to be done by me for this path that was soon to be offered.

It always surprised me at the quickness of a spirit vision; that it could be presented to one and still leave them with a complete detail of all things that were within it.

It was almost like taking a picture of this event and being able to go over and over it again and again until a complete story was achieved from the story that was meant for one to see and understand.

In this case, I had been shown a place that I was to go to, where I was to travel into and stand alone and ask the Ancient Ones for their assistance. I was to ask for their assistance in clearing the clouds from my mind so that I could more clearly see those things that were being shown to me so that I could come to understand what my part in what I was being shown would be.

As this spirit picture was finding a way from the spirit realm where it had begun and into the thinking mind of myself, I heard the sound of Grandfather's truck coming down the dirt path next to my parents' house.

Knowing that what I had been shown by the old ones had found its way to my within place, I began to move from this place where I had been standing.

Before leaving, I silently gave my gratitude to all of the children of the Earth Mother and the spirit wind for their assistance in presenting me with this spirit vision from the Ancient Ones. Leaving my place on this ground, I gave to them a final wave of my hand in an effort of sharing myself with them, as a friend would do for another.

Grandfather had driven his truck to the end of our street. This had allowed him to turn around without his headlights shining through anyone's window and disturb their sleeping time.

By the time he returned, I had finished my farewells to those who had been willing to offer me so much and was standing next to the dirt pathway.

"Good morning, Speaking Wind," came the expectant sounds from Two Bears.

"It is good to see that you have been so attentive to the time for our arrival, little one," was the following of Grandfather's greeting to me.

"I can see that there has already been good move-

=⊕=

ment on this path you are about to seek out. Would you like to share the front of the cab with Two Bears and myself and share with us...or would you prefer to climb into the back with Cheeway and continue your visit with the dream spirit?"

"Grandfather," was my response to his speaking words.

"I have been given much to think on for this past day and one half. But I hold this feeling of great expectation for what is about to take place. And I do not hold an understanding for it."

"What fills you with this expectation, little one?" came the reply from Two Bears.

"Is it something that you wish to share with us at this time?"

"Not at this time, Two Bears. I do not want to give either of you the wrong impression, but..." Hesitating a little to place the correct emphasis on these speaking words to them, I paused.

"It is alright, little one," Grandfather reassured me.

"Put these feelings you are holding into the first set of speaking words that come to you. In this way you will learn many great lessons on your life path.

"And this learning will come to you in the way of those speaking words you will be willing to share. This is how the learning for many of our feelings come to us all.

"First we must hold onto the knowing that whenever we will share speaking words to another, that we are not sharing with them first. But we are placing ourselves first.

"In other words, Speaking Wind, you will be talking to yourself first. And when you receive the understanding for those things that have come to you, then you will be better able to understand what it is you are feeling. And you will hold the wisdom to convey these things to another.

"So do not hesitate, little one. Share those things with us in the first way they will come to you. We will understand."

"Well, Grandfather...," I started.

"It is that I feel that I am about to receive something very important. Something that is so important that it cannot be ignored.

"And who is this something going to be important for, little one?" Grandfather asked.

Looking at the place where both Grandfather and Two Bears were sitting, I only could find one word to describe it..."Everyone!"

With both of their faces filled with compassion, they returned.

"You are most correct, little one. What you are about to quest for will be for the benefit of everyone. Everyone who will have the eyes and ears to see and hear with. And this is the face of truth that we share with you.

"What is about to be shown to you will be a last chance for many who travel in this domain. A last chance for them to understand what it is that is about to happen here.

"For those events that are even now forming themselves into their own life, even now there are many of our wise ones who do not yet hold the needed understanding that you are soon to be presented with. This needed understanding that you will soon be standing in the doorway of seeing."

"Well, Grandfather...I believe that I have already

=⊕=

been given much on this day already. If you and Two
Bears do not mind, I think that I will join my brother
Cheeway in the back of the truck.

"In that place, I will be able to sort through these
events that have come to me a little more clearly.
Then perhaps by the time we arrive at the lands of the
Jemez, I will be more capable of sharing with the both
of you," I concluded.

"We do not mind this, Speaking Wind," came the
reassuring voice of Two Bears.

"We already have prepared a bed for both of you
and it is tied down so neither of you will blow away
from the wind of traveling."

Nodding my head in an up and down manner, I
returned to the back of the truck. And reaching there,
I saw an old and familiar sight, one that I had been
used to seeing.

Cheeway was lying on one of the beds with his
head tilted back and his mouth open. I climbed in and
shut his mouth using the palm of my hand. Then I
found my way through the top and bottom blanket
until I could get comfortable.

Seeing that I had found my place in the back of the
truck, Grandfather began our trip that was taking all
of us to a place where something was about to be
revealed. Something that was going to be for the
benefit of everyone in this domain that was the Earth
Mother's.

Lying back and looking onto the vanishing faces
of the star nation in the last of the night sky, and
listening to the snoring of my best friend, Cheeway, I
was filled with the face of belonging and companion-
ship of friends. This face that was coming to me was
sharing that I was not alone...that I would not ever be

alone.

Taking this knowing with me, I was feeling the return of the dream spirit, a friend of those who come to the place of understanding for themselves and those things that are around them. This spirit friend allows our spirit to soar with him in great heights of learning that will be brought back to our conscious part to be worked through. Thereby we will gain in our next higher level of understanding for ourselves and see how all things are here to share with us...and we with them.

Soon...I had joined Cheeway and the dreamers of our people.

INTO THE JEMEZ

I was awakened by the gentle nudging of Grand-father. Looking up, I saw that while he had been retrieving me from the dreamer's world, Two Bears was doing the same thing for Cheeway.

However, as had always been the case, whenever one would call Cheeway back from the dreamer's world, they would have to do so with great care.

It was not that Cheeway meant another any harm, but when he would return from this place of our ancestors' spirits, he would always be so disoriented that he would bump into things and cause many things to crash around him.

For that reason, whenever we would spend sleep-ing times with either Grandfather or Two Bears, they would always make sure that Cheeway was not ever near anything that would break easily.

=*=

When he would be given his sleeping position, there would always be plenty of room for his usual maneuvers on waking from his sleep. And, when there was not the advantage of having distance between myself and him...such as was the case in the back of Grandfather's truck, then the first one who would be woken from their sleep would be me, to be followed later by Cheeway.

And on this morning of our arrival in the Jemez Mountains, this was no different. Looking at the place where my best friend Cheeway had been sleeping, I was very grateful that I was no longer in the same place I had been, for where I had been sleeping was now covered with one foot and an arm of Cheeway.

This was his efforts of trying to rejoin the life spirit of this domain. And, even though both of his eyes were always open, one could not be too certain about where all of his parts would arrive during this process of waking.

After a third shake to Cheeway, Two Bears looked over to the place where Grandfather and I were standing and smiled.

"I think this will be enough for this little one to come back to us," he said, smiling, while holding one of Cheeway's feet away from his face.

"Yes...," came the speaking words from Grandfather.

"I, too, hold this knowing that we can leave the rest of the waking process to Cheeway. After all, there is still much for us to do and there appears to be another messenger on his way. One that we would do well at finding shelter from."

Turning my head to all the directions that were on

the top of the tall mountains we were in the middle of,
I could not see anything. There was not anything that
I could see that would share with me what it was
Grandfather had been speaking about.

Seeing my face when I turned it back to him, he
gave me a warm smile and said,

"You must learn to not only look with your eyes
that have come into this domain with you, Speaking
Wind, but you must learn to listen to the calling voice
of the spirit within you.

"This is where the face of truth to those things that
you will have a great need for will come to you from.

"Now little one, close your eyes and see the ocean
of life that is all around us on this land. Feel its
presence and accept those things that it will share
with you. For this is where I have heard this calling
to me from. This is the place of balance from all things
that are within this domain. This is the calling voice
of harmony for all life that is with us.

"With this in the front of your thinking mind, you
will know that what I have shared with you is truth.
But, this is not the reason I have been willing to share
this with you. The reason that has come to the front
of my thinking mind is that this is the way you will
learn for yourself. And, this is one of the greatest
reasons any of us will come to enter this domain that
is the Earth Mother's. However, this is one of the first
reasons that so many who enter forget to remember."

As has always been the case with any of the speaking words that have come to me from either Grandfather or Two Bears, there was always a great truth
shared.

For what Grandfather had shared with me was
that there was a messenger coming over these lands

that would require us to find shelter.

This could only mean that there was a mountain storm coming over these lands. But from the place I was at in the present...this message had been missed by me, and I was now being given a path for another level of understanding. This path would allow me to share on an even higher level with all of the life that was with us. And in the process of sharing...I would receive another way of hearing the calling voices of the spirits of life that had come to know these lands as their home where we were now on as the invited guests.

Turning from my position at Grandfather's truck, I looked over the lands that were near me. Using the teachings from Grandfather, Two Bears, and The Silent Brotherhood that had brought me to this place of seeing now, I silently called my given name to those who were living on these lands that I now held a need to enter.

"I am Speaking Wind, my brothers and sisters. I have a need to share this space with you. To share this space so that I might come to hear the calling voices that are yours to share with clear sight.

"I stand before you. I stand before you with all that is me placed on the outside. In this way, you will know me when I will pass you by again. And, we will once again share our stories of life together.

"But for now, I would ask of you to share a space with me so that I may travel into the silence. Into the silence that is between my understanding and your path of life.

"Share with me this place where I might fit into your home, my brothers and sisters. Share with me a place that I might come to rest among you."

After giving my thinking words to all of these children, I closed my eyes and waited for an answer. An answer that would come to me not in the way speaking words are shared between we two-legs, but in a way that is the speaking of the children of the Earth Mother. A way that would allow me to know through the speaking pictures these children would place within the front of my thinking mind.

Grandfather had shared with me many seasons ago that there was a time when all of us shared the common language. This common language is now the only one these children of the Earth Mother and all of the spirits of the land speak.

He shared with me that this was a time when there was no separation from Great Mystery and ourselves. And it was not until we had come to think of ourselves as being so different from all other life that we had come to begin a new way of speaking.

It was a way of speaking that would not share with us any of the things we had been seeking for. It was, rather, a process of learning to speak that would end our union with all life that was around us.

It was a way of allowing us to be so different that we eventually became separated from all that we had come to know through the spirit of belonging.

And now...now that our paths have been so lost, many of us are on the path of returning to the place we once were. This path is laid out before all who would seek it through coming to understand the speaking words of these children of the Earth Mother. All of these children continue to speak now as we once did in those long seasons of the past.

They are able to maintain their higher levels of understanding and the belonging to Great

Mystery...while it is we who have lost our way.

How often I would think over these kinds of things as I would look and observe those who would come to cross my life path. Those who would always seem to find me so they could unload their troubles.

I could see the face of understanding come over me as I would think on how they would approach me. How they would always ask me for answers and how I knew that they would be the only ones who would be able to guide themselves.

How strange it was, I was thinking as I continued to wait for an answer from these mountain children. How strange it was that we two-legs could have strayed so far from our path of understanding and belonging just because we had wanted to be different.

I did not hold an understanding of why we would have wished for such a thing. Not when the price was so high. This price of being separated from all life.

Thinking over all of the seasons of preparing that Cheeway and I had done to get to this place, I realized that there was a life path for all life that was in this domain. That there was a right to follow one's own life path without the control of another and that there were many great truths that needed to be relearned by all of the two-legs before they would have the eyes and ears of their spirit opened for them.

I was thinking of how much work we had to do before we would be ready to share with even ourselves in a meaningful way. This thinking was giving to me a sad feeling for those many who leave this domain just as they had entered.

I was sad for the ones who leave this domain and their life path that had been given to them still locked into their sleep of illusion, and because they had remained in this sleep of illusion, they did not ever come to know the many wonderful blessings that had been offered to them. These blessings had come to them in the form of events to learn from so they might come to understand themselves and all that is around them in a clear and loving way.

This way would share with them the light of direction that is always waiting for us to see its glow over the path we have chosen for ourselves to travel.

It was beyond me why this decision was made in the first place by all who travel in this domain on the two-legs. However, from those things that had been shared with me by Grandfather, I had learned the reason for this was only because it was time for it to be. This would all fit well into my understanding when I would hold more seasons to the life path I was traveling now.

I was remembering how important it was that Grandfather and Two Bears showed us this meaning of it being time for all things that are. It was a great effort they spent on both of us to see this light of reason. This light of reason was that all that we would ever do could only be done in the right way...and in the right time.

As we continue to travel our circle of life, we will see this meaning and come to embrace its face of truth. And, when we do this, there will come to us a great gift from Great Mystery. This truth would share with us that to worry about needless things that we in truth do not have any control over anyway, would only be a waste of our time.

It would be a waste of our time trying to change, alter, or control those events that were going to be anyway. It would only be when we would be in a place on this life path where we would understand to allow all things to be, that we would find the spirit of belonging. This spirit of belonging would allow us to reside in the way we had once all been given as an equal among all life, and as one who would know Great Mystery is a part of all of us.

Just as I was holding all of these thoughts in the front of my thinking mind, I realized that I had my eyes open all of the time. They were never closed, as I had thought.

And this knowing that had come to me allowed me to see that the place I had been asking permission to be with these children was the one I had been in all the time. And all of this sharing that I had once held the thinking was coming to me from within was coming to me from these children who were in this mountain land.

It was their way of sharing their speaking words with me. But it had become so natural that I did not notice the difference...other than hearing and seeing things that I had not thought of or seen before. And, I felt a feeling of belonging within myself that gave to me a great peace and timelessness to all things.

When this came to the front of my thinking mind, I noticed that even the air that was around me had changed. All of those feelings I had once known as small breezes were, in fact, currents of a life force that was continually coming from all life around me. There was a great abundance that it would carry with it as it would go from one part of the lands that I could see to another.

Before, I had only known the word of the spirit wind. But now in this place that I had been accepted into by all of the children of the Earth Mother, I was not only knowing this term "spirit wind"...but I was seeing the face of this spirit, as well.

I was being shown that this spirit wind that crossed all of these lands was similar to a very gracious host at a party. That as he would touch all life on these lands, he would see which ones needed more of this life force that was his to give...and he would fill them with it. And, for those whom he would come by, the ones who held an abundance of their own life force, they would hold out what they had as extra so he could carry it with him and share this great blessing with the ones who were in need.

All of this was taking place within what appeared to be a large ocean of life that filled everything that was within it, everything that went from the top of the sky nations to the bottom of the places where the rock people dwell.

And, for the first time that I ever remember...I was a part of this. I was also floating within this sea of life. This sea of life that was keeping the balance of all living things so well.

As this feeling of belonging was coming to me, I could also feel myself begin to move in a back and forth motion. One that was not strong enough to knock me over, but one that was strong enough to let me know that it was not coming from myself.

As this rocking was coming over me, I remembered what Grandfather had shared with me about the Earth Mother. That in all of her domain, there was one thing that did not change. This one thing was the beating of her heart that allowed all life to share in it as well.

And, with this beating of her heart coming over me on this new place I had been welcomed into, I could feel something else...a feeling that was well within this feeling of her beating heart.

And once this had become a good part of me and I of it...there was a new motion that was being given to me.

It was not so much in the motion that was a beating of a heart...but it was more in the way of a tempo of this same beating. I had once before felt this while I was on the lands of the mesa.

However, this new motion that was being shared with me was carrying something about it that was very different. Something that I did not hold the understanding for...not until I had recalled another of the teachings of The Silent Brotherhood. One that allowed me to reremember this wisdom that had been shared with me earlier.

It was that within each of the parts of this domain that is the Earth Mother's, there are many other spirits of the land that have been given their portion to look after. And in some of these places, there are specific domains that have been drawn. In those domains where the lines are very obvious...the spirits of these lands tend to be very exacting over the ones who share in it with them.

In the domains where there are not as many lines that are obvious, the spirits of these lands are not as exacting and the lessons that are to be shared on those lands are ones that allow for more freedom of the spirit; because the ones who they have been given charge of are not so much in need of being told what it is they need to do.

And, this was the case on this land I had been invited to in the Jemez Mountains. I had always felt a loving freedom from these lands that have long been considered very sacred to our people, all the way from my short seasons with the Earth Mother until this day that I had been allowed to become a part of them as well.

So it was that while the first thing that had come to me was feeling the beating of the Earth Mother's heart...what I was now aware of feeling was the beating sign of the spirits of the land's own pulse of life. This was being shown to me in the form of a rhythm. A rhythm that would allow me to call on them for their assistance from any part of this domain that is the Earth Mother's.

After receiving this understanding, I could feel my chest grow and expand. I could feel the good feeling that had been presented to me on this day and for it...I was very grateful.

With this knowing and understanding that was coming to me from this sharing that was from the spirits of the land, I now had a way of being able to communicate with them. And this was a way that had been kept by our people for many generations.

It was through the beating of the Earth Mother's heart that the first beating of the drums had come to be known by our people as a way of reestablishing the connection with all that had once been ours. The secondary beating of drums in many of our ceremonies is the connecting with those spirits of the land we are asking assistance from. Those spirits of the lands that have been given their own dominion and gifts to share with those who are in need.

And now, looking into this ocean of life that was before me...I realized that I had been accepted by all life travelers here...as well as the spirits of the land.

I could feel there was a change in the currents of

the flowing life that was passing me by. And it was this difference that had first called my attention back to those things Grandfather had shared with me about the coming of a storm.

From this place on the passing current that was carrying with it a feeling of change, I saw there was a small spirit picture that had formed within it. One that showed me a coming storm. It was from this that I realized this was what Grandfather had been referring to as his message. That this was what had been shown to him when he shared his speaking words with all of us.

Once this picture had been shared with me of those things that were yet to be...I felt myself returning to the place I had begun, the place beside Grandfather's truck.

When I could hear the beating of feet on the back of Grandfather's truck, I knew I was back. And, I could also hear the groaning sounds of Cheeway as he was gaining his vision back...back into this domain of the waking spirits and I knew I had been returned from my journey by these spirits of the land.

Before I turned around to see what progress my best friend had been making, I gave my silence of thanking to those who had allowed me to enter their domain of life.

And with that finished, I turned to the truck...to an ever familiar sight of seeing Cheeway trying to coordinate his body enough to have all of it travel in one direction at the same time.

Grandfather and Two Bears already had their provisions out and were setting them into their walking blankets. Both Cheeway's and mine had been set just to the front of the truck.

=⊕=

Seeing all things were coming along as they should be, I walked over to the front of the truck and began packing my provisions in my walking blanket. Once I had finished, I joined Grandfather and Two Bears on one of the sitting rocks and observed Cheeway as he, too, began his task of packing.

"It is truly an amazing thing to watch, little one," came the beginning of Grandfather's speaking words to me.

"You mean this waking of Cheeway, Grandfather?" I asked.

"Yes, little one. This is what I mean," Grandfather replied.

"Why do you find this so amazing to observe?" I asked.

"It serves, for those who would see, as a reminder to all of us. As a reminder to all of us how we are when we will finally begin to wake from our sleep of illusion.

"When we begin to wake from our sleep of illusion, little one, there is a great mystery that begins to unfold before our eyes. It is a mystery that has always been with all of us...but it is one that has not been recognized yet.

"And when one will begin this wakening process, they will at first feel very lost and alone. Lost and alone because as they will wake, there will be a great feeling of loss. A feeling of loss from all that they had been carrying around with them that, in truth, did not hold any value of truth for them.

"At first, they will feel the emptiness of this loss. But as time will continue for them, they will find there is a great deal of understanding that is coming to them. And this understanding that is being worked by them now has a place to reside. Its place will be among those empty places where the temporary things had once been.

"When this process begins to take place on their life path, they will see how good it is to have room within themselves for all of this to reside. And it will be then they will come to understand why it was that so much of what they held onto before had to be dropped away.

"However, until they will come to that time, they will not see the true value in this. They will only have the feeling as if someone has placed a great curse over them. A great curse that has caused them to lose all those things they had worked for. All of those things they held as being very important to them.

"The wakening process...this wakening from the sleep of illusion, well, it is a difficult process in itself, Speaking Wind. But it does not last for a long period of time. That is if the one who is traveling through it will come to understand what is taking place.

"And, because it is a very difficult process, then it is very important for us to observe it whenever it will be presented to us. It is important because there is not only much to remember for ourselves from this...but there may still be many lessons within this process that we will need to learn from. To learn from so we will have a better understanding for what has taken place within us as well," came the speaking words of Grandfather.

"This is what you see when Cheeway tries so hard to wake from his sleeping time, Grandfather?"

"Yes, little one. This is what I see. For the same steps that Cheeway takes each time he wakes from being with the dreamers, those same steps are what are required for another to wake from their own sleep of illusion.

"And this is why both Two Bears and I do not mind this waiting time for him. We hold the knowing that this process that has come to Cheeway...that it has come through him for a reason. And in many of his actions we both can see something else that we have either forgotten to remember or something new that comes to us from his motions," Grandfather explained.

"Do you think these movements and actions of his are coming to me for the same reason, Grandfather?" I asked.

"Perhaps, little one. But only you can answer your own questions," said Grandfather.

"If you will look at those things that are being presented to you, Speaking Wind, you will find a great secret in them," came the speaking words from Two Bears.

"You will find that all things that will cross your life path will do so in their own time...and for their own reason. And this time and this reason has come because of you."

"You mean this time and reason has come because they had been set into motion by ourselves, Two Bears?"

"Yes, little one. And perhaps within these events that will come to you...you might find the reason for your expectation and feelings of apprehension that have been residing with you."

Looking over to the face of Two Bears, I could see a look of wisdom come over him. It was a look of wisdom that had been presented to me because of a needed piece of knowledge that was within him. A

=⊕=

piece of knowing that I knew I needed and that he would be willing to share with me if I were to ask.

"Two Bears," I said, sitting straight on my sitting rock.

"Yes, little one. What is it that I may assist you with?" came his reply.

"Could you explain why all of this takes place with us. I mean, why all of these events come to us as they do?"

Two Bears turned his eyes from observing Cheeway trying to pack his equipment into his walking blanket to me.

"Perhaps you need to come to understand about the song legend that shares this, Speaking Wind. Would you like to know of this?"

"Yes, Two Bears. I would like to hold this knowing...and I am sure Cheeway would like this, as well," I responded.

"Do not forget the reason for our being allowed to come to this land, Speaking Wind," came the calling of Grandfather's voice.

He continued, "You hold a feeling for it. This much I have already seen within you. But you do not yet hold the knowing nor the understanding. And this is why we have come to this land.

"There is a great event that is about to unfold in this domain that is the Earth Mother's. An event that will affect all who are here. And what Two Bears and I have seen is that you have been one who has been called to hear of it. But there is still much to do...and this sharing of the song legend of the Earth Mother's council may be a very important part of it to you and Cheeway.

"So it is for this reason that we will be willing to

tell you both about this. But not now and on this place. For we still have a long journey into the mountains to travel. And, there will be just enough time for us to reach our destination before the mountain storm arrives.

"Once we have prepared ourselves among the children of sheltering, then we will have the time to share this song legend with both of you. But now that Cheeway is ready, we should begin our journey."

Finishing his speaking words, both Grandfather and Two Bears stood up from their sitting rock and began to walk up what appeared to be a shallow worn path. One that they could see, but one that would not have been obvious to another who did not have prior knowledge of its presence.

Grandfather took the lead with Two Bears behind him and Cheeway following behind me. I could see that Cheeway was back to being himself now and had no trouble in keeping up with me.

I did not know where it was we were being taken to, but from all of those other places Grandfather and Two Bears had allowed us to visit, I knew this was going to be a good one. One that would also be blessed with the balance of life over it, and one that would allow us to enter as friends and long lost relatives to those who had come to live here and call this their home.

THE GUIDING HANDS

Making a journey with Grandfather and Two Bears always took a great deal of effort. There were not any signs of slowing from either of them even though they both held a great number of seasons over them. Seasons that had been filled with learning and understanding for those things that had been presented to them.

Cheeway and I would often speak about their energy levels and would ask them what it was that had allowed them to keep such a pace with this life path of theirs.

They would always smile at both of us and say that it was because they did not hold any of those things called excessive baggage with them that often cause one to feel weighed down and tired all of the time.

In those times when Cheeway and I would ask them what they had meant about excessive baggage, they would look at us and smile. Then they would tell us that there would always be times in both of our life paths when we would be confronted with many events. Events that would come to us with a great lesson behind them. But, if we were to get caught up in the emotion of these events, these emotions would not allow us to work through them to see what this lesson was. We would then end up carrying this emotion of the event with us as another piece of extra baggage. This baggage would cause us to have an even greater weight to us than we should have.

And, as we would enter from one season to the next on this life path, all of those pieces of baggage would cause us to feel their weight. And we would often be found walking with a stoop at first, then we would feel the tiredness of our own life path all over us.

And it would be from this weight that we would see the wrinkles come over our faces and feel as if we could not keep up with those things we would try to do.

It would be when we would no longer carry this baggage with us that we would be able to follow our seasons in this domain, Grandfather and Two Bears would always say. And, if we were speaking to ourselves with words of truth, then we could follow our path if we would come to know how to work our way through these emotions that we could become stuck in.

As this picture was working its way through my thinking mind, I turned to Cheeway and asked him what thoughts he had of this.

"I do not hold any more understanding for this than you do, Speaking Wind," came his reply as we continued our ascent up the face of one of the great stone mountains.

"However, I am sure that if the time will allow...if there will be time for this kind of sharing, then Grandfather and Two Bears will give to both of us another explanation of this," said Cheeway.

"I know, Cheeway. But there is something else that I must share with you."

"What is that, my brother?"

"This feeling that I was given. This feeling that came over me yesterday...the one I shared with you," I said.

"You mean the one that makes you feel as if there is something very big going to happen...and soon?"

I replied, "Yes, Cheeway...this is the feeling I speak of. It is growing within me and all of these things that are coming to me on this day. All of the picture thoughts that have been given to me to share from...and those things that I have been sharing with you. It is as if they all fit into this feeling that has come over me."

"You mean that you are feeling as if all of this is connected, Speaking Wind?"

"Yes, Cheeway. I hold this to be a truth of mine. Especially this part of these events that have led both Grandfather and Two Bears to bring both of us to this land and in the way they have done."

"What do you mean, my brother?" Cheeway asked, still keeping one eye on the rocks we were traveling over.

"From all of the events that took place yesterday in the center of the village. Those events of the men who were speaking to each other before I found where you were sitting. Those events that came to all of us from the speaking words of the one called Standing Tree. And the events now...now that Grandfather and Two Bears have brought both of us to this land now. They have not ever done such a thing on a quick notice as they have now done, Cheeway.

"All of these things seem to be connected somehow to these feelings that something is about to happen. Something that will involve not only myself and you, but something that is going to be a part of every living life in this domain that is the Earth Mother's.

"I just cannot shake this feeling that all of these events are connected together. Connected in a way that will bring me into this picture and as a very important part."

"And this bothers you, Speaking Wind?" Cheeway asked.

"It bothers me, Cheeway, because I do not have any kind of understanding for what it is that is taking place here. It also bothers me because of these feelings that are coming to me. I am getting the feeling like I am being led as a blind person would be, around one object but allowed to run into another so they might get a feeling of what it is like."

Just as I had finished my speaking words to Cheeway, I felt my foot catch a loose stone on this mountain path. As I came to rest my weight on it...too late to shift it from one foot to the other, I felt my entire leg support go out from under me.

The last non-moving picture I remembered seeing was my right foot straight above my head. After that, everything else was a blur. But I could feel myself rolling off of the path we had been traveling on and very quickly.

It was not long before I felt the bump of hitting Cheeway and catching him up in this rolling off the mountain as well. And, when I felt myself hit him, I heard him let go of much of his air.

Together we were rolling down the side of the mountain trail we had been on. But we were rolling so fast that I could not see anything as it went by. There were only blurs and the numb feelings of hitting smaller trees and rocks that had placed themselves in our way.

Suddenly, we stopped. And looking to what it was that had placed itself in our way, I could see that it was a gathering of many of the smaller standing people.

We had gathered many things on us as we had continued our descent over the side of the mountain, and their weight, along with the non-giving way of the standing people, had stopped our motion.

Trying to get some kind of an idea of where we had traveled to, I began to laugh. This was a laughing that was coming to me from a relief and also a great enjoyment as well.

I looked to get my bearings and saw Cheeway first. His head was covered with many small vines and it made him look like a bowl of spaghetti. Hanging off these small vines were many leaves and sticks.

All of this looked so funny to me that I found my laughter growing very quickly. It was growing so that soon, I found myself unable to move at all. The only thing I could do was to look at Cheeway and laugh.

After he saw how I looked as well, he joined in with me. Seeing that I too held the same kind of debris all over me was all it took to set his laughter into the same momentum as mine was. And soon, there were only two lumps of flesh...unable to move under their own power because they were both laughing at each other so hard they could not move.

Between our breathing and laughing, however, we could hear the speaking words from both Grandfather and Two Bears come to us.

"Do not move, little ones. We are coming to you."

Even these speaking words from the two we had come to respect the most in this domain had seemed funny. How strange it was that they were telling both of us not to move. We did not feel as if anything was broken or out of place with our bodies. But when we would try to move from our positions, we both felt like two turtles that had been turned over on their backs. While there was movement from our hands and feet, there was none of it that was being done with any kind of result. Anything that would have allowed either of us to get up from our laying down positions did not seem to be available to either of us.

=⊕=

It was from the weight of our provisions that had been packed into our walking blankets that was keeping us on our backs like overturned turtles. I was sure there were many more riders who had attached themselves to them as well, which was weighing us down even more.

Soon, Grandfather and Two Bears had reached both of us. Reaching down, they assisted us to our feet.

"It is a good thing these spirits of the land held a great liking for both of you," came the first calm speaking words from Grandfather.

"If you had been allowed to continue on this journey just another few inches, I am afraid that we would be carrying your empty shells with us back to the village."

"What do you mean, Grandfather?" Cheeway said still laughing, but not as uncontrollably.

"Look at what is below you, little one. And look how close you are to it."

Both Cheeway and I looked into the direction that Grandfather had been pointing. And when we did, our laughter stopped very quickly.

We saw that where we had been stopped was only a few inches away from the edge of a cliff that emptied itself into a large valley of stone and water below us.

There was a drop that must have been one hundred feet down. When we saw how close we had come to this, both of our legs became wobbly and no longer supported our weight.

It was for the quickness that was in Grandfather and Two Bears that allowed us to not fall down on the earth once again. As they caught both of us, they assisted us in finding a sitting rock that was not so close to the edge we had rolled to.

"It is good that these spirits of the land have accepted both of you little ones. It was they who allowed these other children of the Earth Mother to assist you in not falling over the side of this great cliff."

Looking over to the place where Grandfather was standing, we could see a look of relief come over his face as well, and we knew that we were not the only ones who were feeling such a frightening way of feeling. Looking on the face that was being worn by Two Bears, we could see that this feeling was equally shared by him as well.

"You see, little ones...," Two Bears began,

"It is when the ones who have come to assist us see those things we have come into this domain to perform. Those things we have shared with the Earth Mother that we would do. It is when they will see we are developing our talents and abilities to do them that they will assist in our well being.

"It was they who intervened in requesting this assistance for both of you from these spirits of the land. And it was they who shared with them a spirit picture of those things that need to be done that allowed them to see you for what you will become.

"When the spirits of the land see you...and see you in the way that all who are traveling on the blue path of the spirit. Then they will see that you are doing well on your path and they will step in to offer their assistance.

"This comes to you as a sign, little ones, a sign that you are indeed on the correct path. But this path is one that can truly only be known and understood by the one who is traveling it.

"There will not ever be another who is traveling in this domain that can tell you what path is right for you to travel. Only you will possess the ability of seeing this for yourself. And, when the spirits of the land see that you are on the correct path...then they are pleased with this. And they will continue to assist you in doing those things you have a need to perform.

"Just keep in the front of your thinking minds, little ones, that there will not ever be an event that will come to you by accident. There will not ever be anything that will happen to you by chance....all of these things are done at the right time and in the right place so that you will be offered the opportunity of learning from them.

"However, this is a truth that we will discuss further with both of you when we arrive at our destination. "

Two Bears continued to look at both of us with a knowing look over his face. And seeing that both of us were catching onto these things both he and Grandfather had been willing to share with us...they turned around and began walking up the small stone trail. This small stone trail that was taking us deep into the sacred mountain lands of the Jemez.

Picking up our walking blankets and readjusting them over our shoulders, Cheeway and I began to follow the two we had come to respect so greatly into a place we had never seen before. The place they had been willing to share with us was a sacred place, one where many of these feelings I had been carrying with me would be cleared.

Trying to pick up my step to keep up with their pace and still looking at all the small stones under my feet, I was left with a great deal of time to think. The thoughts that were filling me were not coming to me with any direction I could follow. They were only growing within me now and I was beginning to feel this weight of not knowing what it was that was being offered to me and still having to carry it with me.

We had been traveling for about two hours when Grandfather stopped and called for both Cheeway and I to come up and look at the place we had been brought to.

Grabbing our walking blankets, we picked up our step from a walk to a run, for both of us had become very excited about this new place that was going to be shared with us. Arriving at the same time, we both looked over the top of the hill that Grandfather and Two Bears were standing on and were amazed.

We were looking into a small valley and it was filled with two streams that had seemed to cut a wedge into the great stone that was in the middle.

On one side of the great stone there was steam rising from the water. This was quite amazing to us because though the weather was still cool, it was not so cold that we would have expected this.

"Grandfather...?" I asked, standing very still now.

"Why does the steam rise from the river that is on the left of the great stone. The air that is over us is not that cold, is it?"

"What you are looking at, little one, is something that takes place in this valley no matter what time of year it is," began his response.

"In the times that are not too distant from the ones we now share, our people came to this land to pay reverence to the birth of the cloud people. But this was a time when we were free to travel on all of these lands of the Earth Mother's."

=⊕=

"What then stopped this process, Grandfather?" I asked.

"It was when there were many eyes laid on all of our people, little one. It was when the ones with the white skins began to think that our power was something for them to fear. And, remember what has been shared with you from the teachings of the old ones. That whenever one will see the face of fear come to them in any form, they are not in the place of understanding...themselves or any of those things that are coming to them.

"You see, little one, our people could have offered an explanation to them. An explanation that would have cleared much away from their views of us. But, from what had been shared with us by the old ones and the wise, we held the knowing that for this...it was not time. The time for sharing our many teachings with others was not right. And for any of us to attempt to do this would bring a great disaster on all of our people...from the very old to the very young.

"As it has been taught to many of the wise ones of our people, Speaking Wind, we are to learn to work with those things that have been made available for us to work with. It is when we attempt to work with those things we do not have that we create the illusion...the illusion of being or becoming something or someone that we are not.

"So, instead of pushing for something that was not available to us, our people created another kind of ceremony. One that would allow them to keep the sacredness of thanking the Earth Mother for the birth of her cloud people. And one that would not require us to travel into these lands during the times that I have been willing to share with you.

=⊕=

"We created an Earth Mother ceremony. One that was very similar to what we had long performed on this land. But one that was held in the kivas of our villages.

"Remember how we explained to each of you the meaning of the drum beat?" Grandfather asked.

"Well, this was what had come to our people during this time of being watched by the white ones. We heard the calling voice of the old ones. The ones who have always been with us to provide us with their light of direction. And what they were willing to share was that we should use the beating of the drums to call these spirits of the land to our ceremonies. These spirits of the lands who would hear our giving of thanks for all they were willing to do in this domain.

"This was the reason that so many of our people stopped using this land as a place for conducting our ceremonies. If we had continued with our way of giving thanks to the for these cloud people, then I am afraid that our recent history would have been much bloodier than it has been already. And even more than that, we would not have even been given the freedom of performing our most sacred ceremonies at all.

"There would have been not only a fence built around all of us...but there would have been a complete stopping of our life paths. And all of those things in the way of wisdom and teachings...they would have been lost to future generations.

"This was what had come to the front of the thinking minds of our people, Speaking Wind. It is only when a people become so rigid that they are unable to bend with the ever present changes of life

that they will break. And when they break, they will
no longer be a people."

Grandfather set his walking blanket down and
then sat next to Two Bears. I could see they were
going into the silence to ask for permission of the
spirits of the land. Permission from them to enter
and, looking at this, I knew, as did Cheeway, that we
should do the same.

This was considered to be a very polite way of
entering the house of another. And these spirits of the
land as well as the children of the Earth Mother
considered this place to be their home. It was only
polite to ask to be invited in before walking through.

As we were asking for acceptance on these lands,
I was looking over the valley that was just beneath us.
There were many standing people who had come to
know of a great life here. There were also many of the
hooved ones that had come to these lands to gather
much of what they needed to continue on their life
path.

I was being very thankful for all of the life that had
been allowed to remain here. This life would not have
been so abundant if our people had been stiff of neck
for those changes that had been imposed on our
people by the white skins.

How good it was, I was thinking in the front of my
thinking mind. How good it was that our people had
learned so well the ways of a balanced life path that
allowed them to see what was needed rather than
what was wanted.

Soon, we finished our request for acceptance by
those who had come to call these lands their own and
picked ourselves up from the sitting positions.

We began traveling down another stone path that

had been cut away in the side of the mountain and began our descent into the valley below. This valley had already given so much beauty to all of us...and had given me a feeling of being much closer to the answers that I had been seeking. Answers to those questions that had come to life within me from the events of the past two days.

Reaching the bottom of the stone path, Grandfather and Two Bears stopped to remove their shoes and instructed Cheeway and myself to do the same.

"This is the place where the sacred lands begin, little ones. It is out of respect for all that is within Great Mystery that we take our shoes off. It is out of respect for the continuation of maintaining our contact with the Earth Mother that we will touch her skin with ours," came the speaking words of Grandfather over the sounds of great amounts of rushing water, these sounds of the rushing water that had been caused by two streams that met together just in front of us.

A SACRED LAND

After Cheeway and I took our shoes off, we followed the lead that Grandfather and Two Bears had taken. We followed the path they continued to walk.

However, what we found was something that was a great surprise for each of us that left us both in awe.

When we first took our shoes off, we could feel the coldness from the lands we had been standing on. However, when we took our first step on what appeared to look like ordinary sand, we found there was no longer a coldness about it, but there was a warmth that seemed to be flowing all the way through us.

Both Cheeway and I were sweating from our efforts of trying to keep up with Grandfather and Two Bears on this uphill ascent. Our tiredness was showing by the little beads of sweat that had begun to roll down our foreheads.

From these small trails of moisture, we were feeling the coolness of the spirit wind on this day. It had caused both of us to share a small headache and we knew this to be from the coolness of the wind against our wet skins.

However, as soon as we stepped onto this warming sand, we could feel this pain leave both of us, and it left very quickly.

We knew that this would be explained later by Grandfather and Two Bears...but for now, we must content ourselves with following their lead.

Grandfather and Two Bears had set their walking blankets down by the opening of a small cave. It was located deep within the great stone that had kept the warm river and cold river separated. In what appeared to be a perfect triangle, the sand formed itself in front of the great stone and between both of the rivers.

As both Cheeway and I sat our walking blankets down and waited for Grandfather and Two Bears to exit from the small cave, we noticed that there was a small light coming from the inside of its opening. This light was not bright enough to cause any competition with the fullness of the moon at night, but it was a light that was enough to see with even if one did not have another source with them.

Exiting the cave, Grandfather and Two Bears had

both of their arms full. Grandfather appeared to be carrying a large canvas with many paintings on it. Two Bears was carrying what appeared to be the supporting poles as well as what looked like lanterns attached to other poles.

Setting them down, both made mention to us that we should assist them in setting this up. And, with no other prodding, both Cheeway and I took this task to our path and began our work.

With all four of us doing our part, it did not take very long to complete all of the preparations that were needed. Sitting down in the warming sand, I looked up at the tarp that was now stretched over us and was amazed at the intricacy of all the paintings that had been completed on it.

It was almost like reading a story or some kind of a book, I was thinking, when the speaking words of Two Bears came to me.

"What you are looking at, little one, is actually a picture history of those events that have come to our people. Those events that have held a great weight of importance and meaning to them."

As Two Bears began his speaking words, Cheeway joined me and out of the corner of my eye, I could see that Grandfather had found a sitting place for himself on the sand and was looking at Two Bears with a good smile over his face.

"If you will look at those paintings that are on this tarp, little ones, you will see the almost complete history of our people. An almost complete history of them because it does not include any of the events from the lands we had originally come from. Nor does it include any of those events that are yet to take place.

"You see little ones, our people have been traveling with the Earth Mother for a long time. And this time has been marked by our people in terms of worlds and ages, instead of years, as you have been taught to count in your school.

"When one uses the term of years instead of worlds and ages, they limit themselves in a great way. They limit themselves from being able to look further than the time they will use. And this is what has come to so many in this domain that is the Earth Mother's. This is one of the great reasons for them not being able to see far at all for those things that hold a great need by their spirit.

"Each of these events shares with us what has taken place in the past of our people's life path history. That it is just as important now as it was then. And this is the mark of truth that is shared with us, little ones. Truth that can only come from the Ancient Ones of our ancestors.

"It is this truth that is contained in the sacred tarp of remembering and this is why we continue to keep it on this sacred land. For this land that we are sitting on now is one of the beginning places where our people had come to know this face of the Earth Mother's as it is now. And it will be one of the places where we will return to when she is about to put on her new face."

Hearing these speaking words of Two Bears, I could not hold my silence any longer.

"Two Bears?" I asked with a raised note of concern in the tone of my voice.

"Yes, little one. What is it that I may be of assistance to you with?"

"You speak of a new face for the Earth Mother.

One that is different from the face she now wears. This is what gives me concern. It is a concern because I do not hold an understanding for it and it continues to weigh heavy on me."

"Could this have something to do with what you had heard being discussed by those three men in the village yesterday?" Two Bears responded.

"Yes...yes, this is a part of it. But how did you know of this when I had not discussed it with anyone...not even Cheeway?"

"The spirit travels in many ways, little one. And it travels in complete freedom of those things you may now consider to be limiting. And a sharing spirit will not be limited to those things that hold back our bodies or robes we travel in.

"This freedom that comes to all of us is one that is well known by all of the members of our spirit family. And when an event will come to any of us, it will be shared with all."

"But how have I shared this with you, Two Bears? I do not understand," I said.

"In the dreamtime of each of us, we join with all of the members of our spirit family. We join with them and review all of the events that have been presented to each of us. Those events that have come to us so that we will be able to grow in the ways of our spirit.

"And it was during this dreamtime of yours, little one, that you shared these things with us. With all of us.

"But for now, let us continue with what you had asked of us earlier. Do you remember?" Two Bears asked.

"You mean about these events that come to all of us and how each of them have been designed by us and the Earth Mother?"

"Yes, little one...this is what I am referring to. Would you and Cheeway like to hear of this now?"

"Yes, Two Bears, we would like to hear of this now," came the speaking words of both Cheeway and myself in unison.

"Good then," was his reply.

"It is good because it is time for each of you to hold an understanding for this event. And it is necessary because one who is among us is about to be offered a peek through a great doorway. One that has been on the horizon for our people for many seasons.

"However, as it is with many things in this domain that is the Earth Mother's, we too need to take time to sustain ourselves. And as you will look over to the direction of Grandfather, you will see he has prepared two bags for us to eat from. Once this is finished, then we will continue with the explanation of what we have come to call 'Holding Council With The Earth Mother.'"

A CALLING VOICE FROM
THE ANCIENT ONES

Hearing these speaking words come to us from Two Bears, both Cheeway and I nodded our heads to share our agreement with what had been said without breaking our silence.

Rising from our sitting places in the warming sand, we walked to the place Grandfather was waiting with the two sacks.

However, instead of opening these sacks to begin

eating, he only handed them over to us and said this food would still need to be cooked.

This surprised Cheeway and myself because we had not begun any cooking fire on this land. And without a cooking fire, we could not see how this food could be prepared.

Seeing this look come over our faces, Grandfather smiled at both of us as he handed each of us one sack.

"Do not look so concerned, little ones. You must remember to keep in the front of your thinking minds that when you will be given a task to perform, that it is always given with a path to accomplish it. And this path will come to you when the time is right.

"Now if you will both look over to your left, you will see there has been a small path cut out of the great stone. If you will follow this path, you will find at the end of it will be a great pool. A great pool that is the beginning of the warm water that is forming the steaming stream next to us.

"Once you arrive at this pool, there will be an opening with a large roof. And within this large room with the roof, you will see a place where our people have prepared long poles to hang sacks on such as the one I have given to you.

"Take two of these poles and tie our sacks on them. Then place them into the boiling waters of life that are rising to us from deep within the face of the Earth Mother.

"When the food that is contained within them is finished, they will rise to the surface. This will tell both of you that the time for cooking is over and you may bring them back here where we may all share in this meal.

"Have you both understood my speaking words

to you?"

"Yes, Grandfather...we understand."

Taking the sacks and placing them over our shoulders, Cheeway and I began to walk up the stone trail that had been carved into the side of the great stone.

As we began to climb, we noticed that it was beginning to snow. This was always an exciting time for both of us and even more now that it was a time in the season when there were not many occurrences of this taking place because we were so close to the growing season.

However, as the snow began to come down, both of us were not feeling it at all. This was due to the abundance of warmth that was not only coming to us from the sand we had been sitting on, but also from the warmth that was present in the stone path as well.

This was indeed one of the many blessings that was being offered to both of us on this day, I was thinking, as we continued to travel on this stone path. A blessing that neither of us would forget for many seasons.

Not wanting to take any more time than was necessary, neither Cheeway nor I shared any speaking words on this task. We did want to hear those things that would be shared with each of us about the holding of council with the Earth Mother. It was something that each of us held a feeling for that shared a great need with our spirit.

We reached this place Grandfather had described to both of us in a very short time. And, as was always the case, his description was accurate.

Entering through the last portion of this journey, we had to bend our heads as we traveled through a small tunnel that had been formed by the passing of water many seasons before. Waters that had since left to find another route to the hot stream that passed by the great stone.

Once we had exited from this short tunnel, we found ourselves inside of what appeared to be a great room that was filled with a bubbling pool of water.

Looking up, we noticed the roof was not a complete one, but it had opened up partially on the top giving one the experience of being outside of a sheltered place while remaining within one as well.

We found the long poles Grandfather told us about and tied our sacks on the end of them. Placing them inside of the precut holes made for them, we knew there would be some time left to wait, and we each found a diversion for ourselves.

Cheeway went back through the tunnel from the way we had come and I found one of the openings that the water was running through to the outside.

There were four openings from this pool that were allowing equal amounts of this hot water to enter this sacred land.

I was thinking how much like the four directions and the four chiefs of earth, air, water, and fire this was like. It was as if this bubbling water was sharing itself with those things that are so much a part of all this domain. And for this, I was very thankful.

Finding one of the closest openings next to me, I walked out of the enclosed portion of this place and looked outside.

Running right next to me was the hot water that was filling the stream that would eventually run next to the place we had made for ourselves. To my right was a small ledge. It seemed to be made for one to sit and observe all of the life that was on these lands...and it also seemed to be inviting me to share myself with it.

So, taking it up on this wonderful invitation, I sat on it. I sat in a position that would allow me to hear the sounds of the rushing warm water next to me while still being in a place where I could see the entire valley below me, as well as the edge of the great stone where Grandfather and Two Bears were waiting for us to return.

As I sat down on this ledge, I leaned my back against the smooth stone wall that was behind me and crossed both of my feet beneath me. This was a position that I had become very used to from my seasons with Grandfather and Two Bears. And it was one that allowed me to find a place of rest so that I might not have to be concerned with my body part for short periods of time.

From my sitting position, I was looking over the sky that was above me. I could see the clouds that had come to this land were colored with a light gray. And I knew this to be from all of the snow they were carrying on their backs.

It was giving to me a very restful feeling to observe them as they found their own place over these lands and continued to allow the small snowflakes to drop from their bellies.

I observed them as they would leave their mother's arms of the cloud people and come to cover the face of the Earth Mother, bringing with them many messages from the cloud nations. Messages that would be shared with all the children of the Earth Mother who were with this land on this day.

As they would leave their homes, they would float in an effortless manner to finally meet together on the face of the Earth Mother. As many of them began their descent over this land, there were small movements from the spirit wind that would play with them.

The spirit wind would catch some of them and send them either spinning in a circle or toss them back up into the sky where they would later find their own way back to their original destination. A destination they knew would be theirs no matter what direction they would travel to get to it.

What a wonderful lesson they were offering to those who could see it, came the thought to the front of my thinking mind. How well they walked their path...this path that has been offered to all of us from the Great Spirit and the Earth Mother.

Watching them as they continued on their life path in this cycle, I could not help but reflect on those things that had been shared with me about not worrying about finding our own path from my seasons past.

I could hear those speaking words of Grandfather and Two Bears returning to me from my within place...this place where my spirit resides.

"Remember, Speaking Wind...it is only by allowing all things to be that we will find our path through the light of direction. This light of direction that is first shared with us from the Ancient Ones' council fire.

"It is when we are weak of faith and spirit within that we will attempt to control all things that come to us. And this creates a great cloud over our vision which will cause us to lose our way.

"The further we travel with this clouded vision, little one...the more we will try to exercise our own control over all things that will come close to us.

=⊕=

"This includes other people's lives as well as all events that will come to cross our path. This is a time when we will come to tell others what they should be doing and find ourselves sitting in a place of judging them, as well.

"However, this telling and judging will not be applied to any of those things that we will do, but is only applied to those things that are around us. And this comes to us because we have indeed lost our way on this path of the spirit. This path that is only for us to travel.

"When this takes place in anyone's life path, they do not assist themselves or any others. They either stop progress on all life paths that come close to theirs and they may even cause some to go backwards if they will listen to them.

"Remember, little one...remember, when one will not have the strength of understanding, they will find themselves in this destructive mode of life. This comes to them because they have forgotten how to listen to themselves. And since they cannot hear those things they are asking questions of, they believe there is no other that has any answers that are suitable.

"This causes them to hold a false believing in what they see as truth. They will see this body part of themselves as the only part of life that is important. And because of this, there will not be many things that will be seen by them that are of lasting value or truth.

"They will see all life that is around them as being temporary and in doing so, they will hold their own life as being the single most important thing. This will also create their false believing that the only things that are important are those that will give to their body part a feeling of goodness or satisfaction. And they will fool themselves into seeking out only those things that will do this.

"However, as it is with all things that are within this domain, this body part of themselves will wear out and begin to fail them. And when it does, they will look to another for their needed levels of satisfaction. They will look for another who will be foolish enough to listen to them and do those things they will tell them are right to do.

"When this happens, they will indeed find their gratification through another. But the sad part of this is that the one who has foolishly allowed this to happen to them...they have given up their own seasons of youth and without any gain for themselves.

"Remember, Speaking Wind, these seasons of youth come to all of us for a reason. And that reason is so that we may have the stamina to work our way through the many lessons that are being offered to us. Lessons that cause many of us to fall and hurt ourselves. But with the seasons of our youth, if they are used wisely, we can bounce back from those things that we may call our mistakes and learn from them. Learn from them so we may, in the time that is ahead of us, come to see more clearly and know what our path is.

"However, when we give these seasons of our youth up to another, to one who is as I have been willing to describe to you, there will be a great many lessons that will have been missed by the one who has been so foolish to listen to them. Lessons that are very important to the preparing that all of us are doing so we will be prepared to encounter those events that will soon be upon us.

"This is why we have stressed to both you and Cheeway that it is very important to learn how to allow all things to be. To do otherwise is to open yourselves up to many things that you would not wish to participate in doing...either to yourselves or to others.

"Remember, Speaking Wind, when we allow all things to be, then we have become who and what we are in truth. But, when we will try to control those same things, then we will always be in the state of becoming. A place of becoming that will not ever allow us to be."

With those speaking words of Grandfather echoing away from me, I was looking at the playing that the spirit wind was doing with all of the snowflakes. And as I was observing them, I was thinking on what had just been shared with me once again by my calling of my spirit.

I could see that no matter how much each of these small flakes of snow had been tossed and played with by the spirit wind, they would always find the exact same place they were meant to travel. This place where they would have all of their needs met...this place where they would always end up where they needed to go.

As I was looking at these small ones, these small blessings from the cloud nations, I could see another place that was also of great interest to me. It was a place where many plants were growing on the right side of the warm waters over this land.

I could make out that there were many vegetables growing as well as many stalks of corn, and this had been from the continual efforts of all those who were still allowed to visit this land.

Grandfather and Two Bears had told us of such efforts that were always made on our people's sacred lands so that all who would be allowed to travel to them would leave something behind for the children of the Earth Mother to eat. In doing so, they were ensuring a continuing balance of all life paths on these lands where balance was such a strong medicine to learn from. On these lands where this balance was always being taught to those who held a seeking spirit within them.

Returning my eyes to the top of the ring of mountains, I was looking at all of the standing people who were silhouetted against this gray white sky. The great pine trees that were standing overlooking this valley were the only ones who were not sleeping through this season. Our people had come to know them as the bringers and sharers of peace that is to be found on the path of the spirit. This path of the spirit that has long been known to our people.

As I was looking over them, I could hear the spirit wind rustling through their many arms and backs. I could hear the sounds of this spirit wind that was passing through them echo off the many stone face sides of this valley we were in. And hearing this sound come to me, I was very thankful for being in a place with so much to share...especially the warmth of its own life force.

I knew that if it had not been for the warmth coming to me from the waters as well as this stone ledge I was sitting on, I would have been very cold. On this day, so much of life was traveling around me, carrying the message to all the children that their time was not just yet for waking to the growing season.

They still needed to rest for awhile yet.

Suddenly, the spirit wind stopped its movements and the falling snow was coming down without interference from anyone.

There was a silence over this land, one that I had not heard so completely before. It seemed as if all life had paused for the present and was holding its breath.

This feeling had also taken its effect on me as well, for I found myself holding my breath, too.

Through this silence that was in such abundance over this land, I felt a presence come close to me. But it was not a presence of one such as Grandfather, Two Bears, or Cheeway. It was a presence of one who was in all places and at the same time.

Then...it made itself known to me through a calling voice that was being carried over the blanket of silence that had fallen over all life that was near me.

"Speaking Wind...," came the call from all directions at the same time.

"Speaking Wind, come to us...we are waiting for you.

"There is no longer a need for you to stand at the outside of the circle and look out. The time for you to stand in your own circle and look within is with you...now.

"We are waiting..."

As the calling voice came to its end, I was reaching down with both of my hands and feeling the face of this small ledge I had been sitting on. I noticed the sounds of life were returning over this valley.

When the calling voice had come to me, I noticed that I had lost all of my own feelings of my presence. And now, I was feeling where I was sitting in an effort of making sure that I, too, had returned to myself, as

=⊕=

the sounds of life on these lands returned to me, as well.

Coming out of the silence that had been over these lands, I heard the calling voice of my best friend Cheeway from behind me within the large room of the boiling water.

"Speaking Wind," came his call.

"Come and help me, my brother. The food is done but the sacks have grown very heavy and I cannot lift them out of the waters alone.

"And besides that, there is a pesky dragonfly that is bothering me and won't leave me alone."

Rising from my sitting position, I returned to the inside of the large stone room where the boiling waters were. When I looked over to the place where Cheeway was attempting to take out the sacks of food, I almost laughed so hard that I fell down.

Each time he would attempt to raise one of the poles out of the water, the little dragonfly would buzz his face, causing him to release the pole back into the water. This was not only causing him to feel a great sense of frustration over these efforts he was making, but it was also getting him very wet in the process.

Nearing him, I called out.

"Cheeway, I am here now. Let us both grab onto each of these poles and pull them out together."

But just as I said that, the dragonfly found another one to come to...me.

And holding himself in front of my face and in a very steady motion, I recognized this small child of the Earth Mother as the same one who had visited me earlier this morning when I had been waiting in the front of my parents' house to be picked up in Grandfather's truck.

=⊕=

Surely this could not have been the same child that had visited me then. For that was many miles away and with the weather being as cold as it was, how could one such as this still be alive.

However, as those things were crossing the front of my thinking mind, the little dragonfly flew away. It was almost as if he had been waiting for me to give him his recognition and once I had done this, his quest had been completed.

"Well my brother, it seems as if this small one certainly knows you," came the sounds from Cheeway.

"Yes, Cheeway...it does appear he did.

"Come on now, let's get this food back to the camp. I am certainly interested in those things that Grand-father and Two Bears have found necessary to share with us."

Picking up both of the poles with the food, Cheeway and I sat them to one side of a small stone next to the water. We both knew that much of this weight that was coming from them was only being added by the water that had once been charged with cooking our food and had found a new place of resting.

As we set our sacks on the side of the stone, there was a great escape of water from both of them. And soon, they would be light enough for both of us to manage them very well and without too much difficulty.

"Cheeway...," I said, looking over him.

"You are all wet now, aren't you?"

"I can certainly see what Grandfather means when he tells us that he is very glad we can see the things that are in front of us, Speaking Wind," came the somewhat annoyed tone of Cheeway's voice.

"Of course I am wet. Each time I would try to lift

one of the food sacks out of the water, that small dragonfly would buzz my face and cause me to drop them back into the boiling pool.

"But why do you make such a comment, Speaking Wind?"

"Well...I was outside sitting on a very good place, Cheeway. And as I was sitting there, I could see the top of our camp place from my ledge."

"I am glad to hear that, my brother, but what does that have to do with my being all wet?"

"If you are only half as hungry as I am, Cheeway, then you would be willing to see a quicker way back to the camp place, wouldn't you?"

"Of course I would, but both you and I know the path we came up here on. And it is not very long...especially since we will both be going downhill from here."

Thinking for a few moments, Cheeway looked over to me and said,

"You have found a quicker way back to the camp, Speaking Wind, haven't you?"

"Yes, Cheeway...yes I have and it would be a great journey for us to take. One that will remind both of us of our own child within.

"Do you want to come with me?" I asked, picking up one of the sacks and placing it over my shoulder.

"First tell me how we will be traveling. I do not want to make a decision on only a partial knowing."

"When I was looking over to the place where Grandfather and Two Bears are waiting for us, I could see that the warm stream runs next to it. And, if we were to slide down one of these openings that comes from this boiling pool, we would be able to float our way down to them.

=⊕=

"What do you think, Cheeway...are you willing to come with me?"

"Yea!" came his return.

"It sounds like we will have a great time. After all, the food we are carrying will not get any wetter, will it?"

With our speaking words finished, we both strapped the sacks of food to our backs and walked over to the opening I had shared with him that opened up to the flowing waters that would take us back to where Grandfather and Two Bears were waiting.

We both sat down on the edge of what appeared to be a large stone slide. One that had been formed by the passing of many minerals from the waters over the great stone. And, as we sat down, the force of the water behind us forced us into it.

Plummeting down this water slide, both Cheeway and I were making our sounds of enjoyment. Those sounds that are remembered well by the child that is within us.

Hitting the water, we had expected to sink all the way down to the bottom. Much to our surprise, however, we did not go any further than our shoulders and finishing our descent, we found that we were being held halfway out of these waters for the rest of the time.

Even if we had wanted to, I do not think either of us could have remained submerged for a long period of time. It was almost like laying on a bed of smooth and new grass. This was the feeling we were both receiving from this ride with the blessings of the water spirit.

Once we had adjusted to this new experience, we laid ourselves back and enjoyed the ride.

Placing our sacks of food on the front of our stomachs, we laid our heads back into the top of the warm running waters and looked up at the sky above us.

The flakes of snow were still coming down and as we continued to watch them, they would turn into the tears of the water spirit as they would feel the warmth from the rising steam of the flowing waters we were in.

How wonderful it was to be allowed to share such a great mystery with the Earth Mother and all of her children, I was thinking. Here we were being allowed to float down one of the rivers of life and being supported by the very life that was within it itself.

This must be how one feels as they enter the red path from the blue path of spirit. As they find their own way through the great golden doorway that opens for them onto this red path of life.

However, my thoughts were cut short when we heard the calling voices of Grandfather and Two Bears from the shore next to us.

"If you will not stop your playing with these children, little ones, then I am afraid that we will all continue to get much hungrier."

Both Cheeway and I looked to the sound of the calling voice and could see that we had already come to the place of our camp.

Seeing that both Grandfather and Two Bears were waiting for us to come to them...and with our sacks of food, we turned ourselves over in the water and swam in their direction.

Reaching the shore, it did not take either Cheeway or myself very long before we had gotten out of our wet clothes and into warming blankets we had brought with us.

We set our wet clothes over one of the stones near the sand. We knew that it would not take long for them to dry and, in the process, we would be getting dryer ourselves from the warmth of the sand beneath us.

"Come over here, little ones," Grandfather called.

"We have prepared your eating bowls and places under the tarp."

Neither of us needed any coaxing to respond to this bidding. For both of us were hungry enough to eat anything that had been prepared on this day. And before another speaking word could be spoken by either Grandfather or Two Bears, Cheeway and I were sitting next to them and waiting to give our thanks to those who had so willingly given up their own life path so we could continue ours.

GUARDIAN OF THE GOLDEN GATE

We had finished eating the dishes that had been prepared for us by the boiling waters of this land. As we all finished, we set our bowls to the side of ourselves and went into a short silence that would allow us to give our thanks to those brothers and sisters that had so willingly given up their life paths so that we might continue ours.

Sitting under the tarp, Cheeway and I were looking at the silence that was being carried by the falling snow. A silence that shared with all who could hear how the peace that is the Earth Mother's can fall over all things.

$$=\bigoplus=$$

The peace of being...of being on a land that was in such balance with her needs and all of her children was also filling us as well.

However, this did not last long because soon the speaking words of Grandfather and Two Bears had come to life once again.

"Tell me, little ones, came the beginning of Two Bear's speaking words.

"Tell us why both of you decided to jump into the steaming waters with all of your clothes on."

Looking up from the place we had been sitting in the silence of giving thanks, Cheeway and I looked over to the place where Grandfather and Two Bears were sitting.

"Well, Two Bears...," I began,

"Cheeway was already all wet and I wanted to return to this place quickly. So this is what our decision was. Since neither he nor the food could get any wetter and I wanted to return quickly, to follow in the steaming waters...well, this seemed to be the quickest return for both of us.

"And it also seemed to hold the most enjoyment for both of you as well?" was the questioning voice of Two Bears.

"Yes, Two Bears," was Cheeway's reply.

"This held a great amount of enjoyment for both of us. And...it was also a way of getting out of the boiling waters room so I would not be bothered by another of those pesky dragonflies."

When Cheeway mentioned the dragonfly, I could see Grandfather's and Two Bears' faces light up. There was actually a light that seemed to hold both of them and through it, they managed to smile at both of us.

=⊕=

"There was a dragonfly in the room with you?" Grandfather asked.

"Yes, Grandfather...," I continued.

"It was buzzing around Cheeway so much that it was causing him to drop the sacks of food back into the water. And each time he would do this, he would get wetter."

"Then what happened, Speaking Wind?" Grandfather asked.

"Well...when I entered the room with Cheeway, I saw the trouble he was in. I mean how wet he was getting from those efforts that were being hampered by this small one of the Earth Mother's children.

"However, when I was standing next to Cheeway, the dragonfly seemed to lose all interest in him and what it was he was doing. He only seemed to be interested in my presence then, and held himself in a stationary position in front of me.

"He was hovering in the front of my face and looking into me, Grandfather. It was giving to me a feeling similar to the one I had earlier this morning when this same event happened to.

"I mean...I really thought that this was the same dragonfly that had appeared to me just before you arrived to pick me up. But, I know this could not be...especially not in this weather."

"Why would you say this, Speaking Wind?" came the questioning voice of Two Bears.

"Because when this weather is like it is, Two Bears, these little ones are not active at all. They become like the bear...they only wish to sleep."

"So this makes three times you have been visited by this child of the Earth Mother?" Grandfather asked sitting in a very patient position now.

"I do not hold the knowing if it has been the same child that has come to me, Grandfather. But yes...yes, I have been visited by a child such as this one three times," was my response to him.

"And each time they have come to you, Speaking Wind, they have done much the same thing?"

"Pretty much, Grandfather. Each time they have stood before me and given me the feeling that they were looking within me to the place where my spirit resides.

"Is this important?" I asked, trying to hear what it was that was sitting behind all of these speaking words that were being shared with me at this time.

"It is important, little one," was Grandfather's reply.

"It is important because these little ones...the ones who have been coming to you, once held a great place among all of these children of the Earth Mother's. But now the place they hold is one of great honor. One that has allowed them to become one of the messengers and guardians of the great golden doorway. This golden doorway that is the only opening between the red path, or our life path...and the blue path, the path of the spirits of our ancestors."

"You mean they have lost much to gain this place among all of us in this domain?" Cheeway asked with his usual inquisitive tone of voice.

"Yes, Cheeway," was Grandfather's response to him.

"Dragonfly has given up much, but a lot that has been given up was only given up through their own ego and foolery.

"However, little ones, this small child of the Earth Mother—this one who has been tricked into changing itself into what we may see of him today—still has a great role in Great Mystery. One that is continually filled with honor and purpose.

"Do you both remember the teachings that have come to us from the Ancient Ones? Those teachings that share with us what meaning the medicine wheel has for us?" Grandfather asked, sitting in a comfortable position on the warming sands beneath us.

"When Cheeway and I heard these speaking words of his, however, we were not all that familiar with what those teachings had been. And in a reflection of this place of knowing, we silently shook our heads in a left to right manner so as to tell Grandfather that we did not hold this knowledge well that he was now willing to share with both of us.

"Well, now would be a good time to share this with both of you. By returning to these teachings, it will make more sense to you how this little one called the dragonfly...this little one became the guardian of the great doorway.

"It is from the teachings that were shared with our ancestors by the Anasazi that we have come to know of the medicine wheel. And this term of medicine wheel is one that applies to all things that will come to us, as well as to all of those efforts we are willing to spend our time on.

"The medicine wheel is set into the four directions. These are the directions of the South, West, North, and the East. And each of these directions holds the meaning of what there is for us to learn from.

"First, there is the South. This direction of the wheel contains a teacher and it has been known by our people as the Coyote or the trickster.

"Because this teacher is the trickster for this direction, we are to be aware of the many things that can come of our talents and direction of finding if we take them too lightly and attempt to play with them. If we do this, then we might very well be tricked out of learning anything that will be of value to our spirit's advancement while we are traveling on this direction.

"The color of this direction has been shown to us as one that is red. And this color of red is significant of the child that is within all of us. This child that we all wish to know, but this child that has become so unreachable to many who have crossed our life paths.

"You see, little ones, this child of the south direction on the medicine wheel...there is a very special part to it. One that bears sharing at this time.

"When we are all in our younger seasons with the Earth Mother, we cannot wait to grow up and become the adult that is seen through all of our eyes.

"When we will see the adult from the eyes of our young selves, we will only see that they have many more rights to their life path than we do. That they can do almost anything they want to do and at almost any time they will wish to do this.

"So when we are of short seasons with the Earth Mother, we are in a great hurry to become this adult that we see. And in this process, many will be willing to forget their child part of themselves so they will not be held up on their way to becoming this adult that they believe will bring to them great happiness.

"However, when they finally arrive at this place of becoming the adult they wanted, they find it is not at all what they had anticipated. That there are many more responsibilities for them. And within these responsibilities comes more control over them. More of this control over them than they had as the child.

"And, when they become this adult, there is so much that will come over them, so many things they will have to do in order to maintain their place that they will feel trapped and come to believe that the child within them is dead. That it had only lived with them when they were short of season.

"But this believing is like a false spirit, little ones. It is like a false spirit because it holds no truth.

"What they will find in this place of the adult, in this place they had always wanted to arrive at, is that while there is not the same kind of limitations that had been set on them when they were the child, there are many more responsibilities that will come over them. Responsibilities that will come to them from the ones who will wish to control them. To control them so they will be able to fit into the world they have decided for them already.

"You see, little ones, because there is so much controlling in being the adult in this domain, there is not any room for growth and there is a great amount of restrictions that are placed on all who would buy into this way of life for themselves.

"So, they will sit in the place of being the adult they always wanted to be and believe that there is not any path for them to follow for happiness. No path for them to return to the child they once were. And this comes to them from their own way of looking at things.

"They will see this child they had once been only through the eyes of the others. And those eyes tell them that this place of their child is locked into a time that is no more. A time when they were of short season with the Earth Mother. And to try to return to this place is impossible because one cannot lose their number of seasons they have with them.

"But I will tell both of you that this is not true. It is not true because the child that is ourselves is not locked in a place or a time. It is only locked within ourselves, and in order for it to emerge once again, we only have to be willing to accept it. And once we will accept it from within us, it will emerge and come to live with us once again.

"Remember, little ones...remember these speaking words that I am willing to share with both of you. Remember them and keep them in the front of your thinking minds.

"When one will take the child that is within them, they will grow. For the child will in truth grow in this life path but the adult will only grow old and nothing more will come to them.

"So it is that this color of red has been assigned to the south of the medicine wheel and it is good. For the color red is also the color of the child within each of us and signifies the place of innocence, faith, trust, and humility. All of those attributes that the child within us possesses.

"As it is with this south position of the medicine wheel, it signifies the point of our beginnings. The place that all of us must begin our quests and tasks from. But we will not be able to begin any of them unless we will learn how to become our own child once again. And if one will attempt at beginning anything of value to the spirit from the place of the adult, there will not be any forward movement for them. There will only come to them a feeling of frustration and non-belief for what they are attempting to do.

"You see, little ones, from this beginning place on the medicine wheel, this place of beginning, if one attempts to start from their adult place, then all of those attributes that I have shared with you will come to them in the exact opposite. And because of this, they will not find any advancement...any advancement at all.

"The next point on the medicine wheel is the direction of the West. And this is the second place you will encounter for those things that will be started on your path of questing for the Earth Mother.

"It is in this point on the medicine wheel that we find our second teacher...the Bear. The Bear is significant of the color black and black is symbolic of the female energy. The energy that is common among those who would take the time to find their own place of introspection or thinking within themselves.

"You see, little ones, this second place that is on the medicine wheel is one that those who travel the path of the others say is bad and evil and should not be looked for or tasted.

"And for this, there are many reasons. Many more than I am willing to share with you on this day.

"But the major reason for this is that it is the totem of the female energy and for the last age of the Earth Mother, this female energy has been a major enemy of the ones who have been given permission to travel here and to learn.

"This female energy is one that will be prominent in the next age that the Earth Mother is about to enter...but this is getting away from the point I am wanting to make. The point of explaining what it is that this female energy is all about.

"The color black has been considered to be an evil

color of the others. And it has been considered to be evil because there has not been any understanding for what it brings with it. However, if there had truly been a good understanding of what it held within it, I am afraid that there would have been great efforts at eliminating this color from all things that had been known. For within it, there is not evil at all...but there is a great strength and power.

"It is a strength and a power that cannot be controlled by another and this is the major reason for it to have been considered evil.

"Think over this for a moment, little ones. Do you see any evil from your own mothers? Do you see any evil in the way that the children of the Earth Mother take care of their young? Do you see any evil in the Earth Mother herself?

"All of these things are significant of the color black. This second place that is to be found for all who will encounter the path of the spirit and travel the medicine wheel.

"Now, little ones, think well on the attributes of the female energy that is within this domain. This is the energy that is willing to allow all things to be. In doing so, will then take them back to a place where they can look at and study to see what significant value to their own spirit these offerings hold.

"This is the place that comes to the Bear each winter and while the bear will sleep, many events that had come to it are reviewed and learned from. And they are done in such a way that there are no others around to tell the bear what those events and lessons should mean.

"This allows for the freedom of the spirit within each of us to learn well from all events that will come to us. And this does not hold any place for another who would control us or try to make them like they would wish for us to be.

"You see, little ones, it is not the color black that is evil to the others, to the ones who would wish to control all of those things that you will do or become. It is what it represents and that is the female energy of allowing all things to be and then to take time in the within place of the spirit to see what it is that has been offered.

"This is what has created this illusion of evil for all things that hold to them the color black. But I will tell each of you that unless you will come to see these things that I am willing to share with you clearly...then I am afraid that you will not be allowed passage from the second point on the medicine wheel of life to the third. And this is where you will remain until you have ended the seasons you have been given to travel in this domain that is the Earth Mother's.

"Now the third point on the medicine wheel comes in the direction of the North. And this, too, is a very significant point to learn from for it is the point of the wise ones. Those who have been with our people for many generations and have shared with us the light of direction from the council fires of our ancestors and the Ancient Ones that we call the Anasazi.

"The color that is associated with this point on the medicine wheel is white. This is the color of all colors because in it all colors blend to create this white. But to try to see the separate colors within this one makes one look very foolish because no one who is on the two-legs can do such a thing.

"But this is a truth that has come to us from the old ones. And it tells us that this is what is to be in a time that is not yet born to this domain. That all of those who are now among us...and especially the ones who see so many differences among all of the children of the Earth Mother...will soon come to a time when these differences will not be seen. That all of those things that had once been seen as a difference will not be taken away, but they will be married into all things. They will be married into all things and will make one new oneness. And this new oneness will be such that no one may ever see a difference, or the way things were once before any longer.

"Now this point that I am willing to share with both of you on the medicine wheel...this point that is to the north, it is the place of the elders of the blue road or path of our people. It is here that many of the grandfathers and grandmothers reside and they will wait for their own family members to arrive there. They will wait for them to have been willing to work their way through those other two points on the medicine wheel in order to reach this third one. This third point of the wise place.

"And when they will see the arrival of those other members of their spirit family, they will greet them with a great smile. For they have the wisdom to share with them when they will have reached this place of being. This place where they, too, have passed many tests on their life path and will have the understanding within them to understand the speaking words of the wise ones now.

"For you see, little ones, it is by passing through the first two points on the medicine wheel that you will gain in your wisdom. This wisdom that will have come to you by learning to work your way through the many events that had been offered to you. Those events that had come to you in a way of seeing if you were of strong enough spirit to pass through the first two points.

"And as it is with all things that are in this life path, there is no thing that will ever come to you...there is nothing that will ever happen to you that will be by accident. For all of those things you have gone through, they have come to you so that you may learn from them. So that you may come to a place of understanding the value and strength of your spirit. And when you will have come to this place of understanding, you will have the knowing that will share with you that all is important...that all life is living and that it has a place among Great Mystery. That it is not only you who holds a place of importance in this or any other domain, but you are only a part of the whole and it is this whole that we must travel with and in balance if we are to find our way.

"The totem animal in this place of the north is the Buffalo. And this child of the Earth Mother's teaches us wisdom and gratitude, two speaking words that are like the white color as well.

"If one will discover wisdom, then there will always be gratitude accompanying it. For one does not travel without the other....this is something that is just not possible.

"When you will see one who will call themselves a wise one, and they will not hold the sense of gratitude for those things that have come to them. When they will not hold the gratitude of sharing with all who will come to them those things that have been shared with them is what I mean for both of you to hear. They will not have found the wisdom they have professed to have attained. They will only have found a place of seeing a part of the truth they have been seeking. And without the gratitude of this understanding, they will seek to hide it away and not allow another to see or to know about it. This is done by them in a way of trying to hold onto it. But keep in the front of your thinking minds little ones, that when one will try to hide or hold onto anything, then in truth, they have nothing at all and these are the ones you must learn to keep away from, for they will only hold you back on the path you have been willing to travel.

"For when both of you have reached your full growing seasons, you must always remember this. That when it is the right time for both of you to begin this sharing that you have entered this domain to perform, then all of the fences will have been taken down. And you must not hold onto the ways of the past, those same ways that have shared with our ancestors that they must hide from the whites and the outsiders all of those things we have come to learn from the old ones.

"When this time will come to both of you, you must not keep from any who will come to have the eyes and ears of their spirit to see and hear with any of those things that have been shared with you. You must be willing to share openly when this time will come.

"Do not be fooled by those who would listen to the speaking voices of the past. The ones who will try to tell you that to be open with yourself and those teachings that have been shared with you, that they should be kept behind closed doors. Remember to listen to the old ones who are with you and hear them in what they are willing to share with not only you but

=⊕=

with all who are willing to listen. This will be the place of the white light...the time when all may be shared freely.

"Go among them in this time, little ones. Go among all of them and do not hold anything back. For there will no longer be anything left to fear...the times for that will have been over.

"Now, the ones who will come among you and will profess themselves to be grateful, the ones who will say this to many, but you will not see any wisdom come from them. Then these, too, are the ones you would do well to keep away from. For they have not yet seen anything to be grateful for. They are only holding a blanket over themselves in hopes that there will not be any other who will see them. For in the front of their thinking minds, they have come to believe that if another will ever see them for who and what they are...then they will hurt them.

"These will be the ones who will hide behind themselves and this profession of being grateful for all that will come to them. But to be grateful without having attained the wisdom of what it is to be grateful for, well...this is just not possible. For the ones who would do this would have another plan in the front of their thinking minds and it is most always one that will not serve any good for the spirit.

"So it is, little ones, that the ones who profess to have found wisdom but do not have the gratitude...they have not found wisdom at all. They are still seeking those things they have professed to have found. And the ones who profess to be grateful for many things, but do not possess the wisdom that should accompany this, well...they have not found the spirit of gratefulness at all. They are only fooling themselves and those who would listen to them. For they have something entirely different in them than what they are willing to share with you.

"And when you will come among any of them, little ones, remember that they are still asleep within the illusion and give them their room and time to awaken. For even some of them will do this.

"However, little ones, you will not find any of them at this place we are sharing on the medicine wheel. They will not have been allowed to pass the first point because they have not been willing to learn from those things that have been presented to them on their life path.

"Now, on this third point of the medicine wheel you will find the totem animal or child of the Earth Mother to be Buffalo. This is the child of abundance and this abundance comes to this one because within this spirit lies the wisdom and gratitude for all of those things that have been offered to it. All of those great lessons that have been shared...it has learned from.

"For this child who has been given this third point of the medicine wheel, this child is one who will have prosperity follow him wherever he will travel. And all of those he will touch, they will feel this goodness that will come to them from his wisdom and gratitude.

"They will feel this abundance and will know the color of it is white and it will be good.

"Now there is a place that is connecting the third and fourth points of the medicine wheel, little ones. And it is a place that would do both of you well to remember and understand.

"It is a place of seeing all of those things that had

once been before you and the valuable lessons they have held before you to learn from.

"This is the place our ancestors have named the Trail of Spirits from the Red Path to the Blue Path of the Spirit.

"It is in this place...this place that is in-between the North position and the East position on the medicine wheel that this will take place. And on this place, there will be many who will be seen as having a sad face to wear but some will have a good one over them as well.

"What takes place on this place that I am willing to share with you is this. When all three points of the medicine wheel have been successfully traveled through, there will come a time in all life paths when they will be called on by their other members of their spirit family to prepare.

"They will be called on to prepare for the times that are about to come to them. And these times are those of completion. Either a completion of their life path, or a completion of another circle that has been on their life path in this domain.

"But for whatever reason their preparing has come to them, they will be seen in a place of reviewing. A place where they are offered a chance to review all of those things they have accomplished as well as all of those things they have turned away from.

"It is during this place on the medicine wheel when all who will encounter this review will be the closest to the east point. This last point that is located on the medicine wheel of life, little ones.

"And it is at this east point where you will find the last place I have been willing to share with you. This last place where the Great Doorway lies that is the opening to the Blue Path of Spirit as well as the opening for the Red Path of our earth walk.

This same doorway has been left to the little one that had come to you. This one we have come to call the dragonfly, or the guardian of the Gate Way.

"But, before I will go on, let me take a little more time to explain what is at this last point of the medicine wheel. For what will be shared on this last place has an equal weight of importance to it as well.

"The Ancient Ones have shared with us that it is in this east point of the medicine wheel that is the home of Eagle and it is the place of illumination for all things that have or will ever come to you.

"This is the color of yellow that is over this last point of the medicine wheel. Its color is a reminder of the mirror of the Great Spirit that is in the day sky. Yellow is a reminder of the promise that was made to us of those things that will soon return. As it is with those things that are on their way back to this domain, this return of warmth over the face of the Earth Mother promises continual growth so that life may continue to learn from all those events that will come to it.

"In this last place on the medicine wheel, little ones, this east point, this is where we have come to know the home of Eagle. And the reason for this is what has been found there is only found in its natural state with Eagle. In all others, this awareness must be earned by working our way to it.

"Eagle is known to our people as the connection to the Great Spirit. He has the ability of living in the realm of spirit and maintaining his connection and balance in this domain of the Earth Mother's at the

=⊕=

same time.

"For Eagle, there is seemingly no difference in those places and he keeps the doorway open by allowing us to see how easily it can be traveled through.

"The feathers of Eagle are considered by our people to be the most sacred of healing tools.

"Eagle represents a state of grace achieved through hard work, understanding, and a completion of the tests of initiation which result in the taking of one's personal power. It is only through working our way through all of the events that will come to us that we will ever know Eagle for who and what it is in truth. Only when we will be able to see through the emotions of all events and see their faces of truth and lessons they will bring to us that we will learn of the path of Eagle."

Grandfather paused in sharing his speaking words with Cheeway and me. We both knew what it was he was doing. He was looking into our within places to see if we had been able to keep up with all that he had been willing to share with us.

However, as Grandfather looked into each of us for these signs, he was sure to find a question, one that was forming in the front of my thinking mind.

But as was always the case with either Grandfather or Two Bears, we would always have to surface our own questions to them, even if they had already seen them.

They had explained to both of us that this was for a specific reason. That reason was to allow each of us learn how to speak to ourselves.

They had each taken great care to explain this to Cheeway and I because they would continually remind each of us that the ones who would need our speaking words would not all be at the same place Grandfather and Two Bears had found. From our eyes we had worked to achieve these high places on this path of the spirit.

So, as Grandfather finished looking into each of us, he sat back and made his intentions known to both of us. He was finished for the time being with explaining the medicine wheel of life and was now ready to answer the question that he had seen. He would be willing to answer it if I were willing to make my own efforts in bringing it out from within me.

"Grandfather," I began, adjusting my sitting position on the warming sand.

"Yes, little one...what is it that I may offer you assistance on?" came his return.

"It is on two things, Grandfather. First, there is the medicine wheel of life you have explained to both of us and there is this small one called dragonfly."

"What is it that you are needing assistance on then, Speaking Wind?"

"Well...the medicine wheel of life. This has been a good explanation for it, Grandfather, but there is still a part of all of it that I do not quite understand."

"Perhaps your own speaking words on it may assist me in clearing your vision, little one. Would you care to share these things with us now?"

"Yes, Grandfather...I would.

"As you have been willing to share the meaning of the medicine wheel of life with us, I have received many pictures of its meaning. Pictures that I have recognized were coming to me from my spirit. From my spirit because it was being spoken to by many during this time," I shared.

"This is very good, little one. You have remembered that there is no one who is in this domain that has been given more than they can do. And in doing those things that have come to them, when they are assisted by their spirit, they will come to be seen as great blessings among many. And you have done well to take the self out of the speaking words you have shared.

"It is only when the self is placed into those things that are being shared with you that you will find a great fall waiting for you. A fall that will be placed in the front of you to remind you that for all of these things you have...that they have not come to you to make you look great. But they have come to you because you have been willing to do the required work of preparing in order to allow them to come to others through you.

"This is good, Speaking Wind...this is good and will save you many hard times. Times that would not be needed if you will continue to keep this in the front of your thinking mind.

"But I believe that I am getting away from the first question you have wanted to share with us, aren't I?"

"It is alright, Grandfather, for all of those things that you or Two Bears choose to share with us bring a great blessing to each of us."

"So what is that you are wanting to ask, Speaking Wind?"

"It is the medicine wheel, Grandfather. I do not know if it is applicable to our daily life paths or only to the overall life path that we come to share with the Earth Mother."

"What do you think it is making reference to, little one?"

"Well...I can see how it applies to both, Grandfather. I can see how it applies to all of those things we will come to do each day of our life path as well as how it applies to our entire life path. I can see this because when I think on it, I see us moving in a continual direction. A direction that will bring us to each of the five places you have described to us. And I can see this same movement for each day we have been given to travel through.

"Even in the daily applications of this medicine wheel of life I can see how I have traveled through each of the events that have come to me. And how I traveled through the four directions before I had received the clarity of lesson I had been looking for.

"So then, this is my question, Grandfather. Is this medicine wheel of life applied to the overall life path or is it applied only to daily events?"

"You have done well to look so deeply into yourself, Speaking Wind. And, you have already returned with an answer. Do you know what this answer you have already given to yourself is?"

"It is that the medicine wheel of life applies to both of them, isn't it?" was my response.

"Yes, little one...this is the face of truth that you have seen from within you. And for this, you can hold your head in a good position.

"Now then, what is the second question of yours?"

"It has to do with the little one called the dragonfly, Grandfather. I can see from those things you have been willing to share with us how great this position he holds is, but I do not have a knowing of how he has been given this place among so many other children of the Earth Mother."

"Very well then, I will take this time to share more insight with both of you. And Speaking Wind, keep in the front of your thinking mind that this is not done for idle conversation. It is done because there is a great reason and this reason resides within you," Grandfather stated.

"For there is something that is calling to you, little one. That is why we are making these efforts. Something that will hold a great weight to all who are within this domain of the Earth Mother's. Something that you are being asked to take up on this life path you have been willing to travel," came the speaking words of Two Bears.

"But for now, little one, I will assist you in coming to understand a little better what this small one called dragonfly is. And it will hold a great weight of importance to you since you have already seen him as messenger three times. And these three times are important because he will usually only come to us once," came Grandfather's answer.

As I was listening to these speaking words come to me from Grandfather and Two Bears, I was beginning to feel the expectation of something coming to me come back to life.

During the time that had been spent in speaking of the medicine wheel of life, those feelings and thoughts had left me. But now...now that we had come back to them through our speaking words, I was beginning to feel my body begin to tremble slightly once again.

RETURNING TO THE CHILDREN

I was feeling the weight of importance of those things that had come to me, especially from the little one called dragonfly. I was beginning to feel the weight of importance that had been given to this one from the Earth Mother. This weight he had accepted of "the messenger" as his part of the balance of all life paths.

However, as I was looking for those things that were within me so that I could hold a better understanding of what was taking place within me, I heard the calling voices of Grandfather and Two Bears. They were calling to both Cheeway and me that there was something we would have to do before this sharing would take place.

Looking over at Cheeway, I could see that he had found his place next to me as I was trying to understand something that had come to me.

In all of the seasons we had to share together, this was one event that each of us held a knowing for; and that was whenever either of us would find this place called uncertainty, one of us would always find a place to sit or stand next to the other. In this way, we would assure each other that we were still there.

Rising to the call of Grandfather and Two Bears, I was feeling this thankfulness for my best friend...Cheeway. And as he began rising, he was looking over to my standing place and shared with me a face of his I have come to know well. A face that shared with me that he too was in a thankful place for being able to be my friend...and I his.

But now, we had run out of time for this kind of thinking. We were being expected to attend to those things that Grandfather and Two Bears had called on us to do. And we could feel the weight of their calling with each passing moment of time that we did not respond to them.

Reaching the place where they had been waiting for us, Cheeway and I were surprised to see each of them holding a sack. Each held one of the sacks we had brought back the food in from the pool of the boiling waters.

"We have prepared a sack for each of you, little ones," came the opening of speaking words from Two Bears.

"In this way, each of you will have something to return to the Earth Mother for all she has been willing to share with you."

"And, for those things that are about to be shared, you will each have an opportunity of returning the blessing," Grandfather followed up.

Finishing their speaking words to each of us, they handed us our own sack.

"Go to the far side of the heated waters, little ones. There you will find the place where there are many squash and corn children growing. In this place you will each place...not throw...the contents of your sacks.

"This is our way of returning those things that these children of the Earth Mother have a need for, especially since many of them are only now coming out of the sleeping season (the winter) and need much energy.

"However, when you place this offering of ours, you are not to eat any of those things that have been planted, for they are just as sacred to these children as your spirits are to yourself.

"In this valley, there are no longer any sleeping seasons for any of the growing ones. The balance in this part of the Earth Mother's domain has been restored to what it once was before the first world and our arrival in it.

=⊕=

"As you would honor the spirit, these children honor these blessings that have been planted here by our wise ones for many generations. And, they only take what they need and leave the rest for another. For one who would also come to this land with a need such as theirs.

"When you have finished placing these small pieces of food from our meal then return to this place. Return to this place of the warming sand and we will begin to share with each of you the song legend of our people that will tell you both of this small one called dragonfly...the messenger and guardian of the doorway to Great Mystery."

Cheeway and I both took our sacks and wandered beyond the covering of the ceremonial tarp that had been stretched over our camp place. And, as we left the sheltering of the large tarp, we were both reminded of the playfulness of these small ones we had come to know as snowflakes.

Both of us took a great joy in trying to catch one in our mouths because it reminded us of the transformation that is ever constant in this domain that is the Earth Mother's. This ever constant change that we have come to know as our life paths.

As we would feel the snowflakes melting within our mouths, we would be reminded of the many teachings that had been shared with us by Grandfather and Two Bears. Teachings that allowed us both to see that where there was no change...there would be no growth. And in this process of melting these small snowflakes in our mouths, we felt as if we were assisting them in their transformation that would allow them to enter the realm of the water spirit's tears. Those same tears had always been held very sacred by our people because of their knowledge of the shortage of them in future times.

However, as we both were continuing to catch these small snowflakes in our mouths, we were finding that keeping our balance over these lands was a chore. We had each taken many spills on the other side of the steaming water stream and had become covered with mud that was now very thick.

"It is a good thing we will have to cross through the steaming waters before we get back," Cheeway uttered to me in a rather muffled sounding voice.

"Why do you say that, Cheeway?"

"Well, it is just that I think that Grandfather and Two Bears would really laugh at both of us if they saw us coming to them in this way...covered with all of this mud and all."

When Cheeway had finished his speaking words...the ones that I had found very difficult to understand because of his muffling them, I turned from my position to look at him.

When I did this, I fell once again because I was not prepared to see what was before me.

Looking at my best friend, I thought that he had been replaced by a poor looking replication of a Kachina. From all of the falling, he had been completely covered with mud from his head to his toes. And from keeping his mouth open as he was trying to catch these small snowflakes, it appeared as if he were wearing a mud mask with an open fish mouth.

And to top it off, there were many twigs and sticks that had stuck to him as well. This gave him the appearance of a walking stick man covered in mud.

Falling onto the ground laughing, I noticed that when Cheeway looked at me that he, too, repeated my actions. And within a very short time, both of us were laying in the mud laughing at each other so hard that we could not move.

However, from the back of our thinking minds, we were reminded that we had come here for another reason. And that was to make this offering of a portion of our food for the small ones of the Earth Mother so that they, too, could enjoy a portion of the blessing that had been shared with us.

"It is good to see you laughing once again, Speaking Wind," Cheeway said, still laying among the sticks and mud.

"It feels good to laugh once again my brother," was my return.

"Are you still feeling the heaviness of those things that have been filling you for the past two days?" asked Cheeway

"Yes, Cheeway. Yes, I am still feeling their weight over me and I will be glad when I will see the understanding for them so that I may be rid of their weight. It is like something that is coming at me but I cannot see it and it seems to be growing in me—growing within me as if it were about to explode.

"I am sure that you will see this lesson soon, my brother," was Cheeway's reassuring response to me. As was always the case between us, he had managed to find a way of relieving some of the weight that I had found from whatever it was that was trying to come to me.

"It is good that our paths are so close, Cheeway."

"Yes, Speaking Wind...it is good."

Picking ourselves up from the mud and sticks, we shook as much of this mud off from our food sacks as was possible and continued in the direction of the planted garden for the small ones of the Earth Mother.

Having reached this place, we both unpacked the contents of our sacks and placed them on what appeared to be eating stones, flat stones that had been placed among the growing corn and squash on this land.

Once this had been accomplished, we each sang our thanking songs to the spirits of the land and asked their assistance in letting the children of the Earth Mother know of this offering for them. When we finished this, we began our journey back to the warming sands where Grandfather and Two Bears were waiting for us.

Cheeway had risen before me and had already begun his journey into the stream of the steaming waters. I was not as quick and whether it was because of the weight of these events that had been coming to me or from the weight of those things that were now in the front of my thinking mind, I was moving slowly behind my best friend.

I was thinking of those things that had been shared with me by Grandfather, those speaking words of his that held such a great weight of truth for me...especially now.

"When one will find a friend on this path of the spirit, this path of the spirit that we share together, then it is not only a friend they will find that will come to them, little one...it will be their family and this will fill their hearts for all time that is with the good that is from the Great Spirit himself."

Walking behind Cheeway, these were the things I was thinking on. And, as had always been the case with those things that had been shared with me by Grandfather, this, too, was true. I could feel the caring from this one I had come to know and call my best friend Cheeway and the feeling of having been blessed with such a friend was filling my heart greatly.

However, my attention was soon taken from Cheeway and placed on the standing people of this land. They have always been one of the great keys to opening the doorway to our within place. These ones have always been so willing to share their peace and life force with all who would come to them.

I was wondering how many of us two-legs had gone to them and received their assistance in our time of need. How many of us had gone to them and had been accepted but we did not hold the understanding for what it was they had shared with us.

As I was thinking on these things, I silently began to sing to them a prayer of gratefulness, one that would allow them to see that I was one who understood.

Singing this silent song prayer, I was looking up to the tops of the standing people and could see the cascading of snowflakes coming down over these lands as they would leave their home in the gray white clouds above us to find another home on the face of the Earth Mother.

All of this was causing me to fall into a silence of belonging, for the longer I sang my prayer song and watched the falling snowflakes, I found myself falling into the oneness that was so present on these lands. This oneness that is all life to share because we have all begun from the same spirit.

Just as I was beginning to find myself floating in this feeling of being accepted by these children, my thoughts were cut short by the yelling of Cheeway. From the sounds he was making, I knew he required my immediate attention.

"Aiee haa!" came his voice over the sounds of the steaming waters that were passing me by on the far bank.

When my eyes reached the place he was yelling from, I could see that he had already reached a place in the steaming waters where he was submerged up to his waist. And he was standing very still and continuing to yell.

Seeing this as a sign of his being in trouble, I dropped my empty food sack and rushed into the steaming waters to grab him and pull him to what I considered to be a safer place from whatever it was that had come to him.

Jumping into the steaming waters, I could see there was only his head and shoulders above the waters now, and they were both covered with the mud of the lands as well as many twigs sticking out of his hair that gave to him the appearance of some kind of deer or bison.

Reaching him—this place that was in the steaming waters, I grabbed his shoulders and began pulling him out.

However, just as I was making these attempts at taking him out from this place, he began to shout at me. I took it to mean that he was still being attacked by something that was under the water we were both in.

This filled me with a great feeling of excitement, one that gave me more strength than I would have normally had. This extra strength allowed me to bring Cheeway and myself out of the water with such a force that we seemed to fly out of it and hit into the mud that was next to the shore.

=⊕=

Feeling that I had delivered my friend out of the grasp of danger, I leaned my head back into the cool mud beneath me and sighed with a breath of relief.

However, Cheeway did not share these same feelings with me and began to speak, once he was able to sit up from his position in the mud.

"Speaking Wind...," Cheeway began, "what were you trying to do with me?"

"What do you mean, Cheeway?" I said, rising from a laying position to a sitting one.

"I was trying to save you from whatever it was that was giving to you a fear. The fear that had caused you to yell in such a way."

"It is good to know that I am so well taken care of, my brother," Cheeway returned, chuckling to himself.

"But I was not in any danger at all...as a matter of truth, my brother, I was only playing with the water spirit when you came to pull me so quickly out of the steaming waters."

"But the yell, Cheeway...I heard this very surely. Did this not mean that you were in trouble?"

"Oh no, Speaking Wind. I was only calling on my own thunder spirit for the game that was being shared with me by this water spirit."

"I do not hold an understanding for these things you are willing to share with me, Cheeway. Could you perhaps make them a little more simple so I too may hold an understanding for this thing you are speaking of?"

"Of course, my brother," was Cheeway's response, sharing a smile with me through his face of caring.

"Do you remember how, when we were both of very short seasons on the lands of the mesa, how we would often go to the tops of one of the high places to see the arrival of one of the rain storms?"

Without breaking my silence, I nodded my head in an up and down motion that would share with him that I did remember these times of our youth.

"Well, remember how when the spirit wind would carry the water spirit over our lands and how the thunder spirits would announce this arrival?

"This is what I was doing, my brother. For when I entered this steaming water place, I looked down to the part of myself that was under it. And when I did this, I could see that so much of the mud that had collected on me was being washed away by this giving spirit of the water. And as it would begin to wash off of me, it was giving to me the same picture we had both seen many times from those high places on the mesa.

"It was as if I were the dry lands that were standing before the coming of the water spirit's blessings and for all of those places the tears of the water spirit would touch the dry lands, there would be a great cloud of dust rise as it would give thanks for this blessing.

"And as I would look at all of the mud being washed off from me, this was what I was living, too. For I had become the dry lands that were giving thanks for the blessings of the water spirit. And as I was giving them my thanks, I was calling on my thunder spirit to announce the arrival of another recognized blessing from the Earth Mother."

"It was this thanking of your thunder spirit voice that I heard, then, Cheeway?" I asked.

"Yes, Speaking Wind...this is what you heard."

"Well my brother, I hope that I did not disturb you

in a way that you will not be able to find your way back to this place of giving thanks once again."

"I do not believe this will become a problem for me, Speaking Wind. And if you will follow me back into the steaming waters, I am sure that you will find the same thing.

"Would you care to try?" Cheeway asked.

There was no need for additional speaking words from me, I only nodded my head up and down and followed Cheeway back into the steaming waters that were before us so that we could both give our thanks for this great blessing that had been given to these lands we had been allowed to share in.

It did not take very long for both of us to clean ourselves and the empty food sacks. And within a very short time, we were back on the warming sands where Grandfather and Two Bears were waiting for us.

Placing our clothes back on one of the warming stones, we once again placed our warming blankets over ourselves. When we had done this, we sat in a place that was just before both Grandfather and Two Bears and waited for those things they were about to share with us about this small one we had come to call dragonfly.

"It is good to see both of you have made it back in one piece, little ones," Grandfather said as he placed a warm smile over the face he was wearing for both of us.

"Are you ready to learn about dragonfly now?"

Wiping the water and hair that had come over our eyes, both Cheeway and I nodded our heads in an up and down motion. Grandfather knew that we were now ready to listen.

"Good, little ones, then I shall begin."

=⊕=

THE SMALL MESSENGER
FROM THE DOORWAY

Grandfather and Two Bears would always make sure that we were ready to listen to those things that were about to be shared with us, those things they had seen we held a great need for. For this kind of caring, both Cheeway and I were always very thankful.

Looking over to the place where both of them were seated, I saw the two in this domain who had been responsible for so much assistance for Cheeway and me. These two had taken the time to share with us and allowed us to know that the understanding we needed for all things resided within ourselves.

I was looking at the two who had found the time to raise us when there were no others who could. And I was being filled with a feeling of acceptance from both of them and for all that had come to me.

I was thinking over these events that had been coming to me over the past two days. These events had been making me feel very uneasy because of what they were holding within them and I had not yet reached the place of seeing them for what they were. I had only to look at those who were around me and I would feel better...I would feel the peace of belonging to the ones who had come to walk next to me on this path I had chosen to follow.

However, as I was thinking over these things, Grandfather had come to hear my thinking thoughts. And as was always the case, he reached into my within place and called me back to this place and this sharing so that I would be able to benefit from these speaking words he was now willing to share with Cheeway and me.

"Speaking Wind," came the response from Grand-father.

"It is good to pay honor to those who do honor to you. However, there will be many times in those seasons that are yet to be born to you when there will be made great amounts of time for this. But for now little one, it would be well to remain in the present. For there are great amounts of learning you must attain so that when the time will be right, you will achieve the needed understanding for them. This understanding that will lead you to your place of wisdom so that you, too, may share with the many."

As Grandfather finished these speaking words, I looked over to him and smiled. I nodded my head in an up and down motion and in return, both he and Two Bears returned my nod and smile as well.

"In all of the generations that have been with our people, Speaking Wind, the Earth Mother has helped many of us advance greatly. And now is the time when we have returned to her but on a different journey. It is a journey that is to be in assistance to her and not so much to ourselves," Two Bears began.

"However, many of the dreamers have seen this time coming and Grandfather and I have seen this time that is soon to be from our journeys into the silence as well.

"If you will come to pass the test that will be offered to you little one, then we will be able to offer this learning and wisdom to you, as well."

"What test do you speak of, Two Bears?" I asked with perked attention to his speaking words.

"It is a test that we may discuss more later, Speaking Wind. But for now, I believe that we were learning of dragonfly, weren't we?" Grandfather said.

"I was caught in the moment, my brother, please continue with your speaking words," Two Bears said, looking compassionately at Grandfather.

Hearing these speaking words come from Two Bears was not what I had needed to maintain my calm on this day. And as I listened to them once again, I could feel the sense of urgency rising within me once again, rising and turning over in the small part of my stomach.

Looking over to the place next to me where Cheeway was sitting, I could see him looking at me without any face of emotion at all but only nodding his head in an up and down motion. This shared with me that he, too, held this same feeling that something very great was about to be offered to me. But it was something that he would not be able to assist me in...something that I would have to do alone and this was not giving me an easy feeling.

With all of these thoughts in the front of my thinking mind, I was trying very hard to return to the speaking words Grandfather was waiting to share with Cheeway and me that would allow us to hold a better understanding for this small one called dragonfly.

Just as I turned my head back to the place Grandfather was sitting, I could feel this energy that was being built up within me from the not knowing begin to form a ball. It was forming a ball that would soon begin to bounce me in an uncontrollable motion, one that would not allow me to sit still very much longer if I would not take it into my control.

I managed to look into the eyes of Grandfather and could see that he, too, held the knowing of what was taking place within me.

Reaching over to my head with his right hand, he calmly spoke to me.

"It is gone now, Speaking Wind. Come back to us on this day and listen so that you will be able to learn."

As Grandfather said these speaking words to me, I felt a sudden wave of rushing wind travel through my entire body part and into my spirit part. And with the passing of less time than it would take to blink my eyes, this feeling was gone, and there was no trace within me that it had ever been there.

Feeling this removal of what I did not have a need for at this time was filling me with a new awareness of the role Grandfather had been given to share in this life path with us. And from the look that I could see in Cheeway, I knew that he too was holding this new seeing of Grandfather, as well.

Two Bears made the next move. He reached across from his sitting place and placed his right hand under Cheeway's open mouth. And, with a very gentle push, he closed it.

"Now that we are all back, little ones, I will continue," Grandfather's speaking words came to us across the life winds that had come to live among all of us.

"There was a time when this small one called dragonfly was great in size and many of our song legends tell us that the body part of this spirit was one of an actual dragon. A dragon that could fly and spit fire over an enemy.

"And for all of those things that had once been for this small one of today, none of the attributes have been taken away from it. Not even the spitting of fire.

"Think for a moment, little ones. Have you not felt the pain that can come to you from the spitting of the dragonfly?

"If you are bitten by dragonfly, you will think that he holds a great set of teeth within him because of what you will feel from his bite. But I share with you that he does not have any teeth any longer nor did he ever have them. What dragonfly has done to you is to spit on you and this has given to you the feeling of either being bitten or burnt.

"So for this part, the small one has not lost its power of the flame. This flame that will come to you from its mouth.

"However, in those many seasons of the past, those seasons when the earliest of our ancestors were walking in this domain, dragonfly was great in size and held the domain of the messenger and guardian of the great doorway well. But he was holding it with a sense of pride and it was this pride that had grown in him that opened the doorway to what he has now lost to himself.

"But before I get into this part of our song legend of how his transformation took place, I want you both to hold an understanding of what it is that still remains with this small one.

"When you look at dragonfly, you will see that there is a certain medicine that he brings with him. It is a medicine of the dreamtime and the illusionary parts many of us will come to accept as reality.

"For the time that has been given to this one, he has always allowed those who would have the eyes and ears of the spirit to see him for who and what he is in truth.

"Notice the iridescence of his wings and you will see many colors that are not to be found in our everyday experiences. Colors that do not match any

of those you are used to seeing, and colors that remind us of two great lessons.

"First, there are those who would travel on the
path of the others. This path that leads to the left and
is fed by the body and led by the emotions.

"When they will see these wonderful colors that
are within the dragonfly's wings, they will be reminded that they are still in pursuit of those things
they have been looking for through all of the seasons
of their life path. To them, the only things that are
worth pursuing are those things they have not yet
attained and these continual shifting colors that are in
the wings are a constant reminder that they still do
not have what they have been looking for. And this
will give to each of them a desire to grab for more and
more until they become exhausted and can go no
further.

"For them, there is only what has not been gained
by them that holds any real importance to them. And,
once they attain it, then they will just as quickly let it
go. For to them, it has lost its luster and no longer
brings to them a mystery. This mystery of their
looking in all places for those things they do not
understand...and for those things that come to each of
them continually but they cannot recognize. And,
they cannot recognize them because, in truth, they do
not know what it is they are looking for.

"However, for the ones who have found this path
of the spirit of our ancestors, this path that leads to the
right and is fed by the spirit and led by it as well, they
will see a complete different reminding when they see
the many changing colors that are within the wings of
the dragonfly.

"For they will see those things that are the remind-

ing of the many lessons that are located on their path.
On this path of the spirit.

"What they will see with their own eyes and ears
of spirit from the many colors that are ever changing
within the wings of dragonfly is what we are reminded of when we look with gratefulness at the
colors of the rainbow.

"We have come to know that the rainbow is a
creation of the Great Spirit and has been left for us to
see and enjoy. This creation is left to us as a reminder
of those many great and wonderful deeds that have
been performed by our ancestors...and ourselves.

"Those wonderful colors that are within it are
significant of the directions that I have been willing to
share with both of you that are found on the medicine
wheel, as well as a reminding of what path our spirit
can take. The direction is what I am referring to now.

"As it is with the colors of the rainbow, so it is with
the colors that are within the small one's wings. They
are to be admired and serve as a reminder to all of us.
But they are not to be chased or to be held. This is just
not possible and for those who would do such a thing,
they will spend all of the seasons that have been given
to them in chasing shadows that live in the dark...and
nothing more.

"So it is that this little one is a reminder of all those
things that are around us that will change constantly.
And it is because of all this change that comes into all
life paths that his medicine is very powerful for us to
observe and to remember.

"It is when we will become lost in the emotion that
we will want to have all things remain the same, little
ones. And it is only the very foolish that will come to
the place of believing this is even possible.

"If you will look at this small one called dragonfly, you will see a continual shifting of colors, energy, form, and movement. And when you follow this small one carefully, you will be reminded of a vague memory. One that shares with you a time or place where magic reigned.

"The song legends of our people tell us of a time when dragonfly was once a mighty dragon and that dragon had scales like the wings you now see on him today.

"And as it flew through the night, it brought light with its fiery breath which in turn brought forth the art of magic and the illusion of changing forms.

"However, as it is with all things that have been given power in this domain, if there is not an accompanying understanding of what this power is to be used for and the wisdom to do so, then there will certainly come a time when this power will turn on you. And when it will do this, there will be no going back. Back to the place you once were before this mistake came over you.

"And this is what happened to dragon, little ones. It happened to him because he forgot to remember who and what he was.

"The dragon got caught in his own facade and it was Coyote who tricked him into doing this.

"You see, little ones, it was on a day that was in the middle of the sleeping season for all of the Earth Mother's children when this happened. Coyote had been sitting under a sheltering place trying to get some sleep for the next day.

"Coyote knew that during the sleeping season when all of the domain of the Earth Mother is covered under the white blanket of snow that food would be scarce. And he wanted to save all of his energies so he could find enough to eat.

"However, just as Coyote had begun to go to sleep, dragon flew over him and began yelling in a loud enough voice so that it woke all of the children of the Earth Mother's.

"He made a point of telling Coyote that he was so powerful that he could keep the sun high in the sky so that no one would ever be able to sleep again if they did not do those things he wanted them to do. And this went for Coyote as well.

"Now Coyote knew of the power there was to find in the breath of dragon. And he knew that for short periods of time he could bring light and heat over the lands. But he also knew that in order for dragon to do this, he would have to set many of the standing people on fire, and if he would do this...then there would be no food for him to eat at all.

"Now, Coyote was not foolish and he continually lives up to his name of 'The Trickster.'

"He rose from his laying position that was under the rock and yelled back to dragon that he was sure he could do such a thing. In fact, he was so sure that dragon could do this that he was willing to make him a bet. A bet that if dragon could do something else, that he would make it his duty to assist dragon wherever he could if dragon would go along with him.

"Now dragon, hearing these speaking words of Coyote, left the sky he had been flying in and lighted next to Coyote. He was aware of Coyote's reputation of the trickster, but since he had been so sincere in his word, dragon knew that this was something that Coyote would not back away from. And if he were to win, then Coyote would assist him in all things he wanted to do.

"So, with this on the front of his thinking mind, he agreed to Coyote's terms and asked him what it was he wanted to challenge him with.

"Coyote told dragon that he had become very famous for all of his abilities. But there was one that he had heard of but had not yet seen and that was his ability of changing into another form. One that was so different from any he had ever heard him taking on before.

"With a loud laugh, dragon asked Coyote what form he would want him to change into, thinking in the back of his mind how easy this was going to be and that he would have Coyote for his servant for all time.

"Coyote drew a form in the sand that was beneath them and it looked exactly like the one dragonfly holds to him today. But, Coyote reiterated, the term of the change was to return to his original form and unless he would be able to complete the full circle of change then he would lose the bet.

"Dragon agreed to the terms and in less time than it took to draw one breath, he had magically turned himself into the dragonfly. However, once he had changed his form into this small one, he found that he no longer held the magical powers to change back into what he had once been.

"This then is how dragonfly has come to be who and what he is. However do not forget that from those times you will see him, he will be a constant reminder of how one will learn a lesson the hard way.

"Even now though this small one will carry great messages from the golden doorway that is on the east point of the medicine wheel of life, though his form has changed, his purpose has not and he is one of the messengers that should always be listened to.

"Dragonfly is the essence of the winds of change, the messages of wisdom and enlightenment, and the communications from the elemental world.

"Dragonfly medicine always beacons you to seek out the parts of your habits that need to be changed or at least looked at. And this will be needed by the one he will come to so they will have room to see and hear his message to them.

"This then is the song legend of dragonfly, little ones," Grandfather said as he sat back a little on the warming sands of these lands.

"Grandfather...," I said, placing the most sincere look I could find over my face.

"Yes, little one...what is it I may offer assistance to you on?"

"Dragonfly has come to me three times now and still I do not see what I need to change or even make room for within me."

"Dragonfly has come to you, Speaking Wind, carrying a great message. It is a message that if you will make yourself available for, we will then be able to assist you in coming to see it more clearly. However at the place you are at now, this cannot be done. It cannot be done because there is no room within you for this message."

"Do you have an idea of what it is you can do, Speaking Wind?" came the calling voice of Two Bears.

"Yes, Two Bears...I have an idea of what I should do."

"Then what will it be, little one? What will you do so that there will be room within you to receive this message that is waiting to be delivered?" Grandfather asked.

Looking intently at the places where Grandfather and Two Bears were sitting, I could hear only one word come to the front of my thinking mind. One word that shared with me the path that was being presented before me by my own spirit. The only path that would allow for growth of this kind.

"A vision quest, Grandfather. I hear this word come into the front of my thinking mind very loud now...a vision quest and here on these lands we share with the Earth Mother today."

"We have heard this calling for you as well, Speaking Wind...and, it is good," Two Bears began.

"We will take a short time to explain to you those things you will need on this path if you are to succeed. And I will share with you that I do see you succeeding, little one. And when you do this, you will come to know what it is that has been trying to come to you over these past two days," was Grandfather's reply.

"When you have finished this vision quest, little one," Two Bears continued, "we will find you and explain our part in this great mystery."

=⊕=

<u>CHAPTER TWO</u>

THE VISION

PREPARING

I did not know why I spoke the words "vision quest" to Grandfather and Two Bears, but for whatever reason, I knew this was the path that needed to be taken. This path would allow me to see what it was that was trying to come to me.

For the past two days and nights, there had been many events that had been just to the doorway of my thinking mind, and now it was my spirit that was leading me in the ways I had been prepared for. In the ways of the path of the spirit.

When I shared that it was a vision quest that would be needed by me, I felt as if a great piece of this weight I had been carrying had been taken away from me. And sitting in the front of Grandfather and Two Bears, I held the knowing that they, too, could see what had happened and it was bringing to them a good face to wear for me.

For a few moments of time, they were discussing things between both of them, and as was customary for them, when there were things they did not want Cheeway and me to hear about, they would use the speaking of their spirit thoughts with each other.

However, as both Cheeway and I had gained many experiences on our life paths and had achieved the understanding for many of them...we had reached a place where we could understand some of those things that they would share between themselves. And when they saw what it was we had been doing, they became very pleased.

It was during times such as these that they would tell us that this was the way we had all once spoken and it was nothing that was new to any of the two-legs. However, since the time of the great split, we had forgotten to remember how to do these things, and from this failure to learn it, we had lost our way of speaking to the children of the Earth Mother.

But Grandfather and Two Bears did not ever go into any in-depth explanation about this time. They would only look at us and say that it was good we were beginning to remember what all of us once had learned and would let it go at that.

Both Cheeway and I often asked them to explain many of those times to us, but each time we would bring it up they would always smile at both of us and say that when it was time for us to know, we would be told. And from having shared so many of our growing seasons with both of them, we knew that to pursue this any further would only be a waste of our time. For when they made up their minds, there would be no way of getting either of them to change.

However, even with our limited abilities, Cheeway and I could tell that they were both finished with their mental thoughts to each other. They were now ready to begin with their speaking words to both of us. Those speaking words that would allow me to see a little clearer what it was I had seen to do...begin the vision quest.

Waiting for the speaking words to begin, I was looking at the place where Grandfather and Two Bears were sitting.

They had positioned themselves between us and the valley below. And as they would sit and look into each of us, I could see the playfulness of the falling snowflakes behind them as they fell into the deep valley below where the two waters would fall into each other.

As the warming waters that came from the left and the cold waters that came from the right would meet and fall into the valley below, there was a continual rising of steam coming up. As the steam rose behind both of them, it would meet the falling snowflakes and turn them into water droplets.

Looking at this great space of air that was behind both of them...this air that would carry up the steam of the combining waters, I began to think how similar it was to how we had been prepared to send our prayers up in the smoke. We would place the picture of those things that we held a great need to understand into the smoke as it would rise from the fires of our people and into the sky nation's or star nation's home.

Looking at this rising of the steam behind them on this day, I was receiving the spirit picture of the Earth Mother sending her prayers up to the Great Spirit in much the same way. I was seeing a part of her face as she would embrace this steam and send her spirit pictures of those things that were needed in this domain of hers and allow them to rise into the sky nation where they would then be carried to the Great Spirit who would know of her needs.

=⊕=

Looking past this place that was behind Grandfather and Two Bears, I was allowing myself to fly into the rising of the great stone mountains that were all around us. And, as I would do this, I began to hear the faint calling of our ancestors' spirits. Those who had decided to remain on these lands in their spirit form so that they could assist in keeping the balance of all life here. In a way, this was their way of assisting the Earth Mother in keeping those things that were needed by her children...and herself.

However, my traveling was suddenly cut short by the calling of Grandfather's speaking words to me.

"Now, little one...if you would be willing to remain with us for awhile yet, I would be willing to share with you some of those things you will need. Some of those things that you will need to hold an understanding for about the vision quest you have seen for yourself."

Hearing those speaking words come to me from Grandfather, I readjusted my sitting position and tried to concentrate on those things that were about to be shared with me.

But there was so much that was continually reminding me of the peace that was to be found on these lands that I was really being put to the test.

The sounds of the falling waters over the sides of the cliff wall we were sitting on were calming. The sounds of the rushing waters in both of the streams were making me feel as if I could sleep on these lands forever. The sight of the falling snowflakes and the silence they brought with them was also another enticement of peace on these lands, and the calling of the gentle spirit winds over us as they would pass through the great standing people on the top of the

=⊛=

mountain rims all around us was also calling to my spirit to be still and be at peace with itself.

All of these things seemed to be calling to me to come and join with them in this balance of peace they had come to know so well and been so willing to share with those who had learned to listen to their calling voices.

But with the thoughts of what had been coming to me for these past two days, I found that this was my first calling. And if I did not find the understanding of those things that were trying to present themselves to me, then I would not ever come to know this peace I was feeling on these lands that was presently residing within me.

So with these things in the front of my thinking mind, I tried to place all of this behind me. I held the knowing that when my heart was in the right place, that this would no longer be an obstacle for me...and it worked.

Seeing that I had become successful in returning to this place of hearing, Grandfather continued.

"As you know little one, the vision quest is another form of teaching for our people. And it goes back further than the first gathering of the two-legs after the first separation of worlds.

"This vision questing is one of the oldest tools used by our ancestors who came to see their own need at finding direction to their life paths.

"When you ask spirit for the location, Speaking Wind, you will see a picture of a land that is waiting for you to arrive on it. And once you are there and have prepared your circle of the stone people, then you know there will have to be from one to four days that you will have to wait for your answer. The answer that you will send up in the smoke of our people's teachings.

"This quest that you are willing to take onto yourself will allow you to attain a higher level of understanding for your place that you are traveling. And Speaking Wind, I share with you that you are indeed at a split in the path. A split in the path you have willingly taken onto yourself.

"It is because of this split that has come to you, little one, that you are in need of this assistance and guidance of the old ones. For they are looking into your within place with a great gift. It is a gift that will benefit all who are within this domain of the Earth Mother's more than any other they have come to know of in this time of their traveling.

"Remember, little one, that at this time of the vision quest, Great Mystery will give the Sacred Medicine Helpers permission to come in vision form to you.

"They will come to you in vision form from the spirit that is within them. Within they who are the animals, the trees, the stones, the moon, the stars, the ancestors, and most especially of all...the Ancient Ones. Those who have been called by our people the Anasazi.

"Do not fear them, little one. For they come to you with the heart of goodness and direction. They are what you are in great need of to reach this place of understanding on the path you are traveling.

"Also, because Two Bears and I are of the medicine people, you will not be in any danger. For we will be with you to see that those things that you are in need of will arrive and those things that will only be of an inconvenience will stay away. This is another process that must be taken before you will ever be allowed to enter this domain of the old ones.

"Now when you see those things that are waiting for you to understand, you will know that you have been prepared well for them and see the ones who have come to assist you. They will make themselves known to you and you will come to know the ancestors who appear to you with the name of spirit ally or spirit guide. They will assist you greatly in the earth walk that you will see before you and they will lend to you their assistance so that you will find your way with clarity.

"When they will come to you little one, you will also be shown those things that you will have a great need for. For they will show to you all of those talents and abilities that your spirit has brought with it. And they will share with you the wisdom that you will need in order to use them well for those things you have come here to do.

"And when you will use these gifts properly, you will be allowed to see a new type of growth come to life from within you. A growth that will please you greatly.

"Remember, little one, that a vision quest is only one tool that is used by those who are seeking direction to their life path. Every time one will seek the spirit of silence, this is the spirit who holds dominion over this place, they will find a path that will lead them to the balanced heart and spirit within them.

"And from this process, they will see their own truth come to life from within them. And little one, truth is the final destination of any seeker's path.

"When truth is found inside of yourself, there is no need to look further. For we are here to grow through understanding ourselves and all things that are around us.

"Because each of us is here to grow through understanding, to grow from all of the events that will be presented to us, we find that our path changes many times and can include many shifts in our perception.

"It is from this shifting in our perception that will cause us to have great need of assistance in coming to understand all of those things that will present themselves to us in this path we share with the Earth Mother.

"But the most important reason for pursuing a vision quest is to find our own truth and balance that is always within us. And in this way, we will come to know the path that will allow us to walk in beauty with all of the creations that are among us.

"A vision that is created from the need to control others or from greed is based in lies about the natural order of Creation and will always leave us with a cloud of self doubt. But a vision of the path of the spirit...it is one that is always clear.

"Remember, Speaking Wind, every aspect of your life and every state of understanding is accessible to those who seek the serenity of the spirit of silence.

"It is not necessary to go on a vision quest once this natural balance has been achieved within the spirit who is you. And the original purpose of a vision quest was to assist the seeker in finding a way to contact the state of inner knowing so truth would be present in that person's life...every moment.

"Learning how to stop the world at will is a talent that comes through working on the path of the spirit. This path that both you and Cheeway have been well prepared with. The more you find your connection to the Earth Mother and Great Mystery, the easier this balance becomes.

"In this beginning of your life path, little one, it would not be well for you to attempt to perform this vision quest without the assistance of either Two Bears or myself. For there could come to you great dangers. Dangers that you are not yet aware of.

"However, as you will become more and more familiar with this process, little one, you will become aware that each of the two-legs lives a vision quest on a daily basis. The key is to be aware of it and learn to understand what it is that has been presented to you.

"When you will do this, you will see the signs that will be presented to you. And from those signs that will be offered, they will allow you to make proper decisions, then act upon those signs as a part of your own personal quest.

"Remember, also, little one, that on the path of the spirit...this path our people have come to know as the Red Path, you will see hundreds of lessons that lead to inner knowing. And the goal is to reach that place of inner serenity so that the inner world is equal to the outer world. And, when the two worlds are one...you will have become the living dream of all things. Of all things that are and this will allow you to see the one."

Grandfather finished his speaking words to me and was looking to my within place. This place where my spirit resides.

In those many seasons spent with him and Two Bears, I had become used to this kind of seeing that would penetrate all of myself and allow them to have free passage to all places that were within me.

As Grandfather was looking deep to my within places, I held the understanding for those things he had been willing to share with me. And I could feel their own weight of truth that was coming to me from them.

Grandfather and Two Bears were smiling at me when the speaking words continued.

"Go now and prepare your place among all of the children, Speaking Wind," came the opening of Two Bear's speaking words.

"Go with the path you will see. To the place that has been prepared for you to enter this domain of our old ones.

"Remember the path to preparing not only yourself for this quest, little one, but remember the path for asking assistance and permission of the grandfathers on these lands as well. For without their assistance, there will not be the entry you will need. This entry into the domain of the Ancient Ones...this place where answers to your many questions are waiting for you.

"Remember to take the pouch of tobacco with you and to give your thanks to the old ones before and after this great blessing of light is given to you.

"Also...," Grandfather continued,

"Remember that once you have closed off your circle with the stone people, you are not to eat or drink until you have been allowed to return to this domain."

"And when you will return, little one...," Two Bears continued,

"When you return, we will be waiting for you."

With their speaking words finished, both Grandfather and Two Bears were wearing a smile over the face they were showing to me.

Looking over to the place where Cheeway was

sitting, he, too, was wearing a face that I had become used to seeing many times in our seasons together. For the face he was wearing was one that was holding his mouth wide open and eyes that were filled with more teachings than he could find a place to put them.

Reaching over to his sitting place, I used the palm of my hand to close his mouth and he acknowledged this action on my part with the slight nodding of his head to me.

However, I knew that this time for me to spend among them was over now. It was time to begin my journey to the lands that had been calling me to them.

Rising from my sitting place, I turned to where I had set my clothes to dry on the great warming stone. Once there, I reached inside one of the bags I had brought with me and pulled out a tobacco pouch and tied it around my neck then set the last article of clothing on me, my warming blanket, on top of my clothes.

From the teachings of The Silent Brotherhood, I had learned that before one could go into the spirit quest, there could be no reminder of who they once were taken with them. And this leaving of all clothing behind was a symbolic way of doing this.

However, as I was standing before those who had brought me to this place, I was beginning to miss them already. But I knew this was only my fear that was coming to me. It was a fear of not holding a knowing of what I would find on my journey into the uncertainty of the vision quest.

Turning back to where all three of them were sitting, I raised my right hand to them in a way of sharing with all of them that I was about to begin my path to the vision quest. And seeing this mark of myself, they returned the motion that for what I would find on this path...they were all of a good heart.

As I turned my back to them, I could not help but feel that I was also turning my back on the me who had been. Turning my back on this part of myself so that I could have room for the me who was about to be born new; this part of me that was about to have another birth on this path of the spirit I had found to travel.

And now...now I would have to turn all of my energies to my within place where my spirit resides.

For I knew that it would not be with either the eyes or ears of my outer self that would hear the call of the spirits of the land for the direction to this place that had already been prepared for me for my vision quest. It would have to be from the inner eyes and ears of my spirit. It would only be in this way that I would be allowed to see and hear the ones who were already with me as they would show me the way to the lands I needed to be on.

FOLLOWING THE SPIRIT'S CALL

With only this small tobacco pouch that was tied over my neck, I continued to travel over to the top places of these lands.

As I traveled, I could feel myself as if I had been caught in the in-between times of the day and night. For the snow that was coming down on me, even though it had melted from the heat that was rising from the ground to meet it, was still a very cold form of water. I could feel myself getting very cold on the upper portions of my body while the lower places of myself were being kept warm by the heat that was always living in this land.

However, as I continued my ascent up to the higher places of these surrounding mountains, I could feel that this heat that had been so prevalent in the valley below was now beginning to get less and less. And all the while, the snow was getting lower and lower to the ground and stones that I was traveling over.

It had not been very long before my bare feet were beginning to get numb as I continued my ascent up to the higher places in these mountains of the Jemez and I was afraid that if they were to get too cold, I might cut them and not feel it.

So I would remember to look down to where my feet were traveling every now and then just to make sure there was no blood coming from them.

Just as I lowered my head to look at my feet, I heard a soft and gentle voice call me by name. It was a calling of a voice that had a direction to it. This was one that I could easily follow with my eyes, not like the many other spirit calling voices that I had come to know so well on these lands. These voices would seem to be coming to me from all sides and all places at the same time.

"Speaking Wind...," came the voice once again from a grouping of the standing people who wore the pine robe.

"I am here, little one...come to me."

Looking into the direction where the speaking voice had come, I could see there was a particular part of this small group of pine trees that was calling my attention to them in a way that I could not ignore.

It was the spirit wind of these lands that had made this first obvious to me. It was showing itself to me by the weaving back and forth of the pine trees to the beating of the spirit wind's heartbeat as they would carry the sound of the passing of his breath through their branches.

There was a coolness in the air that was all about me on this place I had come to stand on. As each of the snowflakes would land on me, I could hear their small caring voices come to me and say to follow the direction I was being shown. To follow my path and to follow my destiny, both of which were being called to me by this speaking voice just behind the pine trees.

The sun was more than halfway through the sky at this time, and I knew that if I did not find a sheltering place soon, that the night air that would come over me would certainly be biting at me from every direction. Especially since I wore nothing but this small tobacco pouch that was tied around my neck.

"Before you can see, Speaking Wind," the calling voice continued,

"Before you can see, little one, you must first be willing to open your eyes to what is waiting before you."

Deciding not to mind the fact that I had no clothes to wear and that the sun would soon be finished on these lands for another day, I let the thought of finding a warming shelter for the night pass me by and ventured in the direction this calling voice was coming to me from.

Looking at the dancing of the standing people that were in the front of me, I allowed my feet to begin their own journey. A journey that would bring me to this place that was on the top of one of the highest

=⊕=

peaks of this mountain rise.

I could feel each of the stones that I stepped on as I continued my journey onto this place where the calling voice had come to me from. And, as I felt the cold stones under my feet, I could feel that the sensation of feeling was beginning to leave me.

So, as I continued my journey, I began to pay more attention to observing my feet. I knew that if they were cut too severely, then I would have to find some of the medicine people who were growing on these lands and wrap them so I would be able to continue my traveling.

I could feel very strongly in the front of my thinking mind that this place that was in front of me was the same place I needed to go. Even though these small stones that were under each of my steps were beginning to hurt, and the wind that was carrying the falling snow over me was sharing with me its bite of the sleeping season that was about to pass, I held the knowing that I must reach this place for there was a direction that was about to be given to me. I needed this direction so that I might find the lands that had been prepared for me. They were waiting for me so that I could enter the doorway that held my vision quest.

Continuing my climb to the top place of this mountain, I could feel my spirit getting stronger within me. As it was continuing to gain in its strength, I could feel it begin to make a great change over me. A change that was like nothing I had ever come to experience before.

All of those places where I had been feeling the cold biting at me and the snowflakes snipping at my body warmth were no longer noticeable to me. In fact, as I looked at my arms as they would go from the front then to the back of me as I continued walking up this steep incline, I could see steam beginning to come off of them. A steam that was very similar to that which was rising from the boiling waters in the valley below me.

Then, as I looked down at my feet once again, I saw that where there had once been many small cuts and scratches...now there was nothing. There were no longer any marks or feelings of soreness.

And as I continued to take the additional steps that would eventually take me to the place of the calling voice, I noticed that there was no longer the feeling of the sharpness of the stones and small sticks under me.

Now when I would take each of these steps, I could only feel the softness of them under me. It was as if I were being allowed to feel the softness that is in all of the Earth Mother's skin...and I was being allowed to walk on it.

Where there was once cold over me, there was only the feeling of a warmth; where there were once cuts and scrapes on each of my feet, there was now only the softness of the earth beneath them, and all of the cuts and scrapes had been healed as if they had not ever been there.

From the place where my spirit resides, I could only hear the calling of my spirit's voice to me...."Go now, Speaking Wind...Go now and be with those who call to you..."

Hearing this calling of my own spirit to me, and feeling the softness of the Earth Mother's skin under my feet, I began to step up my pace. As I did this, I could feel another change in the face that is the Earth Mother's that I was now walking on with all of those blessings from her that before now I had only heard of.

As I continued to pick up my pace, I felt the earth beneath me begin to hold a bounce in it. It was a bounce that was allowing me to take even quicker and longer steps without making any effort of my own.

Just as I would place one of my feet down, the one behind me was being bounced up and pushed into the next place that would always be in front of my other foot and always in the direction of the group of the pine trees in front of me.

I was no longer breathing hard on this day. It was as if I were being allowed to sit and observe myself climbing on this tall piece of the mountain I had been called to. And soon...sooner than I had realized, I was at this place that had been calling to me. I had arrived at a place I felt would have taken me more than twice the time to arrive at.

Now I was standing at the very top of this mountain place I had been called to and was taking time to look around me and see all that had come to call this place their home.

I was looking at a flat place just behind these standing people and saw one of the bubbling water places there. It had been located in the middle of a flat place of the stones that allowed the steaming waters that came up from the inside of the Earth Mother's heart to fall into a large valley that was below me. This valley was filled with many generations of pine trees that I could feel the life from.

Looking into this place, I took the time to enjoy the show the small snowflakes were making as they came to dance with the spirit wind. And I was given a thinking thought that for all of those things that were taking place in front of me...they were all being done in a perfect balance. A perfect balance of life that was being lived and understood for what it was.

My thoughts, however, were taken away from this by the coming of the calling voice once again. And this time, it was coming from a place that was just behind me.

When I turned around, I was very surprised to see who the owner was of this same speaking voice that I heard so well from the bottom of this high place I had arrived at.

It was a beautiful woman and she was dressed in all white. Her white robe seemed to give off a radiance of many colors of light and on her sleeves were the marks and colors of the four chiefs of direction.

These colors have represented to our people the four chiefs of direction for as long as I could remember. They have always been used in our sacred ceremonies.

How was it that one so beautiful had come to be on this land with me? I was wondering as I was taking in all of the beauty that was hers to share with me. And how did she arrive at this place without me noticing her?

Then it hit me. I was completely uncovered now. I had no clothes on me at all and I was standing directly in front of one of the most beautiful women I had ever been blessed with seeing.

As this came into the front of my thinking mind, my hands immediately covered the front part of my manhood. For as this thought came to me, I was filled with the feeling of being embarrassed at being in front of her without any clothes on.

All of a sudden, a feeling of cold was beginning to

cover me once again and as this cold was finding itself back to me, I could feel the hurting of my feet being born to me once again, as well.

So here I was, standing in front of the most radiant and beautiful women I had ever seen...freezing, feeling the pain returning to my feet, holding my hands over myself in an effort of not showing to another those parts of myself that were usually clothed, and trying to smile through the shaking I was doing because of the cold. And...all the while...not knowing what to do.

As this woman who was standing in the front of me continued to walk closer to my place of shaking, she placed a warm and tender smile over her face. It was one that caused me to relax more and more as she took each of her steps that brought her closer to my standing place.

"It is good to see you, Speaking Wind...," she began, as she arrived at a place that was very close to me.

"And it is good to see that you have arrived for this vision quest as others have done. And that is without the reminding of those things of your past such as the clothes you have become so used to wearing.

"But tell me, little one...why does it bother you so to be standing in front of me without anything on? Is it something that you are trying to hide from me?"

I could only look back at her and try to smile while nodding my head in a left to right motion. One that would share with her that I did not think this was the reason for my being like this...but I really did not know.

"Would it make you feel better if I were to drop my robe away from myself, Speaking Wind?"

Looking back at the place she was now standing, I could only shake my head in a left to right motion. This was to share with her that this would not assist me in how I was feeling right now, and to also portray to her that I was feeling very cold, and hurting, as well, by the way I was standing before her shivering and breathing in very short patterns.

"There is something I would like to share with you, little one...that is, if I can hold your attention for awhile," the lady said.

"What you are feeling now is the absence of the spirit within you. You are feeling the cold, the hurting of your feet, and the embarrassment of being before me without any clothes on because you have allowed yourself to fall away from the path your spirit has shown to you.

"I do not understand what it is you are saying to me," was my first return of speaking words with her of any kind.

"Then I will place this in a more understandable manner for you to follow. Let us both have a seat on one of the rock places that are beneath us, shall we?"

Following her lead, I found that I had to force myself to sit on one of these places. But as I observed her, I could see that she was not having any difficulty at all in her sitting...it seemed to be only me who was having troubles. I was feeling out of place here and wishing that I had not ever come because of all I was now feeling.

"Little one...," she began,

"What is it that you have come here in search of? Is it to see if you can travel among all these children of the Earth Mother without any clothes...seeing if you can be stronger than the last part of this sleeping season that is over these lands?

"Or is it because you have come here to find an answer. An answer to those things that have been filling you with their weight of calling but not with the understanding you need?"

"I have come in search for those things that have been causing me to feel this great weight," was my answer to her as it came out between shivers of my body.

"Then you will have to keep your eyes and ears focused on those things, will you not, little one?"

"Yes...yes, this is what I have come here for," I responded to her once again.

"Then allow me to take you to a place that was just before you had seen me. Let us both go to this place and see what has happened within you...what has taken place but you have seemed to lose sight of...shall we?

"Go back to the place when you first heard my calling voice to you from this place. Do you remember how you were feeling and what it was that was going through the front of your thinking mind?"

"Yes...yes, I do remember what was taking place then. I was thinking about finding a sheltering place for myself because the snows were continuing to come down at this heavy level and the warming of the sun would soon be gone from this land for another day."

"Yes, Speaking Wind, but there was something else that had come to the front of your thinking mind at this time, also. Do you remember what it was?"

"Well, it was just after I heard the calling of your speaking voice that I decided this was the place I needed to travel to. And when I had made up my mind that I would not seek out a sheltering place, but I would continue to journey to this place...well, that was when I began to feel my spirit grow within me. And as it was growing, I could feel the warmth return to my body part and all of the pain leave my feet that had been cut and scratched in many places.

"Oh yes...I could also see there were no more places on them that were bleeding from those small cuts and scrapes that had once been on them. And...that there were no longer those scrapes and scratches on them either."

"And have you looked at your feet now, Speaking Wind?"

"Yes...yes, I have looked at them and I have seen there are other scrapes and bruises on them once again."

"And what has this shared with you, little one? Does this lesson have a face you can see?"

"I can see that the healing and warming I was receiving only a short time before is no longer with me," was my response.

"You are beginning to see then, little one. And this feeling of the softness that is on the face of the Earth Mother. Has this left you, as well, or do you still feel this with you?"

"This, too, has gone from me and I can share with you that this stone place I am sitting on is very cold and hard to me now."

"Then little one, would you like to return to the place you were once at? It is not difficult at all since you have already seen it."

"Yes...yes, I would like to return to this place, and very soon if you will assist me in finding it," was my response to her.

=⊕=

"But I believe that soon I will not be able to share with you any longer."

"And why is that, Speaking Wind? I would wish to hear this from your own speaking words," she replied, still wearing the warm and tender smile for me to see.

"I feel as if I am about to go to sleep now. If I do not begin to move and find a warming place for my body, I am sure that I will soon fall into the sleep of no returning," I replied as I looked at both of my hands and feet that were turning very blue now.

"Then I will assist you in finding your own way, little one."

"Go back to the feelings that had come to you when you first made your decision to forget about finding a sheltering place and come to me. Allow yourself to return to this time, little one. And as you do this, I will assist you in coming to see the path you need to learn. This path that will allow you to find your own spirit within you and allow for its assistance to cover you once again."

Nodding my head in an up and down manner, I saw that she understood that the time I had left to share with her was getting very short now and that if there was no path for me to find a warming that would come to me, I would soon enter this sleep of not returning.

I saw that this is what she understood and I was beginning to feel a little better because of that.

"Now then...," she continued.

"What has happened is this, Speaking Wind. You have not learned from the steps you have taken in order to arrive at this place. Those steps that have given you a seeing of what it is your spirit can do for you and this body part that has so influenced your thinking mind.

"When you had reached a place of feeling very miserable and cold but you held onto the knowing that you must reach this place that had called out to you, it was then that the body part of yourself saw that it had no choice but to allow your spirit part to come to the surface.

"And it was only when the body part of yourself could not convince you that you needed to find a sheltering place so that it could keep warm that it knew of its futile efforts in trying to convince you to follow its lead. Once this had been known, then the body part of yourself allowed the spirit part to come to the surface and not only give to you the warmth that is still there within you, but to also heal your feet.

"However, the body part did not do this thing out of the goodness of its heart. Remember that when the body part gives way to the spirit within you, that it only does this for a short time; and because it does not understand what the balanced life path is all about, then it will look for ways of reminding you that what you have done was very foolish. It will remind you that had you listened to it, then you would not be in the mess you are in presently.

"This mess that I am speaking to you of is the way you are hurting and feeling the biting cold that is all around you.

"Now, you only felt the part of your body when you saw me standing before you. And this vision of me was what you saw in the front of your thinking mind from my calling your name.

"But once you had reached this place, this place that you considered to be the final destination, then the spirit became weak and the body part of you jumped right back into the front of you. And this is why you have been feeling the cold and pain once again.

"It has nothing at all to do with how well you know the words that have been shared with you, little one. For those words are the only way of allowing you to see what you will and what you will not allow yourself to be prepared with. What makes the difference is when we come to the place of seeing that all things are done at the right time and in the right way for us to learn.

"What will follow then will be the understanding that we will attain when we will allow ourselves to look through those emotions of all things that will come to us and see the face of lesson.

"So tell me, Speaking Wind, what have you learned from this experience so far?"

Looking into the face of this beautiful woman, I decided to allow all of my armor to drop away from me. That armor that is called ego and pride.

This, I knew, was what had been stopping me from continuing on with my spirit. With the one who lives in my inner world.

So raising both of my hands out to the side of myself, I allowed my body part to be completely exposed not only to the one who was sitting in front of me, but to all life that was all around me.

"I hold myself open to all of you who share this same life with me. I hold the knowing that it is I, Speaking Wind, who stands before you and that I am willing to bring my inner world into balance with my outer world so that I can see once again."

Finishing these speaking words to all who were

present with me on this day, I began to feel the awakening of my spirit once again.

As this new life from within me became a blend of balance, I could feel the warmth filling me once again and the hurting leave both of my feet.

"It is good to see you have learned this path so well, Speaking Wind. Not many who I have seen come into this domain that is the Earth Mother's have found it.

"But tell me, little one. Why is it you have come to this place in search of your vision quest. Are you so lost that you do not know your way?"

"If you have come to know so much about me then how is it that you do not know of my purpose?" I asked holding as much respect in the tone of my speaking words as I was capable of doing.

"You must keep in the front of your thinking mind, Speaking Wind, for each time that you repeat your quest, you will come to know it that much better. Does this give to you the answer that you were looking for?"

"But what if I were to tell you that I already know my quest and am only looking for confirmation of it," I replied.

"If you believed this, little one, you would not have entered the world of cold and hurting so quickly, would you? Had you been able to hold your sight on the vision of your path, then you would not have become so distracted by my appearance to you and fallen from the path of the spirit. Fallen away from this path and found yourself as you did... cold...hurting...and filled with the false spirit we have come to call embarrassment."

I could only lower my head and look at my feet

when this was shared with me, for there is nothing that is stronger than truth when it is encountered.

"I can only share a part of this with you. But before I go into this...by what name may I call you and where are your people from? I have not ever seen such clothing or markings worn by any others before," I asked.

"When you have finished with this relearning for yourself, then we will go into this, little one. But for now and at the place where you are, there is not yet the need for this knowledge. Soon though...soon.

"But for now, I am willing to listen to those speaking words that you do hold an understanding for, little one...please pursue them."

"Well...," I began, adjusting myself on the sitting rock that had made itself available to me.

"I do not hold a great level of understanding for what has been taking place within me. And, I will tell you in truth, that I have been feeling the weight of something that is very great which is about to take place in this domain.

"It was yesterday when one who is called Standing Tree came into our village and was sitting in the circle of the elders. He was discussing many things that are about to take place in this domain that is the Earth Mother's, but I did not arrive in time to hear what they were. All I managed to do was to call attention to myself and have him make reference to me and that I would be one who might be called on to learn of these things. To learn of these things that would be so great that they would affect all who will be traveling in this domain.

"And from that time, there has only been the weight of confusion that has come to me. This weight of confusion that comes to me from not being able to hear the calling of the old ones' messages. Those same messages that I am sure hold a great importance to those events that Standing Tree had been discussing with our elders yesterday."

"And this is why you have begun a vision quest, little one?" she asked.

"I have begun this vision quest so that I may see the direction I am to travel. To clear my eyes and ears so that I might see what is being offered to me...those things that have to do with this great event that is on the way."

Looking at me with kindness in her eyes, the lady smiled at me and said, "What you have shared with me is truth, little one. It is a truth that not many until now have even come to dream of.

"And I will share with you that this one called Standing Tree is correct in those things that he has shared with the elders of your village.

"You see, Speaking Wind, Standing Tree is from my nation and I will tell you that all he had been sent to do among your people has been done. You are the proof of this because you are now sitting before me."

"So this event that he spoke of is truly great?" I asked.

"It is greater than anything any of your song legends have spoken of, little one. Greater than any have come to understand...any of the two-legs that is.

"So it is good that you and I have found each other and I will share with all who are with us that you are indeed the one who the message will be revealed to. That you are the one who will bring this message to the many when the time is right."

Hearing these speaking words come to me gave

me a chill up the middle of my back. Now, more than before, I was feeling the weight of something that was great on me. Something that was calling to me but I could not understand.

"The time is right now, Speaking Wind."

The lady continued, "The time is right for you to sit in your proper place among the old ones. But you will do well to remember that from that point until the time is called to you...you will find yourself in a great sleep. But it will not be the sleep of illusion, for you have already passed this. It will be the sleep of preparing yourself for all those things that you will have before you to do. For the ones who will be waiting to hear those things you will be told on this night."

"But I was prepared with the knowing that when one is on a vision quest, there must be from three to four days of fasting. Is this not correct?" I asked.

"When one will begin a vision quest, little one, this is the proper way to conduct oneself. However, you are already in the middle of your vision and this is how I have been able to come to you."

"I do not understand these things, lady...," I said.

"Then I will attempt to share with you what I can for the time we have been given, little one. But when this time is over, then it will be time for you to go onto the flat place that is within the domain of the rock people and ask permission to build your circle.

"Do you hold an understanding for what it is that I am sharing with you, little one?"

"Yes...yes, I do understand. Thank you for having patience with me on this day."

SPIRIT OF THE STANDING PEOPLE

"I am called Telah and I am from the nation of the standing people, Speaking Wind," she began.

"Tell me, little one, what do you think of when you stand before the great tree nation. Do you feel those things that are there?"

"I can only say that I see many of the children of the Earth Mother, Telah," was my respectful reply.

"And now, little one...now that you have seen and heard my speaking words to you, tell me what you see."

"Many things that I did not see before...," I responded.

"I see that there is a part of the Great Spirit within you, Telah, and if it is as you have shared with me, that you are a part of the great tree nation...one of the standing people's spirit, then I will say to you that this is in truth a new knowing for me. A knowing that will not be lost for a place to reside within me."

"This is truth that has come to you on this day, Speaking Wind. For I can see within you a willingness to wake from this sleep of illusion that you and all like you have entered into when you first arrived into this domain of the Earth Mother's. However, I must take this time to remind you to learn to feel the importance of this great gift of sharing that you have come to remember.

"It is in the knowing that we will find our way through to the understanding that all of us are so much in search of. And this knowing that has come to you on this day that we are now sharing little one, this knowing will allow you to understand that all who are within this domain of the Earth Mother's hold a spirit within them.

"For there is no thing that you can see or feel that does not have a life path of its own to follow. The only difference is that these children of the Earth Mother have not become so blind to this truth, not like the two-legs have to now. But for all of this, there is a reason. And the reason is for the best and advancement of all spirits who are with us as well as the ones who are still in the waiting place across the great spirit waters.

"You see, little one, we too have a spirit that can feel and love. A spirit that can understand and be hurt. It is not only the ones who travel on the two-legs that have been given this blessing.

"When you will look around you on this land, you will see before you the great tree nation, the stone people, the sky nation that holds the cloud people, the spirit wind, and the star nation who holds all of those ancestors and their willingness to share those things they have come to understand with us. And you will, in time, come to know that there is another nation that resides beneath the face of the Earth Mother and we have come to know them as the underworld nation.

"They are not there to travel with us, though, for their preparing is much different than ours is. Than all of those who travel on the face of the Earth Mother. But I will share with you that there will come a time when you and many like you will have to go to them and learn. To learn of the lessons that had been lost so many generations before.

"You will have to go to them with your heart held out in your hands so they will be willing to see you for who and what you are. Only then will they recognize you and the path you are willing to travel. Only then will they impart those same lessons that had been lost to the two-legs. Those lessons that have been carried to all of them by the Anasazi, the Hohocum, and the Mogolan people.

"You see, Speaking Wind, what took place in their times...it is about to take place once again. And this will be the direction of your vision quest. This is what you have been feeling from this great weight that has been over you for the past two days.

"This has come to you from the Ancient Ones and they are waiting for you to come to them. For there are many pieces of wisdom they wish to share with you. To share with you so that you will be able to use the time that has been left for you here to prepare. To prepare yourself in ways that will allow you to understand what it is you are supposed to share with the rest of the two-legs.

"For without this knowing and understanding that will be presented to you, little one, I am afraid that there will not be much of a chance for any of them to continue in this domain that we call the Earth Mother's. They will be held outside of a great wall and the floor beneath them will be taken away.

"And for those who will be held behind the great wall that is about to be built, they will find when the floor is removed that there is only a bottomless pit that they will all fall into. A pit that will not allow any of them to find a way out.

"But these are things that are still ahead of you, little one. And I do not want to take any thing away from the Ancient Ones and those things they have been waiting to share with you.

"But for now, let me share what it is the standing people of my nation hold for those who will have the eyes and ears to see and hear it."

"Before you begin, though, Telah, there is a question that I would wish to ask you."

"Yes, Speaking Wind, what is this question of yours?"

"How is it that you can share with me as one of the spirits of the standing people...yet you have not shared with others, as well? Would this not have stopped many who have been mistreating so many of the Earth Mother's children?"

"But we have shared this knowing with many, Speaking Wind. But even for the ones who have come to know the understanding of this great truth, they have not been able to reach many. And the reason for this was that it was not yet time."

"But how could so many of you have been hurt when there were at least some who held this understanding of who and what you are?"

"You have only to look at the history of the two-legs, little one, to know the answer to this. The truth of the reason is not fully known to me, but perhaps the Ancient Ones who are waiting for you will be willing to share this with you.

"All I can share with you is that when you look at the history of the two-legs, you will always know where they have been. For all you will have to do is follow the trail of destruction and misery they leave behind them.

"When you see this as I have shared with you, Speaking Wind, then perhaps you will hold a little better understanding of why they have done as they have.

"Now, if you will be willing, little one, I will continue to share with you what my nation holds

open for all who would embrace us. The many blessings that are within your reach. Then after this time
of sharing, and before you begin to seek your direction of your vision quest in more detail, then I will
share with you a path that will allow you to know
another doorway. A doorway that will bring you
closer to those things that are with the rest of us in this
domain that is the Earth Mother's.

"The standing people, the trees, we are your sisters and brothers, Speaking Wind. We, too, have a
male and female path for our advancement just as the
two-legs do. And it is our path to be the chiefs of all
the growing ones with leaves.

"Think of us, little one, when you will use our
many blessings that we have been so willing to share
with all of you. Blessings that will not stop even from
all of the abuse we have received from the ones of
your kind.

"For it is not our way to hold those things that
must be in a way of trying to control them, little one.
You see, when one will see their path of the spirit open
for them, they will hold the understanding for Great
Mystery.

"It has been Great Mystery that has shared with
our nation many generations before your kind had
arrived, that all is done in the right way and time for
it to be.

"And as you will come to understand from the old
ones, Speaking Wind, as they will come to you on this
night, you, too, will see this truth and it will be
presented to you in a way that only they are capable
of doing. In their way that will share with you
perfectly no matter where you are on this path of the
spirit that all of us are traveling together.

"But when you will come to think of all the bless-ings our nation continues to pour onto you, then you will hold a better understanding of what part we play in this domain. For there is none who are here in this domain that is the Earth Mother's that have been destined to travel alone. If this were the case, then no blessing would ever be needed by any who were here and we would all wither up and die, little one.

"When you breathe in the air that is needed by you, take the time to be thankful for our nation of the standing people. For it is from us that you have this.

"You see, little one, when we breathe in the air that we need, we are thankful to the two-legs and all those who let out what it is that we need to take within us to live. And from this sharing, you can see how we assist each other. The only thing that is lacking is being thankful for those things that have been made available to you. For your kind can be a very selfish lot, thinking that they are the only ones here who merit thinking about.

"When it is in the sleeping season and you are feeling warm from a warming fire, think of us. It is from our shells that you receive this warmth, little one. And it is from our same shells that you have been able to build over you those roofs that keep you dry during the rains and warm during the dark times.

"Think of us, little one, for things such as these and you will come to know your path better. For it is only when we are at one with ourselves that we will see the connection. This connection that has been placed over all of us by the Great Spirit and he has done this so we will come to know that while we can stand strong alone...we will not ever be in a place where we cannot stand without all of these others who travel with us. The ones you can see as well as the ones you cannot see.

"Unless this knowing is held by one who is willing to seek their part of this great path of life, they will not ever be able to see what it is they are seeking. For they will be blinded with their wants and not see their needs.

"We share with all who are in this domain, little one. And it is a kind of sharing that is done from the love we have found within ourselves.

"Through our trunks and branches, we give shelter to the winged ones and in our roots, we provide burrows for smaller four-legged ones.

"However, there is a balance that exists between our nation and another nation, Speaking Wind. It is a balance that exists for us much the same way the balance between your spirit and body part exists for you.

"This balance is one that has been forged by the Earth Mother and has been with us for as long as the collective memory can remember.

"We have a balance between the stone people and our nation and this balance continues with the greatest of respect, little one.

"You must keep in the front of your thinking mind that the stone people are the ones who have been given charge for recording all of the events that have ever been. Those events that have been both great and small are located within these record keepers and they remain in their places to share those events with those who would have the eyes and ears to see and hear with.

"These are the ones among all the nations who hold the key to many things that have happened here before. For it is in their collective records that one may find what mistakes they are repeating and how to stop from doing it over again.

"It is the balance that exists between the standing people and the stone people that gives to us a clear meaning for all those things we, too, have entered this domain to perform.

"You see, little one, it is the stone people who are the holders and the standing people who are the givers. What better way to see what mistakes have been made in the past before we will give to those who would come to us. And as we give, the stone people record and remind us of those things that have been...and will be.

"This is one of the many reasons that you will see both of our nations standing so close to each other. It is because we balance each other so well.

"Now, the standing people see the needs of all the Earth Mother's children and we apply ourselves to being their providers.

"Each of us, as well as each of the leaved children have their own gifts, talents, and abilities they have been given to share with others...with those others who have a need and not only a want for them.

"For example, Speaking Wind...," Telah continued to share with me,

"...some of our nation's members bear fruit and some provide healing on the emotional or physical level. And, this is not only to those who are in our domain...but this applies to those who are of the two-legs as well.

"The white pine is the tree of peace and can bring serenity into the life of a person sitting in its shade. The lands throughout the domain of the Earth Mother's carry curative properties and substances such as many of the members of our nation provide for the two-legs to use. Things such as syrup which is from our blood and in other places, rubber..which is used by many of your own kind.

"This domain is filled with the gifts that the standing people have provided. The next time you will see one of our gifts, little one, look very closely at it and see how freely it has been given. But I will ask of you one thing to do...look around and see how many of the two-legs have repaid our people. Have they returned to us any measure for those things we have shared with them? I think that you will see that they have not.

"But let me continue, little one, for our time is growing short and there is still much to share with you.

"Each standing person that you will see in this life path you are traveling with the Earth Mother has a special lesson to give to the two-legs. A special lesson, when if accepted and understood, will assist them in returning to the place they are seeking for themselves. This is the place where they will come to know better the spirit who resides within them.

"The pines are peacemakers and peace bringers. The pine people teach the lessons of being in harmony with ourselves and others as well as the lessons of a quiet mind.

"Rowen or mountain ash brings protection from harm and teaches the lessons of seeing through deception as well as the lessons of how to protect our sacred space.

"Sycamore teaches the lessons of how to reach our goals and make our dreams come true. And walnut teaches us clarity on focusing our mental gifts and how to use our intelligence properly.

"Oak teaches us strength of character and how to keep our body parts strong and healthy. And willow is the wood of love and teaches us the give and take or bending that is necessary for love to be fruitful.

"Cherry teaches us the lessons of clearing the pain of the heart or relating to others in a compassionate manner.

"This is only a part of the great blessings that come to all from our nation, Speaking Wind. Blessings that can be of great value to the spirit side of all life path walkers if they will only learn to see and understand what is being offered to them.

"And little one, there is a great similarity between all of those who live in this domain. And I share this with you so that you can take this back with you when this vision quest of yours is finished.

"For whenever you will think of yourself as being so different from all other creations, think of this comparison that I will share with you. It is a comparison between the standing people and the two-legs.

"As it is with the standing people, the two-legs also have a trunk and it is called your spine. They have branches to them which we call their arms and their hair is much the same as our leaves are for us.

"We all reach for light as the standing people's branches will do, reaching into the direction of the Great Spirit's reflection which is the sun that is in the daytime sky over our lands. And we receive through our antenna, which for the two-legs is the hair and for the standing people is our leaves.

"And each standing person as well as each of the two-legs are very different from the other, for no two will ever be alike.

"Now the two-legs will travel through all of this domain that is the Earth Mother's and as they do this, they see many things. However, the standing people remain in one place and receive nurturing from the Earth Mother constantly so that they may share with all others those things that are theirs to offer.

"The two-legs will also give and receive when they learn to walk in balance and this can be achieved when they will remember their roots...the only physical tree part of them that is lacking.

"Remember this part, Speaking Wind, for it will bring to you a great wisdom for those things that you will find a need for in those many seasons that are waiting for you to arrive in them.

"If you will be willing to walk in balance, you must remember your roots by living in harmony with all of your other relations. You must be rooted in this world through the Earth Mother and allow your spirit to fly through the other worlds and be at one with those realities, as well.

"Without being rooted in this domain, you will not fully understand the purpose of your visions, dreams, potentials, or yourself.

"In time you will look for ways of being grateful for all of the blessings that have been given to you and I will tell you the path that is good to follow.

"When you return gratitude for the gifts you have received from others, you will acknowledge the root of each blessing. The root of anything is its source and if you will return your gratitude to the source of your blessings, you will be balancing your world through acknowledging the gifts you receive.

"You will also be reminded that the ancestors who

rode the wind before you are a part of your roots and that you are here to respect the value of their gifts and their life paths by living in a balanced manner.

"The taproot of all civilizations to come lives in each of us in the present. And to nurture the future is to honor the seeds of the present by allowing them to grow.

"The standing people will ask you, as the guardians of the Earth Mother, to look for the root of every blessing, acknowledge the truth in it, and use that blessing for the highest good so that the giving is not in vain.

"These are my gifts to you, Speaking Wind, as you continue in this dream time that has been shared with you. This dream time that is within this vision quest you have begun and I am grateful to Great Mystery to have been the one to welcome you through this doorway to the domain you have been seeking and the one that has been seeking you out."

"Will I remember all of these things you have been willing to share with me, Telah?" I asked, holding a questioning look over my face.

"You will remember all things that you will hold an understanding for, Speaking Wind," came her reply.

"And what of those things that I do not hold an understanding for. Will they fall away from me and not be seen or heard from again?"

"When the time will come to you, as I see that it will, you will reremember them once again. And when you will have worked your way through another of the many lessons that will be presented to you and have gained the needed understanding from it...then you will find these speaking words that we have shared in this time return. For they will return to you with their own life in them and you will see them as good."

Hearing these speaking words come to me from this one called Telah gave me a good feeling. For these were the same truths that had been shared with me many times before by Grandfather and Two Bears. Truths that shared with me many of their teachings would be remembered by my spirit and when the time was right then I would have them return to me.

I was feeling very good now and the cold that had once been with me from the spirit wind playing with the falling snowflakes was no longer with me.

Looking over to the place where Telah was sitting, I could see that there was something else that she had in the front of her thinking mind. Something more that she wanted to share with me.

Seeing this, I was reminded of the many lessons I had learned from Grandfather and Two Bears when this same situation would occur. I had learned to sit in the silence and wait for them to come forth with those pieces of wisdom and truth they were forming in the front of their thinking minds. And when they were ready...they would begin.

A DOORWAY FOR THE SPIRITS' NEEDS

"The time that is left for us to share with each other is almost over, Speaking Wind," Telah began once again.

"But there is a gift that I would like to present you with. It is a gift from my nation and I have been given permission to release it to you so that when the time is right, and you will be shown this time, I am told...then you may share this gift with those others of your kind who will have a great need for it so that they, too, can find their way through the many events that will soon be on them.

"My gift to you will be a doorway that will be made known at this time. This is a doorway that will allow your spirit within you to seek assistance from the domain of the Ancient Ones. The ones who have been with all who possess life in this domain and provide us with their light of direction from the council fires of the old ones.

"There will be many times when you will be faced with situations that will not make you comfortable. Situations that will cause you to feel alone and confused and sometimes even lost.

"But I will say this to you, Speaking Wind. This comes to all, but it is only when this comes to the ones who are still trapped in their own sleep of illusion who feel they are the only ones who are going through this. The ones who have learned to travel on this path of the spirit...they will not feel this way because they have come to know that all who are within this domain that is the Earth Mother's will have to go through these things. And they will have to go through them in order to learn the many valuable lessons they have entered here to learn.

"You have been prepared with the understanding that there is only one path of the spirit, but on this one path there are thousands of alternatives that will be presented to you. And each of them will cause you to look at things in a different way.

"In a way, this is like learning to see yourself

through all of the aspects that are you. But in this process of learning to understand this, you will be confused at times and will require the assistance of not only the standing people of my nation, but of the Ancient Ones as well.

"This gift that I am willing to share with you will allow you to see how well all life relates to each other and how much a part of all of it we are, in truth.

"Just as it is true that one cannot walk without having two feet, this I am making reference to is for the two-legs, little one. It is just as true that one cannot come to understand those things they will need without seeing the relationship of all life that is around them. This relationship will share with them that they are only a part of the whole and not the whole themselves.

"When they come to understand this, they will begin a great adventure for themselves. It will be an adventure that will not allow them to return to the place they once were...this place we have come to know so well as the sleep of illusion. But from this time on, they will become a balanced part of all life that is on this side of the great spirit waters as well as the life that is on the other side.

"So when you find yourself in the middle of many changes or events that will come to you, remember this gift that my nation has offered to you, Speaking Wind. Remember it so that you may receive the assistance for those things that you are holding a need to see clearly what is before you.

"When you hold this feeling, Speaking Wind, then take the time to travel to one of my nation's people. One that will assist you in finding the open doorway that you will need to travel through.

"If it is peace that you are seeking, then come to one of the pines and ask its permission for entry into the domain of the Ancient Ones. If it is love that is bothering you, then come to one of the willows and ask its permission. But whatever the reason, come to us for this first step even if there is none available to you that is directly related to what it is you are requesting assistance for.

"Remember, little one, that all of our nation is within the bond of understanding and because of this bond that exists between all of my people, we are capable of assisting with those things that are not presently a part of us. And we will do this from the understanding we have been given of our other brothers and sisters.

"When you will come to us with this need then, seek out the oldest and strongest standing person that is living on the land you have returned to. Seek them out and know that they are the grandfather of all who are living near them.

"It is this grandfather of the standing people on this land that you will first have to go to and ask permission for this request of assistance that you desire.

"Walk up to them and make them an offering of tobacco as you ask their permission of entering this domain that all standing people hold the key of the doorway to. Offer them this tobacco as you ask them to recognize you for who and what you are and when you do this, they will see if what you bring with you is a need...or if it is only a want.

"Our nation will accept you if you bring with you your needs. And as you have come to understand that needs are those things that hold a value of learning for the spirit, while wants are only something that is temporary at best. Temporary and serving no need of the spirit in any way.

"When the grandfather will see you for who and what you are and will also see if you bring with you a need, then you will be accepted by them and they will tell you this in a way of allowing you to feel their peace of belonging among them.

"When you feel this, ask them which of their children they would like you to work with. And they will answer you in a way that will not be mistaken. They will cause you to have your attention drawn to one of the standing people that is near your place and cause you to feel a sense of pulling over to where they are living.

"However, if they do not accept you, then you would be well to examine the reason you have come to them. Look at this reason that you are carrying within you and determine if it is truly a need or only a want that you have.

"If it is a want then it would be best for you to do your own work for no other will assist you with this. But if you will look closely at this thing you are carrying with you and see that it is truly a need of your spirit, then the reason for their non-acceptance will be simple.

"It is that the grandfather you have asked permission of entry from does not see that any of his children can assist you. And when this happens, then offer him tobacco in gratitude and walk to another place. One that will be capable of offering to you the assistance you are seeking.

"When you will follow these speaking words that have been set into motion within you, there will be a place that will be made available for you to use. A place that will share with you those things that you are seeking assistance for.

"However, you must keep in the front of your thinking mind that there will be a complete different way of speaking to you on this plane. It will not be as clear as the way you and I are sharing our time and speaking words together on this day. For what you have been allowed to enter here, Speaking Wind, is what we have come to call the walking vision. And this is one that has allowed you and your body part to participate in this vision quest that you have been willing to take part in.

"You see...this is a place where many of the two-legs and almost all of the children of the Earth Mother will reside when we will enter the next place. This place that will be better explained to you by the Ancient Ones. Those who have been waiting for you to arrive at this place you are now at. Those who have been waiting for you for a very long time, I might add.

"But when one is in the level of the two-leg's domain, this level that has not yet found its way to the higher levels of understanding that have always been available to them, they will have to use their thinking minds, their eyes, and their ears in much different ways than they have become used to.

"They will have to hold an understanding of what it means to listen with the heart. To hear with the heart, and to see with it, as well.

"For in the beginning, these grandfathers that you come up to and ask for their permission to enter their domain, as well as the ones of their families, will see and hear you very clearly. This has not changed.

"But it will be the two-legs who will have to learn

=⊕=

to listen to these children of the Earth Mother as they will return to you in their own speaking words their answers to what it is you are asking of them. It will be the two-legs who will have to reremember how to speak as they once had learned in those times of long ago. But because they had once held the knowing and the understanding of how this was accomplished, then all they will have to relearn is how to sit still and listen once again. And for some of them...this can be a very difficult task.

"Think of this process in this way, Speaking Wind. When you come across another who you hold a great deal of caring for, and you see them once again after not having seen them for a few days and nights, when you will first meet them, there will be many exchanges of speaking. Exchanges of speaking between both of you that will not be done by the mouth.

"There will be a held knowing of what has been taking place in their lives and they will hold this same knowing of what has been happening in yours. But this is not shared between the two of you through your speaking words of the body part. Rather it is something that has been shared between both of your spirits and this is the same way that all of the children of the Earth Mother continue to speak.

"As both of you meet, there will be a knowing within you if all has been going well for your friend. This knowing comes to you from somewhere on the inside of yourself, and depending on how well you have traveled on this path of the spirit...you will come to recognize where within you this knowing about them is coming from.

"You see, Speaking Wind, when you and your good friend come together once again, there will be many things that will be shared. And they will not be anything that any of the body part's speaking words can explain.

"You will know if they have been good, or if there are many things that are bothering them from all of the events they have been passing through. But for most of the two-legs, this is not a valid part of sharing, for it cannot be explained by them in their world of the great illusion. And because it cannot be explained by them, they will tend to ignore it and only believe in those speaking words that they can hear from their friend with the ears of the body part. And I will share with you that these ears of the body part were not meant for listening with, they were only meant to be used as a warning giver for times of approaching danger.

"When the two-legs came to believe that these ears of the body part were meant to be used to listen to messages of another...messages that would share with them great meanings, then they came to know this feeling of falling away from the path that had once been given to them to follow. This path that would have allowed them to remain a conscious member of our family of all life.

"So it is that when you will experience this knowing without having the understanding of why it is there, it is good to explore this rather than ignore it. For it will be in exploring this feeling that has come to you from another that you will find a clue of how to remember what had once been done so easily by all of the two-legs. How to share with all life that is within this domain as well as the life that is on the other side of the great spirit waters in the waiting place.

"So when you come to the grandfathers of the

standing people's nations and ask them for permission to enter this place they share with their family, remember how you felt from one you cared for...how they shared their love and how it was revealed to you. Remember this, because it will be the same way this grandfather will answer you. It will be in the same way because this is the true form of sharing. It is a sharing that is from the heart and the spirit, rather than from the opening of the mouth that so many of the two-legs have come to value so highly.

"Now, Speaking Wind, when you are accepted on this place by the grandfather of these standing people, keep in the front of your thinking mind that he has already seen within you what you have a need for. He already has a knowing of what his children can offer to you and when you will receive his acceptance, you must come to know that it is good. It is good because in this place, you will find many of those things you have come to him for.

"Once you will have received this acceptance from the grandfather you have walked over to, the next event that will be presented to you will be where to go. And this, too, will be shown to you by this grandfather.

"It is the grandfather who knows his children very well, and with this knowing and understanding that he holds for each of them, he will share with you which one to go to. Which one of his children will be best prepared to assist you in finding those things you are seeking assistance on.

"And this will come to you in much the same way the original acceptance of your need did. For there will be a deep urge to look into a certain direction on this land, and as you do this, there will be one of the

=⊕=

standing people who will appear to you a little more clearly than all of the others.

"The one who you are being guided to will appear to you either brighter than all of the others, closer, or more accessible. But in any case, it will appear to be different than all of the others who will share on this land you have come to. And when you will see this difference from your within place...when you will feel this difference that you are seeing, then go to it. Go to this one who is calling you to them.

"Remember, Speaking Wind, you do not arrive in a land that you seem to be lost in and try to give directions to those who know their way. This would be foolish to do.

"However, many of the two-legs hold this close to them because they feel it gives them power. But I tell you in truth that it does not.

"So when you decide to travel among the children of the Earth Mother and come to them for their assistance, then do not turn away from those things they are willing to share with you. Listen to them...they do know the way.

"Now, when you see this one standing person calling to you, this one who has been asked also by the grandfather to assist you, then you would do well to go to it. Go to it for there is still much to do...for both of you.

"You must hold in the front of your thinking mind that it is the standing people who carry all of those messages that are to go to either the Earth Mother, the Great Spirit, or Great Mystery as well as the other nations that are in between.

"The standing people will listen to your requests with their heart of the spirit and it is this heart that does not become bothered with any unnecessary emotions that might get in the way. And because they have learned to listen in this way, they see you for what your needs are, rather than the you who merely has wants to be satisfied.

"You will come to understand this more completely as you pass through more and more seasons of your life path, Speaking Wind. So for now, let it remain that it is from the tops of the standing people's highest branches that they will hold all of those needs that have come to them. They will hold them far into the highest places where the spirit wind can pass by them and carry them off to the ones who would be willing to assist.

"Now, when you walk up to this standing person who has called to you, come to a place where you can look straight at the trunk before you, but in a position that will also allow you to look high up into those top places that I have shared with you.

"Then with your left hand, place it on the part of the trunk that you feel the most comfortable with and with the right hand, begin to stroke this trunk of the standing person gently and lovingly.

"For simplicity, think of caressing one who you are having deep feelings for from your own kind. In this way, there will be the proper feelings that will come from you and be shared with this standing person.

"When you do this, you will be showing this person that you care for them. Care for them in a way that they may return this same feeling to you.

"It will be when this feeling that is called love enters this standing person that they will respond to you. And they will respond in a way that will come as a great surprise to those who have not yet learned the way.

"When the standing person finds the love that you are offering to them acceptable, they will move your left hand for you. You will think that this is movement from you, Speaking Wind, but it is not. This is the returning of the love the standing person holds for all life, and when you stop trying to control or analyze it, you will feel this love that is in great abundance throughout this domain of the Earth Mother's. You will feel it and as you accept it, there will be a flooding of this love that is the bond between all life...this is the acceptance of an unconditional love for another life that truly exists for all of us.

"It will be then that you will picture the need that you have come to this standing person for assistance. Picture this need in the front of your thinking mind and allow it to be seen by this gentle one of our nation.

"There is really no other process that you will have to perform after this place has been reached by the two of you. This is where the acceptance of the levels of love through understanding that both of you possess will have been attained.

"All you will have to do is to picture your need and allow it to travel through your right hand and into the trunk of this standing person.

"It is important to remember that it will always be the right hand that will give and the left one which will accept. This will apply no matter which hand you will use to do most of your work with.

"When you feel this picture leave your right hand and pass into the standing person, then your task is completed. You have finished what you had intended to do and you may either sit down under the shade of the standing person, or you may leave and come back in a short time.

"However, remember to return to this same place, Speaking Wind. For if you will not do this, then when the assistance you have requested arrives, it will have to be held by this standing person until you return to retrieve it. Until that time, it will become like an additional piece of baggage for this one to hold for you because it does not have a need for it...only you do.

"This becomes much like putting away your toys when you are finished playing with them. If you leave them out and around, they will either get lost, broken, or someone else will use them. But in any case, they will no longer be yours to play with and you will be left with fewer and fewer until there are none left.

"When the standing person accepts your request for assistance, Speaking Wind, they will take it and place it in a spirit bag which will be carried to the topmost parts of themselves. Once it is there, it is hung on the most outer branches where the spirit wind will pick it up and carry it away.

"The spirit wind continually has many of these spirit bags held over himself for this is what he has entered this domain to do. And when he passes by many of the other spirits who are willing to assist you on his many journeys through all of this domain and through all of these nations, they will see those spirit bags he carries and will know which of them they are capable of giving assistance to.

"Then, taking these bags from the spirit wind, they will add their medicine to them and give them back to the spirit wind who will then return the spirit bags to the standing person that offered them.

"Once all of this has taken place, and I will share with you that it will be from one minute to three days, the standing person will hold onto your spirit bag for you...waiting for your return to it so this standing person may pass on this additional blessing to you.

"When all of this has taken place, Speaking Wind, you will be called once again. It will be a calling that will come to your within place of spirit from the standing person who has received your message.

"Just as you learned to see this standing person out of all of the others, you will be called back to him in much the same way. You will receive this calling much the same as you would recognize that someone is standing behind you before you see them.

"This call will request your presence before this standing person once again. And no matter where you will be...how close or how far, because you opened yourself to this standing person of my nation, they will find you. They will find you because you have shared a piece of your spirit with them and they with you.

"Because this has taken place, there is now a bond of understanding that exists between the both of you and what you choose to do with it will depend on you.

"Now when you arrive back at this place where you once began, return first to the grandfather of the standing people and give to him your thanks for all that has been done on your behalf. Do this with a good heart and a face that is filled with truth. This truth that will come to you that understands that all that has ever been done by you is good.

"Once you receive this recognition, leave another offering of your tobacco and travel to the standing person who has been calling you that holds your spirit bag filled with the assistance you are in need of.

"When you are in the same place as you were when you first made this request of him, enter in the same way as you did before. And that is to use the left hand to receive and the right hand to send, remembering to place the picture of your need into the front of your thinking mind and let it travel into this one through your right hand.

"You will find that assistance you were requesting filling you, and this process will be very quick. However, do not make the mistake of thinking that all of the work for you has been done and you are standing with a completed package, Speaking Wind. For this is not the path of truth you would be following if this is what you believe.

"You will only be given those pieces to the understanding you are seeking that would not have come to you through normal events in your life path. These pieces of assistance will come to you only in a way that will allow you to see the direction of the path you are traveling. And this direction will lead you through other events that will, in time and with the proper understanding for them, lead you to find your own answer.

"Always try to keep this in the front of your thinking mind, Speaking Wind, that all of us are brothers and sisters, but not all of us have come to the place yet of becoming friends with one another.

"A friend is one who will make their presence known to you while giving you the freedom of doing your own work for those things you need. For those things that you will need to learn from so that you may gain the higher levels of understanding that will allow your spirit to advance itself to the next higher place among all of Great Mystery.

"Understand how to be thankful for all that you have now, Speaking Wind. Do not fall off the path of the spirit and onto the path of the others who only consider all of those things they do not have. This will bring you to no place that will serve any benefit to you or any other.

"This is then my offering to you...this understanding of how to use all of the members of my nation of standing people to seek out a doorway to the spirit. Does this hold well for you?" she asked, still sitting in the same position of a peace giver that she had begun from.

"Yes, Telah," I returned with a tone of reverence in my speaking words that had not been heard by me before.

"This sits well with me and for all that you have been willing to share with me, I give to you my gratitude. I know that I will take back with me on this day many things that will assist me greatly with my traveling on this path of the spirit.

"However, there is a question that I would ask of you at this time that we are sharing. It is one that I would greatly appreciate an understanding on, if you would not mind."

"Of course I would not mind, little one. What is this question you would ask of me?"

"You have shared with me that I am already in my vision quest. Is this not so?"

"Yes, Speaking Wind, this is in truth what I have shared with you. Why do you ask such a thing?"

"It is because I do not have a full understanding of what or where I am. Am I in spirit form and that is how I am able to see you? And can others see me, the ones who have not come to seek a vision quest?"

"Yes, Speaking Wind...," came her response.

"You are in this vision quest that you have been seeking but you are only now standing in the doorway of it. And as for seeing me and others seeing you, I will say to you that if another would pass both of us by at this time, they would see both of us sitting on this piece of the Earth Mother sharing those things that they, too, might even hear if they held with them the proper levels of understanding."

"And if one would pass us by, Telah, who was not traveling on the path of the spirit...if one of the others were to come near to us, then what would they see?"

"They would only see you sitting in the cold of the snow without any clothes on you. And seeing this, they would most likely pass you by very quickly thinking that whatever is wrong with you might rub off on them.

"But they would only see you, Speaking Wind... they would not see nor would they hear me. And for that fact, they would not hear your speaking words in any way that would allow them to understand what it was you were sharing."

"And why would this be so, Telah?"

"It is because they have not yet learned to open their own eyes and ears of their spirit, little one. Remember that while one is still traveling on the path that leads to the left, this path we have come to call the path of the others that is led by the body and fed by the emotions; this is the path that one is lulled into and kept trapped within the sleep of illusion.

"This sleep of illusion does not allow any who travel with it to see anything for what it is. It only allows them to see all things for what they would wish for them to be.

"And because they would only have the eyes and ears to see and hear those things they would want to see, or be capable of recognizing, then they would not have any understanding of their own spirit; and if there is not an awareness of their own spirit, they cannot see the one that is within you nor me...for I am completely in spirit now with you.

"As far as hearing these things that you are saying and what they will see on you, I tell you that they will only recognize your body part of yourself and this will be what they will come to see as something that is strange for you to do...to sit in the cold snows without any clothing on and speak in ways that are not understood by them. Ways that are not understood by them because we are sharing in the speaking of our spirits and they will only come to hear this as unintelligible sounds that are being uttered by you.

"Does this give you the answer that you have been seeking?"

"Partially...," was my return. I was still groping with my thinking mind so that I might place these concerns of mine into intelligent speaking words.

"Then what is the rest of this question of yours?"

"Well, if I am already in my vision quest, do I have to go further or have I already received those answers I have been seeking but have not yet come to the place of fully understanding them?"

"There is still much for you to do, Speaking Wind. I am only the one who has come to you for this beginning, but there are the old ones who are now waiting for you to arrive. Waiting to bring you to them on this vision quest you have begun.

"You see, while I am the beginning...they are the completion of all that you are seeking.

"Our time now is over, little one, and now you must enter this land that has been prepared for you and this vision that is soon to be presented."

"I will not forget you, Telah," I said, looking deep into her eyes.

"We have traveled many roads together, little brother, and we will travel many more in those times that have not yet been born to either of us.

"Be well, Speaking Wind. Be well and know that this path you travel is done for many who would be lost without those things that will be shared with you on this day."

I rose from my seated position on the stone and turned to look into the direction Telah had pointed out for me where there was a great place of the flat rocks.

However, when I turned to pay one last respect to her, she was no longer there and neither were any of the marks one would leave on the earth they had been sitting on.

But as it was with so many things that had come to me on this path of the spirit, I knew there would be another time when this one called Telah would return to me when I would once again have a great need for her counsel and wisdom.

So turning myself back to where we had shared many speaking words, I opened my small pouch of tobacco and gave my thanks to the standing people who were here with me on this day; also to the stone people who had also shared great wisdom with me, as well.

Finishing this, I then turned to travel into the great

=⊕=

flat stone land. This land that had been pointed out to me by Telah where I was to begin my journey to the Ancient Ones who had been waiting for me to come to them.

ENTRY

As I traveled into the direction I had been shown, I could see that these mountains were beginning to open up into a clearing. This was not far from the place where Telah and I had been allowed to share so many things from the teachings of her nation...the standing people.

Looking just over to the place where I was traveling to, I could see that there were small clouds of steam that were filling the air on this land.

I could feel something new, though, as I entered this land of the flat stones. Something was calling to me, but not in any way I had come to know before.

For this calling was coming to me not only from my within place, but from all places at the same time and at the same levels of intensity.

This was giving me a feeling of no longer being in control of my actions; but as soon as this feeling had entered the front of my thinking mind...it left. I was left with only the knowing of direction and procedures that I was to follow once I had arrived in the place that had been prepared for me.

I had not gone more than a few yards from the place where Telah and I had been allowed to share those many things that I could feel taking root deep within me and being carried safely by my spirit.

And just as soon as it had taken for me to remember those things she and I had shared together, I looked onto the lands ahead of me. These lands that had been prepared for my entry to the domain of the Ancient Ones, those who were now awaiting for my arrival with them.

It was not from any knowing that I knew these to be the lands where my journey to the old ones would begin, but it was more from a living of truth that was being shared from within me now. Now that I had finally arrived at the place where I was to be.

As I looked over these lands, there was something that was vaguely familiar about them. But as I allowed this feeling to come to life, it was just too far buried for me to find an understanding for it. Too far away for me to reach.

I allowed this feeling to be but not to be in a way that would stop my direction to this path that was being shown.

Setting my first step onto this land of the flat rock, I could once again feel the softness that was all about it as had come to me once before when Telah had called to me and caused me to walk with my spirit.

Now, this feeling was coming into me once again, but now it was even stronger than it had been before. I then thought that it was as great as it would ever become.

Looking over this land that I had been called to, I could see there were many standing people and rock people that had come to call this their home. And as I looked further into each of them, I felt the calling of speaking words that had been shared with me by Telah and they were explaining a deeper understanding for all of life that is within this domain.

≡⊕≡

Whether it was from the teachings of Grand-father and Two Bears, or from the sharing that had just taken place by Telah, I could feel the welcoming by all of these people of the many different nations of life. A welcoming that was allowing me to feel as if I had been one who had been on a very long journey but who had just now remembered how to return.

As I looked over the far distance of these lands, I could see there was a deep valley below me which rose into tall mountains beyond.

Standing on the edge of this outreaching place of the flat rock, I could hardly make out the bottom of the lands below, for they were so far below me that it would have taken a stone thrown into it a very long time to reach the bottom.

Then I looked over to the west and saw the reflection of the Great Spirit going down once again. I knew there would not be much time left for me to prepare those things that were needed before I would begin.

So using all of the time that had been left to me, I began to set about preparing all of those things that were necessary so that I could enter this vision quest in the way I had been prepared from the teachings of the spirit path I had been traveling and learning from.

Looking for the largest and seemingly oldest stand-ing person on this place, I walked over to ask for their permission to use some of their discarded pieces to build a fire with. And when I received their permis-sion, I placed a few pieces of tobacco over their root place, knowing this would signify my appreciation for that which they had given me permission to use.

Next, I walked over to the greatest stone on this land and asked for permission to use some of their

other members to create a spirit circle. I had been
instructed on creating a spirit circle many seasons
before.

And once again, when I received permission to do
this, I placed another few pieces of tobacco at the foot
of this grandfather of the stone people. I then began
my task of constructing my spirit circle that would
keep my body part safe while I would begin my
journey to the old ones. A journey that I was already
beginning to see in the back of my thinking mind.

Gathering the needed pieces of wood that would
serve as my fire, I stacked them in a way that would
allow them to burn very slowly but steadily without
making too much smoke. For among these teachings
that I had been prepared with, smoke was a form of
life that would be seen and interpreted by the nations
of the Earth Mother; and to send it up without any
meaning would be like telling another something
very important when they were not willing to listen to
you. With this completed, I located two sticks that I
could rub together to begin the ceremonial fire.

Once this was accomplished, I reached for the
small pieces of sage that I had found on one of the
nearby stone places. And even though it was not a
common thing to find on these lands anymore, I knew
the sage had come here for a reason. It was to be the
messenger that would carry my calling to the old
ones. I had prepared myself to the best of my abilities
and I was now willing to begin my journey to them.

Picking up the pieces of sage, I tied them into a
rather tight bundle. One that would allow them to be
lit and carry with them a smoke of requesting from
the spirit prayer I would soon share with them.

Next, I looked for all of the stone people who

would be willing to share in this vision quest with me. They would be formed into the spirit circle I was needing to construct with their help.

As each of the stone people who would be a willing participant called to me, I placed them into a loose pile. One that would allow me to share with them where I was going to place them in the spirit circle.

It would be in this way they could see where they would like to be placed and by doing this, all would be able to assist in the most beneficial way possible.

For it had been shared with me by the teachings of the path of the spirit that when one is in a place where they know there is good, they can contribute; then all of their talents and abilities will be utilized as they should be. This will always create an environment where all will be able to contribute greatly and feel a part of the whole that is needing to be built.

There was a small steaming pool of water that was very close to the place I had piled the stone people and this looked to me to be the one place in all of this land where I could build my spirit circle.

So, placing this picture in the front of my thinking mind, I shared it with the grandfather of the standing people and of the rock people and waited for their reply.

It did not take much time before I held the knowing that they, too, felt this was a good place to have my spirit circle; and turning to the small steaming pool of water, I then asked its permission as well, to use its place for my vision quest and entry into the domain of the Ancient Ones.

Pleased with all of the goodness that had filled me from these separate nations of our relations, I looked over to where I had stacked the smaller stones and shared this with them, as well. And as I did this, I was asking them where they wanted to be placed, allowing them the same amount of freedom as I had been given on this journey.

As I looked at each of the places that would soon be made into the spirit circle around the small steaming pool of water, each of the stone people I had gathered would call my attention to them in a way that shared with me where they each would wish to be placed for this ceremony.

When one constructs a spirit circle of the stone people which allows them to enter the crack in the universe and find their path to the Ancient Ones, they will have a great need for those who are within this domain to take care of their body part that will soon be left behind them. This is much the same was as when one drops their robe at the end of their seasons with the Earth Mother.

However, this is not as final as dropping one's robe in this domain. The final destination of the vision quest is not to return across the great spirit waters to the waiting place. The intention is much different. For when the spirit circle is completed, there will be one or several great spirit messengers who will come to assist you in traveling into this crack of the universe.

But in order to do this, the body part must be left behind for there is not any way that it, too, can enter this place of the old ones; at least not that I yet knew from all of those things I had been prepared with.

So it becomes necessary to not only ask the other nations of life for their permission to use their lands for this vision quest, but in the process, one has to ask for their assistance in keeping away from your body part those things that are not desirable while you are away.

When one completes their spirit circle and begins their great journey to the place of the Ancient Ones, they will have entered another dreamtime. One that is sacred on the path of the spirit. And when one enters this domain, there is no telling how long they will be gone because time, as we have come to understand it in this domain, does not exist.

So it is with wisdom that one will ask all of their brothers and sisters in the many other nations to be kind to them while they are away and to assist them in keeping their body part safe for their return... whenever that will be.

As I went on with the business of placing all of these stones in a great circle around the steaming pool of water, these were the things that went into the front of my thinking mind. As I finished the spirit circle, I had placed all of the stone people in a perfect circle, except for the last one. This was to be the one that would be last placed in the east position of where my body part would be staying while I traveled my spirit journey to the Ancient Ones.

Once the east stone had been placed on this spirit circle and the asking of the spirit blessing had been performed, then I would not be allowed to leave it. For once it has been sealed in the east position, then this was my saying to all who were with me, as well as those who were on their way, that I was now ready to begin. And I would remain within this small circle for as long as it would take.

Holding these things in the front of my thinking mind, I shared them with the last of the stone people who I would finally place in the east position, closing the circle. I shared with these stone people what their purpose was to be so they would not feel left out of this ceremony and then went onto the next step that I needed to take. The step of starting the fire I had laid all of the wood for.

Walking over to the edge of this flat rock place, I placed the small spark of beginnings into the smaller pieces of wood I had piled together and soon there was a good start for this fire.

The fire was very symbolic of those things I had been prepared with as I had learned to travel on this path of the spirit. It represented the direction of light that was shared with all who would look for it from the Ancient Ones. They would share this light from the great council fires of our ancestors to show us our way.

And there was another reason for this fire on this land. One that was coming to me from deep within me now, and it was allowing those speaking words of Grandfather and Two Bears to come back to life from within me.

"Remember, Speaking Wind. When you will begin a spirit quest, there is a need for building a small fire of your own. This serves many reasons but the greatest of them is to allow yourself to ask to be connected to the light of the ancient council fires of our ancestors.

"It will be from this light of your one council fire that will light the way for the old ones to see who and what you are. And this will be done from the light that you have started being joined with the light of their council fire. This joining is a bond that will be maintained throughout all of the seasons that will be left to you on your life path with the Earth Mother. And this light will serve as a reminder to you of what it is that you will be seeking from them. The kind of assistance that is needed by you during this time.

"Also, the light from this small fire will allow you to have a place to see when it is time for your return from the great crack in the universe, this crack that is in truth, the opening of the doorway to the Ancient Ones.

"The use of this fire will also be the source of your prayer time to them, as well, Speaking Wind. For it will be from the flames that you will have brought into this fire that will be used to ignite the small smoke offering you will be required to make to the Old Ones. This small smoke offering that will begin to carry with it your pictures of the spirit prayer of assistance you are asking for.

"The process of the fire is no different. For the light of direction you will use from this fire will be the same light that will begin to offer your prayers of acceptance to the Old Ones, and it will be this same light that will allow your spirit helpers to find you and assist you in finding your way back, as well.

"There are many reasons for all of this but for now just remember to be thankful for all that has come to you during this time of opening your spirit prayer to the Old Ones. Be thankful for all of the wonderful blessings that you have been given to carry with you. For if you are outweighed by the things you are not thankful for, then you will become too heavy to lift from this domain of the Earth Mother's. You will be too heavy for even the greatest of spirit helpers to assist you into the great crack of the universe and you will have to look for your answers from another place. One that is not within the realm of the Ancient Ones."

Hearing these speaking words return to life from within me was giving me great comfort. One that would calm me now that my vision quest was about to begin.

And they were allowing me to receive this confirmation for those things I was to do next.

Reaching out to the place I had set the small bundle of sage, I picked it up and set one corner of it into the flames of the fire. This fire that would be my one connection to where I was at now.

I allowed a corner of it to catch on fire, then blew it out which resulted in a long and curving trail of smoke rising from it. Even though there was still a small whisper of the spirit wind over this land, it did not seem to alter this course the smoke had chosen to follow and it continued on its journey into the great sky nation as one straight trail.

Seeing this take place, I knew that the time had come for me to share my spirit prayer with this small messenger to the Old Ones. Calling to them in a way that had been shown to me many seasons before, I allowed them to hear my request of assistance.

Hear me, you four great chieftains
Who hold the keys to the seven directions

See me for who I am
And these needs that have come to life from within
   me

What I am being asked to do
I do not hold an understanding for
And it is giving to me a weight of uncertainty

Show me the light of the council fire of the old ones
So I may see the direction of travel I must take

Show me the light of the council fire of the old ones
So I may join mine with theirs and become one

Allow those who have come to assist me to show
*   themselves*
So that I might see where they will wish to have me
*   travel*

I call on them as I call on you for this
It is I, Speaking Wind, who now stand before you
Stand before you as a part of the life that is one.

Placing this speaking prayer of assistance into the front of my thinking mind, I allowed it to travel into the rising of the smoke from the sage.

I continued to watch this smoke rise into the great sky nation until it had finished its course. Then I knew that it was time for me to enter the spirit circle and close it off with the last stone in the east position.

Walking over to the spirit circle, I could see that the sun had already gone down in the west and there was only the clear sky that was over me.

As I neared the place of the circle, I could see glimpses of the fire within the steaming waters before me. And as I looked over to them, I could feel a lightness filling me. A lightness that was causing me to feel like one of the small cloud people from the sky nation.

Reaching over to the place where I had left the last stone person, I closed off the circle and sealed it in the proper way. This allowed me to give my gratitude to all who were with me for those many blessings that had been shared with me already, and for those which had not yet come.

Also, as I closed off this last place in the east of my spirit circle, I once again thanked all of my brothers and sisters from the many nations for the safe keeping of my body part. For I held the knowing that soon I would begin a great journey. One that I had no way of comparing to any of my past experiences.

With the east stone finally in place, I positioned myself in the western portion of the spirit circle, facing the east. It was a position that placed this small steaming pool of water between me, the east point of the spirit circle, and the fire.

Looking at all three of these places, I was feeling my body part getting lighter and the substance of my spirit within becoming more alive as it seemed to be receiving a new kind of life within it. I could sense this as being familiar, but not so familiar that I knew where this knowing and feeling of it were coming from.

From my sitting position in this circle of friends, I was looking at the steam rising before me.

As I looked at the steam as it rose, I could see that it, too, was following the same course as the smoke from the sage I had used just a short time before. It was traveling into the sky nation and was as straight as the eye can see.

Looking at the rising of the steam with the glowing from the firelight within it was allowing me to see why the entry of dream time for our people had always been held so sacred. For as I looked into the rising of the steam with the glowing of the firelight, I was continually reminded of the oneness that is within all things in this domain. The oneness that is within all of us because we have all come from the same source. And it was a part of this source that allowed such a wonderful thing of beauty to be seen by me on this night. This beauty was sharing itself with me from so many whom I had asked acceptance from on this land.

When the firelight caught the rising steam in a certain way, I could see there were many small rainbows being formed. And as I looked into each of them, they all held a great story to share with me. But it was being shared with my spirit part and I could only hear bits and pieces of it.

I was becoming lost in this portrayal of life. In the way one life will always compliment another when there is a balance existing between them, this balance that is so sought after by the two-legs.

And just as I was in the middle of this thought, there was the appearance of a great glowing light all around me. As I looked up from my place of sitting in this spirit circle, I saw that it was the rising of the moon in the east.

Looking over to her, I saw that she was early in her rise and her full and rounded size seemed to be larger than all of the night sky above me.

As I continued to watch her rise from the east, there were a few of the taller standing people that were being silhouetted against her light. This reminded me of those many times when one thinks they

are alone, only to find another or many others standing next to them, and the surprise of relief they experience when they see them for the first time.

Feeling her presence as she shared her light over
the night sky above me was a reminder of a promise
that we are not ever alone. I held out both of my hands
in an upward motion and offered all that was me to
her for those things that she, too, was in need of.

We have been prepared with the understanding
that this light that is from the moon is another of the
reflections of the love the Earth Mother holds for all of
us. And that when the moon appears to one in the
night sky, we should be just as open to feeling the
Earth Mother's love as we would be when the Great
Spirit's reflection is with her in the daytime.

As I continued to observe her night climb in the
sky over me, I saw no other members of the sky nation
with her. All of the cloud people had gone to another
place for this night and as the light of the full moon fell
over all of these lands, I could see the brightness being
returned to her from the snow covering that was all
around me.

As she continued to climb into the night sky, I
could see her becoming smaller and smaller until she
had arrived at the size that I was used to seeing her as.
And once she attained this size of her normal self, she
remained fixed into the top of the night sky overhead
and continued to watch over all of her children through
a silence only she could understand.

I was becoming lost in this presentation on this
night when I was called from it by the sounding of the
spirit wind crossing the many standing people all
around me.

Behind this passing of the spirit wind, I could hear

many drums and flutes being played from a distance. The sounds were from the high reaches of the many mountains that were towering over me.

Behind all of these drums and flutes, I could hear many voices singing a spirit song, one that I had heard before but in the dreamtime that I had traveled through.

As I listened to them, they began to share their faces that belonged to the singing, the drumming, and the flute playing. And I knew they belonged to the Old Ones who had traveled on these lands many generations before and were still here to assist in their own way of keeping the balance of life available to all who would seek it.

This was something that was remembered well by all of our people...when a spirit walker would become successful in the quests they had come to the Earth Mother to perform, then they would be offered a place of great honor with her among all of her children. They would become one of the guardians over those lands.

When they accepted this place of guardianship, they would find their new homes within all of the lands they had come to know and love so well.

This was what was being called to me then on this night. This calling of the voices, faces, drums, and flutes were coming to me as a reminder of all those who had come before me and had succeeded with those things they had come here to do. And now, they were in a place of great honor. A place where they could continue to offer their assistance to the Earth Mother, the spirits of the land, and all of the children of the Earth Mother from the many talents and blessings that had been shared with them.

But there was something else that was coming to me and it was still further behind those voices and spirit calls than I could see.

Even though I could not yet see it for what it was, I could feel it, bearing a great power of its own. A power that was much stronger than any I had come to know so far on this night.

I could feel the sense of purpose that it was carrying and the direction it was traveling. It was coming to me, and as it got closer, the sounds of the old ones were becoming louder.

There was a new life that was being born into the air that was all around me. It was a life that I could feel but could not see for it was not yet time for this to take place, even though I could tell it was very close now.

As I had been prepared from the teachings of Grandfather and Two Bears, when one will allow things to be...they will be. And from what was being presented to me, this was the path I was now willing to take that would allow me to see the entry into the domain of the old ones.

I turned my head away from the fire and mountains that were all around me and looked up to the place where the reflection of the Earth Mother, the moon, was sitting.

She was looking down on all of her children with a full face now and there did not seem to be anything that could remain hidden for very long.

As I was looking at her, that same feeling was coming to me once again, only this time it was getting much stronger and I could no longer allow it to pass by me. The feeling of another life form taking place on this land was so strong now that I was tempted to move from my position to make room for it. This thought had come to the front of my thinking mind because it was so powerful that I could not help but think of it as having a great mass. One that would make more than ten of me.

I allowed this thought to leave me and continued to look onto the face of the full moon above me, trying not to think of this new feeling of life that was approaching.

I tried to fill my thinking mind with the sounds the spirit wind was making through the tall standing people that had come to call this land their homes. And as I attempted to listen carefully to them, I found the music and spirit calling chants were becoming that much louder and more pronounced.

It seemed as if there would be no looking away from those events that had made themselves known to me on this night. And I could hear them getting stronger and stronger as I continued to sit on the inside of my spirit circle.

Then something told me to look up at the place where the reflection of the Earth Mother was lighting the night lands. As I did this, I was filled with awe. For where there had not been anything filling the night sky, there was a lone and small cloud.

I observed this small one as it came to form itself directly between the full moon and me. As I looked at it, I could feel that it, too, had been given a path to travel. One that was beginning to make itself known to me.

As the small little white cloud passed through the night air, it suddenly came to rest in front of the moon. Then it began to form itself into eleven smaller clouds and they were circling the moon much in the same way the stone people had been surrounded around me in my spirit circle.

Watching them as they were forming themselves into what appeared to be a large spirit circle in the night sky, I was surprised to see that there were only eleven small ones.

Then they began to all move into another direction. One that was sharing with me a new face for the life and direction they had taken on themselves. Within a few moments, there was no longer any resemblance of what they had been. For they were no longer formed into a spirit circle around the moon, they now seemed to have been directed to new positions around her that I had not become that familiar with.

Their movements were slow but they were sure, and what they were doing next was to move themselves from the spirit circle formation back into the oneness of the small cloud I had seen earlier on this night.

Once there was only the one cloud in the night sky, it once again began its separation. Now, it was no longer one, but had become the same eleven smaller ones and they seemed to have been told into what direction they were to move.

With the sureness of a seasoned traveler, they began to go to the places they had been assigned. There were three of them first and they moved to the top of the full moon and remained stationary but next to the other small clouds.

Then this process was repeated by three more and they moved to the bottom of the moon. Next another three positioned themselves to the left of her and finally, the last two moved to a place at her right. Once they had achieved their position, I recognized their face as a star circle of clouds in the night sky.

I could feel there was a significance to all of this movement and the forms that had been created by these small ones of the sky nation, but I could not find the understanding that I needed to see it clearly. And this was clouding my vision of what was being presented.

Just as this had come to the front of my thinking mind, there appeared to me a night rainbow. Though it was very faint at first, as time passed, it became much brighter and more pronounced in the colors it was reflecting back to me.

As I looked at these colors, I was receiving a new meaning for what it was that was being shown.

As soon as the colors became evident in the star circle of the clouds, I saw that the three on the bottom had become a bright red. Next, the three that were on the top of the moon became a brilliant white, while the two that were to the right became an almost iridescent yellow.

Then as I was waiting for the ones that were on the left of the moon to gain their color, I was surprised to see that what had once appeared as a gray outline on them disappeared and their color was now a complete black. One that allowed me to see them as three dark holes in the night sky.

When all of the colors had been formed into these eleven, I could see what they had come to remind me of. It was the medicine wheel of life and they had separated themselves into the four basic directions that are measured by this. Each with its own purpose and path to teach from.

However, I was still perplexed by their numbers. I did not have an understanding of why there were only two that had come to position themselves in the east while all the other directions had three members to them.

As I pondered this question and placed it in the front of my thinking mind, I held the knowing that this was not the time for this answer to be revealed to me. Not yet, at least, because as I was looking into this direction of the sky nation over me, I saw this medicine wheel of life began to lose its form. And as it was doing this, it was becoming something else. Something that was coming to me with another message that once again I could feel but did not have an understanding for.

Looking at these eleven little ones begin their movements, I first expected them to disappear into the night sky. But as their movements became more pronounced, they were not disappearing at all. Instead, they were coming back to the one they had all begun from. And as they did this, the one they were gathering into was becoming more and more brightly filled with the color white.

Now, all of the original eleven had gathered themselves into one. And this one was now reflecting its own color of a clear and brilliant white light. One that did not pale against the fullness of the moonlight that was continuing to fall over this land of our peoples.

As soon as these eleven had become one and made their radiance known, I noticed that there was another change that was beginning to take place within them. A change that would soon come to me, for this was the feeling of knowing that I had received.

The flute players, the drum players, and the spirit chanters were all very loud now and even if there had been a great highway noise near me, I do not believe that it would have been loud enough to be heard. For what was taking place in this night sky was that the one cloud, breaking the silence of the night sky with its brilliant color of white, was beginning to move itself another time.

The one small cloud that had been the eleven was now moving itself to a place that was just under the reflection of the Earth Mother in the night sky above me. Once it attained its desired position...it stopped. And as it stopped, so did all other events that had been so much filled with a life of their own.

The small cloud was now sitting just underneath the full moon and there was nothing that was stirring over these lands but the silence all of us are born into. Even the spirit wind had stopped his nightly movements and the drum players, the flute players, and the spirit chanters had all gone into this great silence that was now flooding all of the lands that could see this place of light. The light was becoming brighter from the inside of this one small cloud who was now sitting under the Earth Mother's reflection.

As this was taking place among the cloud and all that were within this domain of the white light, there was something that called my attention to the place where I had built my calling fire. Something that was telling me that now was the time for me to look on another great change that was coming to this land. A change that would involve me, as well.

FROM SEPARATION TO ONENESS

When I turned my eyes from the place of the cloud in the night sky and into the direction where I had built this small fire on the place of the flat rocks, I was filled with yet another surprise. It filled me with an excitement and an expectation for what was about to take place.

Looking over to this small fire, I noticed that it was beginning to burn much brighter now. Brighter than would have normally been expected from any that I had ever come to see, even when there had been great amounts of fast burning wood cast on them.

For the small fire that I had built was beginning to release a life path of its own and this path it was following was one that led up to the place where the bright cloud had positioned itself in the darkness of the sky above me.

The silence held for a short while longer, only to be broken by the sound of a very long exhale of air. One that was similar to breathing out in a very strong manner, but without the shortness that is held within our own efforts.

This sound was the only one allowed to break this silence. As it began, I could feel the heat and light that was being held within this small fire began to increase. And as it did, there was a sudden whiteness of glowing that was beginning to be born from within this small fire.

It was not the usual glowing of a fire's light that was being shared with me, rather it was a white light that was being formed from the reds and yellows that I had become used to seeing for those many times I would share my prayers with the fire ones of this

=⊕=

land.

Now, as the white light became large enough to almost take over all of the other colors of the fire, I could hear the rustling of the spirit wind approaching as it was coming from the four corners of this land.

Soon there was another calling, but it was not one that was coming from the approaching of the spirit wind. It was one that was coming from the inside of the firelight itself. As each moment of time would pass, I could hear it more and more clearly. It was a calling similar to the one of a child who was ready to be born into this domain. Like the calling of the child to the mother who is about to bear him that the time is now right and all that has been needed...has been done.

As this calling reached my ears, I saw the face of the spirit wind as it approached this small one of the fire who was calling for the release of its life into this domain.

It was a face that was filled with a love and under-standing for what this small fire had been requesting. I was also reminded of the look that comes over a mother's face as she looks down on her new child and sees that all is as it should be.

This was filling me with a great love for all that was being shared with me at this time. This great love was accompanied with an understanding for what was now taking place here.

I was filled with this understanding that what Telah had shared with me was true, and because I had been allowed to listen to her speaking words and come to a place of partial understanding of them, I was now able to see what she had only spoken to me about before.

I was looking at the sharing of the balance we had all come to know at one time. For in this balance of sharing, there were none who would ever stand alone. None of the life that is within this domain was ever left in a place where it might be made to suffer the silence of no other being close to it or of another with whom it could not share all things with.

And within this balance, there was the knowing that for whatever the reason of need, there would always be the right one who would come to assist. The one who would have those abilities and talents that would be shared with the one who was in need of them.

How wonderful, I was thinking in the front of my thinking mind was this caring and nurturing that was being shared with me. What blessings there are within this domain that is the Earth Mother's that are so available to all who would be willing to see and hear them with their eyes and ears.

And as this newness of understanding was coming to me, I felt another change filling this space I had been allowed to share with all the spirit nations of the Earth Mother. A change that I knew deep within myself was meant for me.

Within the glowing of the small fire I had built, there was another color change that was coming to it. It was one that allowed the presence of the white light to blend into other colors and they were beginning to make themselves known to me as I was observing them.

For within the small place that was the center of this fire, the white light was becoming laced with colors of yellow, red, and black. And all of them seemed to be dancing with each other within this small circle that had been created by the hot coals from the burning wood.

They began to dance around each other in a small clockwise direction as their small circle was becoming larger and larger.

As the circle of dancing light was growing, I could hear the beating of the drums and singing of spirit chants begin to echo off from the sides of the mountain walls once again. Soon after that, there were the melodies of the flute music once again that seemed to be playing the message these new four colors were dancing to.

Once all of those things that had once been were back again...the flute music, the drum beating, and the spirit chanting...I heard, felt, and saw the face of the spirit wind as it, too, was gathering itself from the four corners of this land I had come to be accepted on for this ceremony.

And as I continued to feel all that was taking place around me, I could feel the beginning of birth take place. It was a beginning of a birth that I knew I would not ever forget for as long as I would be allowed to travel with the Earth Mother.

Within three heartbeats of mine, I noticed that there was no longer the sounds of many flutes playing this spirit melody of the dancing light. For now, there was only one, and it was not coming to me from the echoing of the mountain walls, it was living in all of the air that was around me.

And within another three heartbeats of mine, the spirit chanting had done the same. For it, too, had left its home and was now willing to live in this same air that was all around me.

Then, after another three heartbeats, I heard the

same sequence of events take place from the drum beating that was calling the rhythm and tempo of the dancing lights. It, too, had left its home from the far reaches of the mountains and had come to live within this air that was all around me.

Next, but only after two beats of my heart, the spirit wind gathered itself from its four places of living and made itself into the one. Into the one that was also filling every corner of this land I could see and feel.

As all of this was taking place, I could see that the dancing of the four colors of light had become very quick now and as their quickness increased, they grew from their place within the circle of the fire's flame.

I was being shown that as the four colors of light would dance in the beginning, all of them seemed to be holding onto each other, much like the dancers of the great unity circle will hold onto each others' hands or arms.

But as time and events continued to make themselves more and more known, there was no longer a separation between any of these four colors of the flame.

There was no longer any need of only holding hands now, for this time and this need for them had seemed to pass, for reasons that were only known among them.

As they continued to grow in size and increase in speed, I saw they were making attempts at leaving this place where they had first found their life.

As they spun faster and faster within the fire, they would make sudden jumps...movements that allowed me to see that they were trying to free themselves from those things that once contained them. And as they would free themselves from those things that once held them within their limits, they would begin to change once again.

With every attempt at leaving this fire of their beginning, they would seem to become stronger. And with their increasing strength, their own colors became more and more pronounced within themselves and this made them even more determined to leave this first home and travel into the second.

For every attempt that seemed to fail for them in their effort of leaving this place they had once known, they were left with a more pronounced color of their beginning. Every time they would attempt to jump from the fire and return, they would become more white, more yellow, more black, and more red.

As this was taking place, I could see that their individual colors were causing them to have an additional weight. A weight that was stopping them from traveling fast enough to leave the bounds of the fire they had begun from.

But also, with each of their attempts of reaching up and out, they would seem to blend into the one color of white once again. But this would only be for a short time and when they would return, they would all return to their own original colors that would be more pronounced and give to each of them more weight. This weight would cause them to work even harder for their next attempt at leaving this place of their first home.

This did not seem to stop them, however. For every time they fell back into this fire home of theirs and their colors became more pronounced, there was something additional they would receive either from the drum beating, the spirit chanting, or the flute playing that would cause them to try again.

And for each of their tries, there would be an additional point of altitude they would always seem to reach...a place that was just a little higher than the one they had reached before.

With each of these additional attempts to go higher, I could see that the higher they would go...the more of a blend their four colors would be.

I did not have an understanding of what was taking place at the time, but later I came to understand what was being presented to me. When this came, I knew that this lesson was not for the spirits of the flame to learn from...it was for me. This was the beginning of what was to be my message.

Now the small flames of the four colors increased their speed once again. But there was something that was much different in this attempt.

There were no longer the four colors that I had once seen. Now, there was a blending into the one white color once again. This white color that is the acceptance of all colors.

And this time, as they reached out with the exhaling sounds of their breath of life, the spirit wind saw what had taken place within them and came to them to offer them his assistance.

It was at this time when I noticed the column of light was engulfed by the spirit wind. As soon as this happened, the tempo of the drum players increased as did the spirit chants and flute playing.

Now, in the middle of all of this assistance that had come to the flames from their willingness to share themselves in a more complete knowing, all their efforts were united and allowed them to share their own individual strengths and talents.

This then was the key that the others of this land had been waiting for, was the thought that came to the front of my thinking mind. This then was what all had been waiting for from these small one who were attempting to reach out to a new place of life. A new and more free place to have their existence known from.

When they increased their speed and made their one attempt as the one color to reach out...they were successful in attaining a height of great proportions. A height that would not have been attainable had they remained as the four colors they had once been.

As they spun out of the ring of the fire place, the spirit wind then picked them up on the back of his hand and assisted them in being carried deep into the night sky that was over all of us. As the night sky was being lit by their presence, they were being filled with their newness of life they had found within themselves.

When this happened, I knew it was good. This was the combining of all that is into the one, and when this takes place there will be no limitation that will ever impede the arrival for any life into a new domain.

It was not long after the spirit wind allowed itself to assist in this process that I sat back within my small spirit circle with the steaming waters and observed one of the most beautiful sights that I had ever come to know.

For before me, there was the lone night sky that had embraced all of the children of the Earth Mother in its darkness of sleep while the light that was in the reflection of the Earth Mother's moon was flooding all it touched with its gentleness of love and caring.

And through all of this, there was a lone but very great column of light that was spiraling into this darkness that had been born to this land. A tall and spinning life of flame that spread itself out through the night, bringing brightness and warmth to all who would be in need of its sharing.

The spiral of the spinning light that had once been trapped as the four colors of its origin was now wrapped within a knowing and understanding that what had once not been possible of attaining as the four colors was now within reach when all became one.

And as all became one, there was a new awareness. One that would share with all who would see and hear it that there is no thing that is not possible when there is an acceptance of all that is...of all that has come from the one will, in time, return. And with this returning, then all is possible.

Higher and higher into the night sky this spiral of the white light would reach. And just as I was about to think that this would be the highest place it could attain, it would go even higher.

This continued to grow into the night sky. There was a purpose and direction that had come to the spiraling column of the white light. It was one that had been presented to me as I continued to sit and observe this new birth taking place from this light that had come to know its way out of entrapment.

For each of its continued efforts at attaining the higher levels of existence that were shown to me, there was a reaching for the one who had come to rest just beneath the fullness of the reflection of the Earth Mother that had remained stationary, high in the night sky.

=⊕=

The moon did not seem to move for this entire process that had been shared with me on this night, and as the moon did not move...neither did the small cloud that was now sharing the same brilliance of the color of white the spiraling flame shared for those who were present.

But now, as all of these events were allowed to share their assistance with this rising of the spiral flame, the column of light was still rising into the night sky. But it was doing so at a slow but steady rate now.

There was no longer any jumping as it was trying to escape the confines of where it had once been held within. There was a knowing that I could feel from it now. A knowing I shared with this small one that soon it would be at the place it was wanting to reach and this would be accomplished without any additional effort on its part.

So looking at the rising column of light, I could see that it was no longer trying to make those things happen that it needed, but it was now allowing them to be. As this was clearly focused into the front of my thinking mind, the column of light gently rose into the darkness that was about this night sky.

As it is with all things that are within this domain, when we allow ourselves to be, we are.

And this is what had taken place for this rising column of light. When it reached a place that was known to it as being where it needed to be, the upward movement stopped. All of its movement to rise to a higher place was no longer happening and now, the only movement within it was the clockwise spinning of the white light from within.

As this column of light came to the place it needed

to be, there was another movement that was called to my attention.

This new movement in the night sky was coming from the small cloud that had been stationary during the time of the calling of the rising column of light from the fire.

Now, this small cloud still radiating its own colors of a brilliant white light seemed to be reaching to the place where the column of light had stopped its upward movement. It was doing so by extending parts of itself, small at first, but in the form of long fingers that seemed to be reaching from within itself toward the place where the rising column of light had stopped.

All of this reminded me of a child who was reaching for the nurturing of its mother being returned by the gentle caressing of the mother's hand as she allows her small infant to hold onto one of her long and large fingers.

Then, and just as suddenly as the small cloud had changed its form through this night, there was another great change that was taking place. It was one that shared with me that all things, no matter what form they may be in, are of the one. That there is no thing that is not without spirit and that spirit within all things has the ability of becoming all that is needed.

As what looked to be the long and reaching fingers of the small cloud continued to reach into the direction of the top of the spiraling flame, I could hear the faint sounds of the spirit wind crossing the tops of the tallest of the standing people. And as it would cross over them, I could feel an acceptance of all that was taking place on this land...on this night.

The spirit wind was sharing with all life that was

with me that all which was taking place now was designed for a specific reason. And that reason was good.

JOINING OF THE SPIRIT TOTEMS

Returning my eyes to the place where the spiraling flame and long, reaching fingers of the small cloud were reaching for each other, there was a great call of the spirit eagle. This call was so pronounced that it literally shook all of the sides of the surrounding mountains and even some of the rock people who had given themselves to this spirit circle I had constructed.

Following this sound of the spirit eagle, I next heard the spirit call of buffalo, followed by the spirit call of bear, Both of whom had come just behind the eagle on this night.

Even though I could not see anything of them with the eyes I had been looking through, I could feel that there was a great connection to them...and to me. And this connection was in the touching of the spiraling column of flame and the reaching of the long fingers from the small cloud.

Then, just as suddenly as the spirit calling of the three spirits had come to me, the fingers touched the top of the spiraling flame. And as they did, there was a sudden hush that enveloped all of the lands as well as those spirits who had come to lend their assistance.

For as the two of them connected, there seemed to be a great and brilliant light evolve from this union. And from the time they touched, I held the feeling that there was a new life that had come forth for me to see as the result of this union of the ones from above and from the ones below.

At first, there was only a small piece of this round and brilliant light that I could see, but with the passing of a few breaths, I could more plainly see that it was beginning to gain in size and nature. It was taking those things it needed from the two who had come to allow its life to be born in this domain. And as they continued to share with this new one, it began to take on its own form.

But it was a form that was not recognizable to me yet. For as it continued to grow, there was only a small spinning ball of light. This new ball of light seemed to hold the qualities of both the spiraling flame and the cloud above.

Soon, it had become large enough to leave the place where the flame and cloud had been touching. It was almost like observing a new life come down the birth canal as I watched its new life begin on its own.

Then, as the spinning circle of light was becoming larger, it left the care of the two who had given it entry into this domain and set itself aside from them.

It left the confines of their meeting together, but as it left the place where the cloud and light met, they did not lose touch with each other. For their embrace was just as sure as it had been in the beginning. The thought that came into the front of my thinking mind at that time was that it was more than likely stronger because of what had come from their union.

Now, the small circle of light began to rotate faster and as it did this, it began to grow. And the larger it became, I could feel more and more that a presence was living within it.

Seemingly stationary in the night sky now, this circle of light shared many things with me. Things that would allow me to search deep within myself for many experiences that I would need in order to relate more fully to those things it was going to present me with.

And for each new experience it would share with me, my spirit from within would call up for me one that was similar to what was now being shared. From this union of my experiences and the ones that were floating down to my place in the spirit circle, there came an understanding. It was an understanding that was too clear for me not to see.

For whatever it was or whoever it was that I was feeling on the inside of the glowing ball of light...it had but one purpose and one direction. And that purpose and direction was me...it had come for me.

When this came to the front of my thinking mind, the first reaction I had was to get up and run away. However, there was a calming that came over me from my within place, the place where my spirit resides. And this calming that came to me allowed me to hold the knowing that if the life within this glowing ball of light had intended to do me any harm, it would have done so before now. There were many reasons for all things that are in this domain of the Earth Mother's, and none of them will do us harm if we will only take the time of understanding our place among them.

And what my spirit was sharing with me was that this, too, was one of those times. That until I had come to understand my place in this event that was being shared with me, I would only see all of it through the eyes of fear. Those eyes of fear are the ones who do not hold an understanding for what is being presented to them.

I was very thankful for my spirit's calming to me on this night. For there had been many reasons that I chose to listen rather than to run. The one that was in the forefront of all of them was that I had allowed myself to be prepared for this meeting. That all of those seasons that I had been given to travel a life path, and all of those seasons that I had been given to listen and learn from the teachings and speaking words of Grandfather and Two Bears...this is what had allowed me to be prepared for now.

Because of the understanding that had come to me through those many teachings, I would now be willing to listen to the call of my spirit from within rather than the emotions that were flooding me now from my body part.

At the same time this understanding came to the front of my thinking mind and I resigned myself to remain seated within the spirit circle I had put together...there came another change in this spinning circle of light that was above me on this night.

It began to move at a slower pace and the growing of its size had now stopped. And as these changes were coming to it, I could see a sudden direction change.

It was no longer remaining in a stationary position in this night sky. But this small one of newness was beginning to move toward me now. And as it was doing this, I could feel a great power that was surging from within it come to me.

It was as if all that resided within this glowing ball of light was being offered to me. And because of the greatness of whatever it was that was within it, I could feel the weight of its being and its presence as it neared the place where I was sitting.

Soon it was over my spirit circle, no longer calling the sky nation which it had been born to its only home. But now it was coming to this place where I was sitting. A place that resided where one-half of the one who allowed it entry here called their home. And I could feel a familiarity come to me from it also.

It was almost as if this small one was calling to all of the great chiefs and all the directions for their permission to do what it had come to perform. To make complete its life path and to share with me a destiny that would be a great part of those feelings I had been receiving for the past two days.

Hovering only a few inches above the land I had come to sit on, the glowing ball of light appeared to be waiting for something that it knew would have to take place before it would be allowed to continue with what it had come to do.

Not wanting to detain those things that the time was right for, I began to look deep into my within place to see if there was something I had missed from the calling voice of my spirit. Something that I had not seen that was for me to do.

For now, looking at this glowing ball of light that was directly in front of me, I no longer felt any kind of fear. But I was being filled with a new sense of direction and a great peace. These things I knew to be good and would not ever bring any kind of harm, or force me to do something that I would not be willing to do.

Just as I had taken this thought to my within place,

there was a sudden break in the hushed silence of expectation that had now filled this land. It was broken by the beautiful sound of a woman's voice and she was singing a spirit chant of seeking.

Oh, Great Spirit,
You who have allowed us all to be
You who are so much a part within each of us
Allow us to see that which is you
Allow us to see that which is me

Oh, Great Mystery,
Out of your love we have been born
From your wisdom our spirit will grow

Let us see those things that come before us
For what they are
And not for what we would only want them to be

When she finished this chant, I saw there was a shaking movement from within this glowing ball of light that had come before me.

She then began this spirit chant once again, but this time there was a male voice that joined her and when they had finished the second time, there was another shaking movement from within this glowing ball of light.

This process repeated itself for eleven times, and each time, there would be another voice that would be joined with the others. Each time another voice joined, it would alternate between the male and female until at the end of the eleventh time, there were eleven voices that were singing this spirit chant.

Each time they would complete this spirit chant, the glowing ball of light would shake once again.

=⊕=

And for each additional time of shaking, I was receiving the knowing that whatever it was that was living within it, these repeated chants were allowing it to take on its own form. A form that I knew would soon be shown to me.

Now...it was done. All of the singing of the spirit chant was completed and what had taken place within the glowing ball of light was still unknown to me, but I could sense there had been a great change within it.

Then, as the air became filled with another silence of acceptance, there began a drum beat. It was similar to the drum beating that had been with me earlier that had filled all of the places where there was air and life.

But now it had a change to it. While it was still beating in the same motion as I had come to know, these same motions that were significant to the beating of the Earth Mother's own heartbeat, there were many different tempos within it. I had come to know that these tempos were the calling on the different spirits of the lands in this domain.

As the tempos began, I recognized some of them from my travels with Grandfather, Two Bears, and Cheeway. They had brought to me an understanding of who and where these spirits of the different lands resided.

And it was through the speaking words of Grandfather and Two Bears that I gained my level of understanding that for all of the different places of lands in this domain, there were various spirits who were given charge over the land by the Earth Mother.

And it was from the different tempos that would be heard through the beating of the drum beats that we would come to know which spirits of the lands were being called on for assistance. Since the spirits of the lands are much the same as all life is in this respect. In the ways they hold their own understanding on how to assist you in your requests.

But as these different tempos were coming to me on this night through the drum beatings, there were so many that I did not have a knowing for. So many of these I had not either heard of or felt from what I had come to consider as my wide travels over many lands.

However, the one or ones who were living within the glowing ball of light did seem to know them. For as each of the new tempos would come over the beating drums, there would be an immediate recognition of those spirits of the land that were being summoned. And as each new set of tempos were being shared with all who were on this land with me on this night, the glowing ball of light seemed to take more and more attributes into itself.

This process continued until all that had been needed had been done. Then it was the glowing ball of light that would be next to share with me.

For just as the beating of the drums stopped, there was another beating that was over this land. And it was coming to me from the glowing ball of light.

Listening to this, I knew that what I was listening to was not the beating of a drum any longer, but it was a beating of a heart. One that was great enough to fill all of this night sky that was around me.

Then, there was a sudden division from within this ball of light. It was one that shared with me that there was not only one who was within it, but there were three and I could hear each of their heartbeatings come to me from within itself.

Suddenly, and as the three beatings of the heartbeats grew in their sound and strength, there was another change. One that I had not been so well prepared for, but one nonetheless that I was intent to observe and not run away from.

As I looked at the glowing sphere of light that had come to set in front of me, it slowly and with the grace of a falling leaf with no wind, sat itself down on the same flat rock I was sitting on.

As it sat itself down, there began to be a growing and shrinking as each of these heartbeats continued to call its movement and rhythm.

As it set itself down on the same piece of land I had been sharing, there was no longer a clear and defined form of a sphere in front of me. Rather, it was beginning to lose its defined form and turn into a fuzzy ball of light. One that would no longer have a need for form.

As I continued to look at the changes that were coming to it, I could see that this form was dividing itself into three, then back into the one. And this process would repeat itself several times.

The first time that it did this, there was a clear and distinct form of an eagle in the top portion of itself. The form of a great eagle that bore the color yellow.

The second time this was repeated, there was the clear and distinct form of a bear in the top portion of it and it bore the color black.

And the third time this process repeated itself, there was a clear and distinct form of a buffalo and its color was white.

Then, and for the final time that this repeated itself, there came a complete separation of all three of them. Once this separation came, each of these three spirits came to rest in a particular place around me.

On my left was the bear. Its color was black and it seemed to float in a place that was in the middle of the night air in the west.

On my right, there was eagle and the color it bore was yellow; and it was holding a place in the night air that was equal to the one bear had taken.

Above me was buffalo and its color was white. The position it had taken was one that was twice the distance as was between either bear or eagle from the place where I was sitting.

And then, I saw another change that took place. It was one that filled me with a knowing that I, too, was a part of this vision; that I, too, held a role to play in these events that had been presented to me.

For as I looked at myself in the sitting position within this spirit circle, I saw that I had taken on the color of red. And this color was radiating from within to very far places outside of me.

And for all of this, I knew it to be good.

It was a good feeling that had come to me from the forming of this great circle with the spirits who had come to me on this night of my vision quest.

Then there was another movement that took place from this circle of the many colored lights that had formed with me. It was a suddenness of movement that called my attention to the spirit of eagle who had been in a place that was on my right.

Looking over to this place where eagle was, I saw there was a sudden movement within him that called my attention to the changing of colors that was taking place.

For as I looked over to this place on my right, I saw that as he was weaving his great wings in a back and forth manner, there was a changing of colors that was becoming more prominent with each of his moves.

As this process continued, I noticed that I was no longer glowing in the red color that I had over me just a short time before, but now I was glowing in the yellow color and eagle was glowing in the red color.

I did not have an understanding for this occurrence and was searching within myself for an explanation of this when I heard a beautiful voice call to me.

"Speaking Wind...," came the lady's beautiful, soft, and embracing voice over the air that was surrounding me and all that had been formed on this night.

"Before you entered this domain for this earth walk of yours, there was a great shift in the colors of the medicine wheel of life.

"It is this shift that has allowed many of the spirit children of the before time's entry into this domain that you call the Earth Mother's. And it was through this shifting in the east colors of yellow to red that gave birth to this new energy.

"However, this time has been completed and all who have come to enter for this great change that is about to take place...they have arrived. But many of them are still sleeping.

"And, with all of their arrival, the colors of the great medicine wheel of life have returned to their original positions.

"In the time that was needed by so many of the spirit children who were returning, the color of yellow was needed in the south direction of the wheel. It was needed in this place so that much of the wisdom that had been left here could be found by the old ones who returned.

"Because of the nature of the south direction, it was decided by Great Mystery that this would be a good place to keep it until those who would have a great need for it could come back. Until they would return and claim those things unto themselves that they would need in order to take their part in this great change that is soon to be upon all who are here.

"And you, Speaking Wind...you will know your part well when you have finished this waking process that you are going through. Then you will have the eyes of the eagle, the power of the bear, and the heart of the buffalo to lead you and many who will see the path you travel."

As the beautiful voice was carried away by the passing of the spirit wind, I once again felt myself gaining the weight of not understanding what this part I was to play would be. And this was a weight that would have to be left behind me if I were to continue in this vision quest that had been given to me on this night when so much had already been shared.

However, from a place that was deep within me, I held onto the knowing that this was far from the end of this vision; for I could feel there was still much further to go and many more lessons that would be taught on this night.

So, keeping this in the front of my thinking mind, I allowed this to fall into one of the small stones that I had set next to me. When the time was right, I would once again pick it up from this small record keeper of the Earth Mother and carry it with me, but with a higher level of understanding which would make it not so heavy.

Returning my eyes back to eagle, I saw that the original color of yellow had returned to him and I was once again glowing in the red color of my beginning.

However, as eagle saw that I had returned my eyes to him, he began to wave his wings in a powerful motion. One that had allowed him to leave his seated position on the wheel of life and come to the place I was sitting.

For a few moments, eagle held a stationary position that was only a few feet in the front of me. Looking deep into my eyes, I could feel that he had left me with something that felt very powerful.

However, as was the case with so much that had been shared with me on this night, I did not hold the understanding of what it was that I had been left with. But I knew that when the time was right and I was prepared to see what it was, that would be the time I would understand.

As this was crossing my thinking mind, I could feel eagle smile into me and hold a look of great pride in the front of his face.

Once this exchange had taken place, I saw that eagle began to rise above me and passed white buffalo who was in the highest place on this wheel of life.

And as eagle rose just to a place above buffalo, his wings grew greatly and so did his body until he filled most of the night sky and the many lights that were now sharing this new life with it.

As eagle grew to this great size, he began to fly in an upward motion. This motion took him above buffalo and the spiraling flame of light, then on to a place that was even above the small cloud who had joined in this union with the column of the spinning white light that had come to bring all of this into a life of its own.

Then with a strength greater than any I had ever

come to see, eagle continued to rise into the deep and dark night sky and headed into the direction of the full moon.

As he continued his journey into the dark night sky, his size only lessened by a little, for it seemed the higher he would travel, the greater he became.

I was receiving the knowing that as one will begin their spirit path while they are in this domain of the Earth Mother's, they too will continue to grow in strength and size as they take each additional step that will ultimately lead them to the place they need to be.

And for eagle, this was no different. For now, even with his great height, I could see that his form was not being lost to me because of the distance.

I saw eagle was flying into the face of the full moon which was lighting his path.

Within a few short breaths, he had arrived. Eagle had come to a place where he was dancing directly in the front of the pale pearl white of the moonlight and this made him seem like a passing shadow before her.

However, just as eagle arrived at this place in the night sky, there was another feat that came to him. One that will remain with me for all of the seasons that will be left with me in this domain that is the Earth Mother's.

Eagle did not just remain in a stationary position in the front of the full moon, but he rose once again to a place that was over her. And as he remained there for a brief moment of time, I could see his size growing once again, until he had the fullness of one who is standing only a few yards away.

And this was the face eagle was presenting to me now. A face that was in truth his to share and one that would not be lost no matter how great the distance would be.

As eagle gained in size and became the one I had seen sitting in his place of the medicine wheel of life, he then slowed his wings to a pace that allowed him to set on the top of the full moon. And when he had set himself on her, he let out a great cry...one that I had become familiar with from the teachings of both Grandfather and Two Bears.

For through this silence of the night sky, there was but one moment that it was filled with the spirit of wisdom that is eagle's to share. His call of the spirit resounded against all life that was with me, and there was a newness of awakening that I could feel take place through all of this domain...not only the part I was sharing, but with all that is.

When this spirit cry of eagle came to its highest place, there was a sudden rush of the spirit wind over the tops of all the standing people and all the way to the place where I was sitting. As it was crossing itself over this land, I could hear the message he was carrying to all who would listen.

The eagle has landed on the moon,
It is good

The eagle has landed on the moon,
It is right.

The eagle has landed on the moon,
It is time.

Spirit wind carried this message on its back to repeat it seven times on this night. And for each time he would sing of this event, there was a new feeling of awareness that would fill me and all who would listen. A new awareness that would later be followed by an understanding for what this event was signifying.

For I knew there was a great message that was being shared with me on this night, one that had been completed by the spirit of eagle landing on the top of the moon. However, once again I was filled with the knowing that I would come to understand the significance of all of this at a later time. At a time when I would be prepared to see this face that had been presented to me.

WHERE SPIRIT LIVES

This sharing of eagle had caused a great stillness in all of the life that was around me. Even in the nature of the spirit wind who, for as long as I could remember, had not ever been affected by any of the visions I had been presented with.

But now, and in the stillness of the night sky over these lands, there was a new level of seeing. It was one that seemed to be very obvious to all but me.

Looking over to the places where buffalo and bear were sitting, I saw that their eyes were also focused on eagle. As I looked over to the places of the spiraling light and small cloud, I could feel their attention was also on eagle and that they had been filled with a great pride. But it was not the same kind of pride that we two-legs have come to know so well, for it was nothing that was so selfish.

It was a pride for one who has come to complete their task for the Earth Mother, for one who has come to the successful completion of doing those things they had come here to do.

As I looked over to the standing people and the rock people, I could see that they, too, were feeling this goodness that had come to them by eagle's actions. That they, too, were being filled with the same pride of knowing that another of their brothers had come to succeed in doing those things he was meant to do.

Returning my eyes back to eagle, I saw that he had already lifted himself from the face of the full moon and was beginning his return to this place of the flat rocks where the rest of us were sitting and waiting for his return.

And as his form continued to cut through the night sky above me, he would periodically share another of his spirit cries. These spirit cries were now being responded to by all within this domain.

I could see that while it was the sleeping time for all of the children of the Earth Mother, none of them were veiled in their nightly sleep now. All of them were completely awake and were being filled by all of the events that were being presented to them, as well, on this night of seeking. On this night of my beginnings for the path I had willingly chosen to travel.

With each of eagle's cries through this night sky as he returned to the place of beginning, there was another layer of awareness that would fall over me. A new layer of awareness that was also filling me with a kind of understanding that was now allowing me to see more clearly those things that were being presented.

=⊕=

Eagle had made it back to the original place on my right, this position I had come to know as the east; and as he rested in this place, the color of yellow left him and was replaced with the color of white.

I looked to the place on my left, this place I had come to know as the west where bear was sitting, I could see that bear was also letting the color of black leave and as it was doing this, the color of white was taking its place.

I looked to the place that was above me, this place I had come to know as being north where buffalo was sitting, and I could see that he already held the color of white, so there was no change needed.

But as I looked to the place I was sitting, I could see that I was continuing to glow with the red color. All three of the ones who had come to sit in the three corners before me seemed to be looking at this color very intently. They were looking at this color I was wearing and I could feel them waiting...waiting for this color of red to drop away from me and be replaced by the color of white.

From my within place, I was fed with the knowing, but not the understanding, that while I would wear this color red there could be no further movement for this vision quest that had come to me. And until I would change this color from red to white, we would all have to wait. That we would have to wait because while there was even one who would not be willing to learn, then there would be no further learning...it would just not be possible because of the weight that I would give to all who would wish to fly.

And it was the word "fly" that entered my thinking mind from a place I did not know that perked my attention to this difference. To this difference that was not allowing any of us to advance any further.

It was then that I was given an understanding for why I, too, needed to change from my color of red to the color of white. I needed to understand how to let go of those things that were no longer needed by me.

This much I then held the knowing for; that while I would wear this color of red, there would be an additional weight that would be with me. And this additional weight would cause me to be too heavy to continue with my brothers and sisters who had come to me. The ones who had come to allow this form to take place.

I could see my need in this time as well. For all of the events and feelings that had been coming to me...the ones who had been filling me with a sensation of something that was very great in importance...they would not leave me if I were to remain locked within this color of red. They would not only remain with me, but would grow until I would most likely end up walking with a great stoop over my back while I was still of short seasons.

I could feel the weight of something being offered, but I could not see what it was yet.

I also knew that until I was able to continue with this spirit journey that was being offered to me by these three wise ones of our nations...I would not find those answers in another place. The only place where I would find those things that I held a great need for was the one place they would be willing to take me. And I could see this from what they were placing in the front of my thinking mind. Those things were being presented to me over and over as I sat and looked at myself glowing with this red color of mine.

Sitting in my original position within the spirit

circle, there was a great amount of sharing and understanding that was filling me at this time. And those things that were being allowed to come to me with their understanding attached, were sharing with me that there would only be one who would be able to allow this color of the red weight to leave...to leave and be replaced with the color of white which would hold all colors within it.

That since the color of the white would hold all of the colors within it, there would be the additional sharing of talents and attributes that were associated with all of the other colors that would allow this color to have no weight to it. And when I would hold this color of the oneness to myself, this would be the time when all of the weight that had been holding all of us back would be taken away. But it would be taken away because of the collective understanding that would be present not only within the color, but within me as well.

And as this was flooding my thinking mind, it did not share with me how I could change from the color red to the color white. I was not shown steps to attaining this direction other than being shown where I needed to be.

This direction that was pointing to me was doing so in a way that I could not mistake. It was telling me that this was a task that only I could do and if I could not find the path to make this take place, then perhaps I was not prepared for those things I was seeking. That this was the place where the vision was to end.

As this was allowed to be born within me, I felt as if there was a sudden injustice to it. For I knew that I had prepared myself for what was to take place next, but I only needed a little assistance for doing my part of it.

As this thought was crossing my thinking mind, I heard the calling voice of Grandfather come to me once again from my within place. As it was doing so, it was gaining in its own life once again.

"Always remember who your friends are, Speaking Wind. This is a very important lesson for all who would come to enter this domain of the Earth Mother's to learn from. And I will tell you in truth that this is the only reason any of us are here...and that is to learn so that we will have more to share with those who would wish to see.

"If you will always keep in the front of your thinking mind that the mark of a true friend will be one who will make their presence known to you, then you will have half of the picture. The other half of this is that a true friend will also stand next to you and allow you to have the freedom of doing your own work through your own efforts. They will not wish to do this work for you because they will have the knowing that this will not assist you in any way. For this would only do you a great harm, and that harm would come to you in not giving to you the freedom of learning from those things you need...on your own.

"There will be times when you will wish that there was another who would be standing next to you. That you would wish they would take over all of those things that stand in your way, little one. But remember, that if they will do this for you, then you will have learned nothing for yourself and will have to do them all over again. So what has this false friend who has been willing to do so much for you accomplished? They have accomplished the fact that you will just have to go back, and in another direction, to learn what you were supposed to learn in the first place. And because of this false friend, there will always be a great deal of time that will have been wasted.

"There will not ever be any other who will have the needs that you will possess, Speaking Wind. They will not have the same needs because they are not you.

"For all of those who would enter this domain that is the Earth Mother's, they will all have their own spirit. And because this is truth, then all of their lessons will not be exactly the same as yours are. And to think otherwise would mean that if there is a face of truth in it, then there is truly no reason for you to be here in the first place. And from the teachings of our ancestors, we have all come to know that this is not truth. That the reason our spirit has for being here is one that will be revealed to all of us in time...in the time when we have become prepared to listen to ourselves.

"Now little one, when you will find yourself associated with those who would not be willing to give you the freedom of learning from your own lessons by allowing you to do your own work, then there will only be a partial understanding for yourself and who and what you are.

"Any time you will come across another who only has this partial understanding for themselves, there will be one facet that will stand out among the rest. And this part of themselves that you see will be associated with what little they have come to know and understand of themselves.

"However, because this is not a full and complete understanding for those things, a fullness that will only come to another when they will have learned to do their own work, then they will become like the plant that will trap the flies inside of it, the fly that has become its food.

"What you will see from them is only the outside, and this has nothing at all to do with the inside of themselves and what their true intentions are.

"Even when these people will begin with the best of intentions, they will always end up with efforts that will control another. And those efforts they will display will only be coming to them from the fact that there is not a complete understanding for all that they are. This lack of understanding that has begun from having another do those lessons that had been presented to them.

"So when you come to a place where you are being offered the freedom of doing your own work, the freedom of learning for yourself, then be grateful and travel forward on this path with a good heart. For what you are being given is the chance to be free within your spirit, and I tell you this in truth...there is no greater gift for any who hold a spirit within them.

"And keep in the front of your thinking mind, little one, that when you will be given this freedom of learning, then remember to allow all things to be. For when you will do this, then you will be. It is only when one will be in the place of trying to be that they will find themselves on a endless journey of becoming. One that will not ever reach its destination and because there is not a destination that is attainable, then they will not ever be. In this place of trying to be, they will always hold the believing that by becoming, they are succeeding and this is not truth, little one. This is not anyone's truth, it is but a false spirit who is keeping you from attaining those things you have entered this domain to be.

"So it is that by allowing all things to be that we will find our pathway lighted, Speaking Wind. And it will be lighted by the Ancient Ones who have traveled this way long before us. Those same Ancient Ones who now sit next to the council fires of our ancestors and allow us to see our own way."

Hearing these speaking words come back to life from Grandfather allowed me to see what was being offered. They were sharing with me that what eagle, buffalo, and bear were offering was my freedom. They were offering this freedom that was within me and because they had also found it, they were willing to wait for me to do the same.

As this found its way into the reaches of my heart, I was feeling grateful for all they had been willing to share with me. And as this feeling grew within me, there were great water drops that were forming in my eyes and rolling down my cheeks.

I held the knowing that for what was being shared with all of them on this night, that there was a gratefulness that was filling them. And looking into the places where they were, I could feel the warmth of their knowing and understanding love fill me from the furthest reaches of my existence to where I was now living...to the front of my thinking mind.

As I continued to observe this color of red that was still radiating out of me, there came a thought. It was one that had been presented to me from my within place...this place where my spirit resides.

I now held the knowing that while I held the color of red within me, I was different from the others who had once held a color of their own, but now wore only the white color of all colors.

=⊕=

And as I allowed this thought to be born within me, there was another clarity of vision that was shared with me. Another way of looking at those things that were now being presented to me and their willingness of teaching.

I suddenly realized that this color of red that I was now wearing was only one of the many colors. And it was not important to see that this color was one that was allowing me to keep my identity separate from the rest, but it was one that was keeping me from joining with them as well.

So I had to come to a place within me that would allow me to make the choice. This was a choice of being separated from them and having my own individuality or allowing myself to come to a place of seeing myself in the completeness of all things. In the completeness and understanding that all life is from the one.

I was holding the understanding that when we enter this domain that is the Earth Mother's, there is a great need for us to hold onto this individuality of ours. And this reason is so that we can learn from the many lessons that will be offered to us. These many lessons will allow us to learn how to prepare ourselves for even greater truths—these greater truths that are of ourselves and where our place is within the whole.

But as we continue to learn from these lessons, we have less and less of a need for exhibiting our separate color. And this less of a need will come to us each time that we allow ourselves to come to the place of learning and understanding from those many events that would present themselves to us.

Soon, as we continue to learn from all of these

things that will be presented to us, we will find that our levels of understanding for ourselves and all things that are around us will be of a level where we no longer have a need to hold onto this separateness. This is a place where we will be at peace in the knowing and understanding that we are all a part of the one. This one that we have all begun from and where we will all return to...those who would be willing to find their way of returning, that is.

It was when I came to understand that in giving up those things that had made me different that I had truly found myself among the whole of life. And in doing this, there was nothing that was lost at all. There was only the knowing and understanding that I had returned to where I had been seeking. To a place and a time when I was a part of all life and all life was a part of me.

I was considering myself to be a little on the short side of understanding when I understood what it was I had been shown by my spirit.

And, I felt a little embarrassed when I came to understand that what I had been seeking was the oneness of all life, but I would not let go of my separateness because of the fear of being lost.

But now...now that I held this knowing and understanding of what it would mean to me in truth, there was no longer a fear of becoming the one with the one. There would not ever be a time where I would know more of myself than now because in allowing myself to be, I no longer feared losing those things that were not me.

As this thought was filling me from within, I heard the calling voice of the one I had met before...Telah. And as she spoke to me, I was hearing her from every corner of the lands and sky that were around me.

"Remember, Speaking Wind, it is when you will fear the loss of anything that you must remember that you do not own it. For what you fear losing is, in truth, not yours to begin with. It is only something that has come to you for a short time and its purpose was to allow you to learn from it.

"When you have not learned from it, you will try to hold onto it. But I tell you that this is not truth in what you will attempt to do. Because the harder you will try to hold onto anything that is not you, the less and less you will come to understand what its purpose was in the beginning. And this will continue to cloud your seeing eyes until they will be blinded and see no more.

"When you are afraid of losing something, then take a good look at where you are at that time. When you do this my brother, you will find a great lesson. One that will allow you to release from you those things that are holding you back. To release them so that they too might find another who would have a great need to learn from them.

"And when you release them freely, you will be given a great gift. One that will allow you to see that there is nothing that we can claim ownership over in this domain. For all things have life to them and in being so, they each have their own separate life path to follow, just as you do.

"It is by letting them go, Speaking Wind, that you will find your freedom of being...this freedom that so many will search for. But so many will search for this freedom by trying to hold onto their past and this will not work. This will not work for them because they are still trying to control those who have come among them.

"And as long as there is a controlling by any, they will not be allowed to advance their spirit through understanding, little one.

"When you come to the place of understanding this, Speaking Wind, release those things that you hold onto. And as you do this, wear a good face over you for what you will be shown next will be the freedom that will allow you to grow as one who is...and no longer be stopped by becoming one who is always in the process of trying to become...as one who is continually frustrated because they have yet to arrive...as one who feels this frustration and tries even harder to become."

Hearing these speaking words come to me from Telah of the tree nation, I held the confirmation of those things that I needed. The confirmation that what had come to me from my spirit within, the speaking words from Grandfather, and now the confirming from Telah...I knew that I was following my path. This path that I had begun and this path that was now about to advance within itself once again.

Holding those things in the front of my thinking mind, I looked once again to the places where bear, buffalo, and eagle were still sitting. There was a great deal of patience and knowing coming to me from them.

And as I looked to their places, I saw this color of white that they wore as one that no longer poised a threat to my individuality. As one that was a process of becoming one with the one and for this...I knew it was good.

Now...now as I returned my eyes to the place where I was sitting, there was a change that was coming over me as well. One that I had been seeking the path to, for it was the changing of my color.

Where there was once only the color of the glowing red, there was blended with it the colors of black, white, and yellow...the colors that the three who were in front of me wore. And this came to me that I, too, was a part of their directions and understanding. That I, too, was a part of this path they had found to travel, but now I was being shown the direction to it. This direction of my journey on this earth walk.

Next, there was what appeared to be light bands and they were forming themselves all around me in an upward motion. This motion reminded me of how the column of flame had come to reach the small cloud above it.

Now, as I continued to allow myself to become at one with the one of all life, there was a spinning of these different bands of light that had formed their column over me. And as they began to spin, there was a sudden blending of all of them.

For where there was once only the red, the yellow, the black, and the white, there was now only a single column of white and it was spinning over me faster and faster until I could feel the air of its presence filling all of this land that was around me.

While this was taking place, I could not see them, but I could feel the heart and mind of approval from all who were with me on this night. For I was being filled with their acceptance for what was now taking place within me. And what was being shared with me by all those whom I could not see but could feel was their acceptance of me, no matter where I would wish to travel among them. For wherever I would travel, they would always be with me and would make their presence known.

=⊛=

It was when this spinning column of white light came to a place of completion that it stopped. It stopped its spinning and settled all around me on this place I was sitting.

Then, as I looked over myself, I found a face that was good for me to wear. It was one that had been presented to me when I saw that I was no longer wearing the glow of the red, but now I was wearing the glowing of the fullness of the white color. And looking over to the place where the other three had been waiting, I could feel that there was a good heart they were showing to me. One that allowed me to see myself for who and what I was meant to be.

Then another change came to me on this night. One that allowed me to hold the understanding that we were about to begin our spirit journey to the domain of the Ancient Ones. Those who I had been told were waiting for me. The ones who had been summoning me to come to them.

And now...now that I had come to the place of understanding those things that had been holding me down, I was filled with the understanding of belonging. Of belonging to all that until now I had only come to hear of and observe.

ENTERING THROUGH THE CRACK IN THE UNIVERSE

Having seen all of the four colors come to blend together on myself, I could feel the lightness that was being offered. This blending allowed all of the positive aspects of each of the colors to come to assist me.

=⊕=

And, as this blending of the colors came to me, I could not ever remember a time when I felt more a part of myself, a time when I could see and feel myself more completely.

This calmed the smaller parts of myself that had been thinking of how much I could lose if I considered myself to be a part of the one. And by my doing such a thing, I would no longer be able to find myself among the whole.

However, this was not the case. What I had found was myself, and it was a part of all that is.

All of these wonderful recognitions were coming to me very fast now, and as they did, each of those things I once held a false believing in were being washed away. They were being allowed to fall away...by me. And this is what I had come to know at this place of seeing, that for all things that will ever take place within us or around us, they will have been designed by ourselves.

This is the great truth that is within spirit...that there is not ever anything that will come to us that will be forced. That all those things that will be shared with us will only be done in a way that will allow us to make up our own minds. To do all things in a voluntary manner.

And when one will force another to do anything, then they have in truth, fallen from their own path. From this path they have come to believe in and feel they are very strong on.

Now, as I was looking at the newness of color that was glowing from me, I could see another change that was coming to me on this night of visions. This was sharing with me that it was time for a new direction to begin. It would require all of us to take flight into a place I knew nothing about.

Eagle had returned to his place in the east and was sitting with the look of wisdom over his face. And looking at buffalo and bear, I could feel this same look of wisdom coming to me from the face they were now wearing as well.

Suddenly, all three of them turned their heads into the place that was just between eagle and buffalo. This place where once there was only the night air and a feeling of a part of a circle of something...something that I could not see but that I could feel.

As I turned my head into this same direction, I saw another change that had come. And with it, I was receiving the knowing that it was one that would mark the beginning of this journey we were all about to take together. I had no knowing of where this journey would take me, but I was now more than willing to travel with them.

Looking to this place that was between buffalo and eagle, I saw that there had formed many small but very bright lights between them. They were giving to me their colors of a shiny blue and red that seemed to be glowing as they followed a path that had been set for them. A path that they alone seemed to hold the understanding for.

I observed them as they began their journey from the place of buffalo and made an arc of themselves until they reached the place of eagle.

And when they had reached this place in the east, I saw they were beginning to gather themselves and form another image. One that seemed would take over this place of eagle if he would not move.

But looking to the face of eagle, he shared with me that all that was taking place in this circle of the spirit was very necessary as it was another step to the preparing for what was to come next. And if this preparing was not be allowed to be...we would not be able to continue with our spirit journey.

Eagle did not move from his place, and there was no need for him to do so.

For as these small bright lights of red and blue found their way to the end of their rainbow, I saw that what they were beginning to form was to be located at a place that was just under eagle's feet. A place that was still within the spirit circle they had formed in front of me, but one that was in no way interfering with those who had come to form it.

As they continued to gather unto themselves, these small bright lights began to form what appeared to be a doorway. This doorway was very large, but yet it was not so large that it took away from any who were near it.

Then, as I saw the form of the doorway completed, there was another change that came to it. For as I was looking at all of these small and bright lights of the blues and reds come together and form this image, they began to change colors once again as all of us who were here had done.

But this color change that came to them was not the same as had taken place within me and the other three. It was one that allowed all of these small ones to take on one singular color.

It was the color of a bright and brilliant gold. A color that is usually associated with the weight of spirit from the many song legends of our people.

And as it formed itself into this new form and new color of gold, it began to glow and radiate a life form all of its own. One that shared with me that there was a great connection to the beating of the heartbeat of Earth Mother as well as one that was in connection to the heartbeat of Great Spirit.

When this thought was born to me, I held the understanding of what had just been formed. Of the meaning and purpose of this new event that had come among all who were present with me on this night of the spirit vision.

I was in awe as this knowing swept its way through all parts of my being. It began to form itself into the places where I could recognize those things that were being presented to me on this night.

For in front of me, what had been formed by these small and bright lights, was the great doorway of our ancient song legends. This great doorway was the only passage point into the domain of the Ancient Ones and Great Mystery from the teachings that had been shared with me from Grandfather and Two Bears.

This was the great golden doorway that had been shared with me from many of the spirit paintings that Grandfather and Two Bears had shown me on the walls of our most ancient ancestors. This doorway was the only access for me to Great Mystery and would allow one to see the place of entry...this place we have come to know as the crack in the universe.

Now as this golden doorway had formed itself and was in the place it wanted to be in, I could feel eagle, buffalo, and bear looking at me. I could feel them observing me and those things I was placing in the front of my thinking mind to see if I was ready to begin.

And as I felt this questioning of me by them, I had to admit that I was nervous about what was to take place next on this vision quest. For I held no knowing or understanding of what would be waiting for me once I entered this great golden doorway.

However, I did have the understanding that none of this that had been allowed to be shared with me on this night was of my own doing. None of it had anything at all to do with any effort that I could have made.

And looking at this, I held the knowing that there had been a good bond that had been developed between these three of the spirit helpers and me. This bond had given me a great level of trust in them and all things that would be presented to me. That they would be shared with me and not forced.

So this was the thought that had come into the front of my thinking mind on this night. That there had been no thing that had shown itself to me with the face of fear and that was because these three who had come to assist me had given to me the time I needed to understand what had taken place before me before allowing me to continue.

And I did not have any reason to believe that this entry into the great golden doorway would be any different, as well as the seeing of the location of the crack in the universe.

Just as these thoughts were coming into the front of my thinking mind, there was another silent voice that came to me. And it came to me from the place in the east...this place that is the home of eagle.

"Do not be concerned with those things that you hold no control over, Speaking Wind. For they have been foretold of their being in this path you travel long before there was a time to be seen.

"There is no thing that has been presented to you

on this night that you did not have the understanding for. And there will be no thing that you will yet encounter that you will not have already been prepared for.

"Remember, Speaking Wind, that when spirit calls...answer. When spirit comes...accept. When spirit leads...follow. For all of those things that will be shared with you in this time will be those same things you have been seeking.

"And the only reason you will at first hesitate will be because these things you have been asking assistance on will be coming to you from places you have yet to remember. Yet to remember, but those same places will be the ones you have spent a great deal of time in before. And this is why they have returned to you now.

"They have returned to you now to assist you in coming to the place on this path you have a great need for. And this is the place of understanding. This place of understanding that will assist you in seeing those things you will need to see and learn from.

"Follow the spirit, Speaking Wind...follow the spirit.

"It is only leading you to a place where you will see, once again, who and what you are and where you must travel."

Hearing the spirit pictures that had come to me from eagle, I no longer held any of the fear that had once been within me. The uncertainty had fallen away, as well, and now...now I could feel the willingness of myself as I began to rise from my sitting place on the flat rock within the spirit circle.

I was beginning to rise into the air that was filled with this newness of life all around me. And soon, I could feel myself becoming as one of the three. As one who was no longer held by the weight of those many things that had once been carried by me. Those things I carried without the understanding from them was what had given them their weight over me, this weight that had kept me from rising before now.

But now as I was rising into the night air, I was told that those things had been taken away...those same things that had once given me weight from my lack of understanding for them would not be a permanent loss. For when I would return, they would be waiting for me.

And when I would return, they, too, would remember me and attach themselves once again to me.

The reason for this was that they had come to me as lessons to learn from and until I would be willing to do the necessary work of learning from them, they would continue to remain with me.

It would only be when I would have the willingness of spirit to learn from them that I would feel the freedom of them no longer being attached to me as a weight. And it would be then, and only by my own working through them, that I would be allowed to enter this path that was being shared with me on this night once again.

For all of this, I did not have a bad feeling. And as a matter of truth, I was very thankful for being allowed to take a break from them and be shown the places that were coming to me very soon now.

For in the front of my thinking mind, my spirit was telling me that I would now be much better equipped to work with these weighted lessons that had come to my life path. That I would have more understanding for what I could not work with before, once I had traveled into this place that was about to be opened up for me.

On my return from this spirit journey, I would see the value of those many things that I once only held as an inconvenience to myself. That when I would return, spirit would find a new path of coming to me. One that would allow me to have a clearer way of seeing those things that I needed to learn from...and prepare myself with.

I could feel this weightlessness come over me as I continued to float in an ever upward motion. This was allowing me to see that soon, I would be in the place where bear, buffalo, and eagle seemed to be waiting for me to arrive at.

As I continued to allow myself to let go of many of those things that had come to me with their weight that comes from all things we carry without understanding, I could feel an increase in my speed. This speed was being shown to me as something that was necessary for me to learn from in order to enter this great golden doorway.

When I came to a place that was half the distance between the great golden doorway and where I had been sitting position on the flat stones, I was given another change. It was a change in the positions each of us would now take. And I knew this was for a reason that I would soon understand.

For as soon as I reached this floating place in the night air, eagle positioned himself in a place that was just in front of the great doorway. And following his lead, bear took the position to my right and buffalo took his position that was to my left.

This left me directly in the middle of bear and buffalo and just behind eagle. This change in position caused them to wear a good face as they each took their turn to look at me and make sure I knew that where I was, was were I needed to be.

Once this had come to be, we all began to move in a forward direction. One that was bringing us closer to the great golden doorway that had made its appearance just moments before.

However, there was one thing that I did not hold the understanding of. And that was how all four of us would be allowed to fit into this place we were heading into...this place of the great doorway.

From what I could see of our positions, and that of the size of the great doorway, there was just no way that was possible for us to enter if we were to hold these positions that had been formed.

And just as this thought entered the front of my thinking mind, there was an enormous growth in the size of the pathway through the doorway.

The doorway, or at least the opening to it, seemed to grow from something that was not large at all to an opening that was bigger than a mountain top. And all of this took place within a few seconds of time...or at least this is as close as I could put it.

Now as there was an ample amount of room for all four of us to pass through without altering our positions, we began. As we began our entry into this place, I could see the other side of the lands that had been held here.

Just as we were about to enter, there was another event that came. One that I once again did not feel prepared for. And that was of another picture that was now lying just beyond the opening of the doorway.

In a place that was just to the middle of the door

passage, there was a line that had appeared. And it appeared at first to be one that would be moved by the smallest of breezes, but as the moments passed and we came closer to it...I could tell that this was as far from the truth as I could have been.

As we neared the opening of the doorway, I could see that what had first appeared as one single line was in truth, not a line at all. It was another doorway, but one that I had not ever come to know or see before.

Nevertheless, this is what had been placed within my thinking mind by spirit as we neared it. And the closer we came to the opening of the first golden doorway, the larger this line became.

Now, as we approached this first entrance, there was a sound of rushing water and wind. This sound was so loud that it drowned out all of the other sounds that had been with us to now.

Just as we passed through the great golden doorway, I could see that this once small and horizontal line that had appeared was now growing. I could hear the sounds of the rushing wind and water get louder, as well.

Soon, there was no longer a horizontal line in front of us, but now it appeared to be another doorway, one that seemed to be born on its side. For as tall as the golden doorway was, this one was just as long. And as wide as the first doorway had been, this one was just as tall.

Inside of this second doorway, I could see that there was some kind of distortion. One that appeared to be similar to the heat waves that would cross our lands and try to carry the heat back up to the sky nation so it would not give so much harm to our lands.

However, besides the rippling of what appeared

=⊕=

to be heat waves, there was another appearance that had made itself known to me. And it was coming to me in the form of colors. Colors that I knew had a great meaning from what I had been prepared with.

Getting closer to the opening of this horizontal doorway, I could see there were what appeared to be ribbed colors within it. There were still the four walls of this doorway and they continued to go back further and further. And as they did this, they appeared to be getting smaller; but I held the understanding that this was only because of the distance they held within them.

However, the thought that had come to my thinking mind was that as these ribs of light went from wide to narrow, there did not seem to be an ending to them at all. I knew this doorway was going to be a very long one. One that would not be as easy to travel through as the first one had been.

Looking at the colors that had come into this doorway, I saw that there were blends of blacks and whites, and each of these colors seemed to form itself just like a rib of light.

Grandfather and Two Bears had once shared a similar picture with me from one of the older spirit paintings in a cave. And it was they that had explained why this color of the black and white had become so relevant to our people.

They told me this color of black and white had come to us from the teachings of the Anasazi and the black represented the sleep time where we would learn from the old ones and dreamers, while the white represented the time when each of us would wake to find ourselves as we are in truth. This is where we find ourselves as a part of the one...no longer separated by the sleep of illusion.

Just before we entered this other doorway...this one that appeared to be on its side, eagle stopped our forward motion and made a great spirit cry. One that seemed to be even louder than the one he shared with this domain when he had landed on the moon.

And as his spirit cry echoed through the long and seemingly endless corridor of the doorway in front of us, the colored ribs began to move, slowly at first but picking up speed as we stood our position and observed.

They were moving in a direction that was toward us, and as we entered this place, I could see that these colors seemed to be moving much faster.

I did not know if we or the ribbed colors of black and white were moving faster now. But whatever the case, there was the feeling of a great movement now that we were within this doorway—a great movement that shared its purpose. This purpose was known to eagle, bear, and buffalo, but was not clear to me...only that we would soon be at the place we had been destined to arrive.

As we continued to travel deeper into this great doorway, I noticed many other passages appearing in front of us. As we came up to them, there would be another spirit call of eagle that would go ahead. And when he would hear an answer, there would accompany this answer a direction that shared with him which passage we would need to travel into.

During all of this time, I could feel the strength that was within eagle. For it was his strength of wing that was allowing the rest of us to follow him on this journey. It was his strength of wing that was giving us flight on this time and place, and had it not been for this, I do not believe we would have been able to do as well as we were all doing now.

Continuing on with what was appearing to be an endless journey, I could see eagle flying in the front of us and bear and buffalo just to either side of me. I could feel no tiredness coming from eagle. There was only an increasing in his strength the further we would travel through this ribbed corridor of the doorway's tunnel.

Then, and from what seemed to be out of nowhere, there was no longer a tunnel from the doorway. It had left us in less time that it took to blink an eye.

We were flying very closely to the lands of the Earth Mother now. And as I looked around myself, I could see that we had come to a place that was similar to the lands of the mesa. Yet there was something that was different about them. Something that was just beneath my awareness.

However, as I had come to understand, that when spirit would lead, there would always be the best of reasons for what would take place. And it would be my quest to understand...and not to control.

As we continued to fly close to the face of these lands, I could feel the air rushing past my ears and pushing against my face. And turning to both my right and left sides, I could see bear and buffalo had not lost their positions. They were still with me and in their same place.

Looking to the front, I could see that it was eagle who had been shown this direction we would need to travel into. And I could feel a great sense of understanding that was covering him as we continued to fly forward.

The sun was very bright on these lands as I looked

over them. I could see that all of the children who were growing here were well kept in balance. Well kept in this balance of the life path all of us seek to find.

Then, just ahead of eagle, there appeared a rainbow. It was one that seemed to be larger than the sky nation and the closer we got to it, the larger it would grow.

Once again, and without decreasing our flying speed, eagle let out another spirit cry. And as this sound reached the great rainbow, it began to rise. It rose out of the earth that it was touching and into the sky nation, the place where it had come to know as its home.

We continued to travel into the direction of the great rainbow, and as we did, there was a continual rising of it from the place it once occupied.

Now, I could see that with its rising above the face of the Earth Mother, that it was not one rainbow, but it was four. They were all spinning in a clockwise motion, showing off all of the colors that were theirs to blend.

Looking into the center of this four-legged rainbow, I could see a place where all of them held their beginnings. It was in the form of a small circle with four lines leading out of each direction.

Then these lines that led out of the small circle grew in size and turned into the four direction rainbows that were spinning around.

I noticed that in each of these four places of the rainbow, there seemed to be two for each of the four directions they were reflecting. That instead of only one rainbow on each of its legs, there were two. But it was very difficult to know if this was truth because they would always be in a pattern of blending into themselves and those colors they held with them. And this made it very difficult to see if, in fact, there were two...or only one.

However, there was not a great deal of time that was given to me in looking at this whirling rainbow. For as we continued our approach, it was moving ahead of us, as well, keeping a measured distance between eagle and itself.

But I could also see that it had now taken over the place of leading us to wherever it was we were meant to go.

I knew this...but I did not understand it. So as it had been with so many of the events that had come to me on this night, I allowed myself to be...and be guided. For to do anything else now was just not possible. Not if I wanted to see what was waiting for me at the end of this journey.

Looking to the far horizon that was ahead of us and behind the great four-wheeled rainbow that was leading us now, I could see what appeared to be a rising of mountains. Mountains that seemed to be very familiar to me, but in some way they were now very different.

As they appeared in the far horizon, I could hear a spirit chant that was being carried over the air that was around me. And hearing it, I carried the under-standing that they were calling to me with this chant. They were calling with those things that were being shared with all who had come to assist me in finding my way to them.

I could only hold in the front of my thinking mind that this was the place where the old ones had come to meet me. I had been told so many times before that these Ancient Ones were willing to share with me the meaning of what had been coming to me from the past two days, but were weighing me down because of my lack of understanding for them.

As I listened to these calling voices of the spirit chant, I could hear many flutes and drums beating with them. But for whatever reason, I knew they were not coming from the same place as the voices had come. But nevertheless, there was still the oneness that was about them as they were being carried over the great gap that was still between them and us.

Hey Yaw Hey,
Hey Yaw Hey,
Hey Yaw Hey,
Hey Yaw Hey...Ah Yea!

Over and over this spirit chant and the accompanying melody would repeat itself. And the closer we would come to the place I could tell they were coming from, the spirit chant did not gain nor decrease in its intensity. For it would remain the same no matter where we would travel.

There was only one thing in the front of my thinking mind now, and that was to go to this place where they were calling to me from. Looking over to the faces of buffalo and bear, I could feel that they, too, were of the same mind as was eagle, the only one of our council that I could not see the face of, but could feel him very well.

Then, just as the mountains became very clear, we began to rise. It was the kind of rising that came very quickly for all of us.

It had begun from the rising of the four-legged

rainbow and as it climbed higher and higher into the sky that was above us, eagle would follow...and we would follow eagle.

Soon I could see all of the face that was the Earth Mother's on this land. And from this great height, I could tell that there was a group of mountains within another group of them.

However, as high as we were, I was beginning to feel that we would not ever be able to get back to these mountains. For as I looked down on this land that was beneath us, it continued to get smaller and smaller as we rose further and further away.

Then, as we were climbing into the air so quickly, there was the repeating of the spirit chant to us once again. When this happened, rainbow allowed itself to begin a fast descent into this place that was far below us.

As we continued with our descent, I could feel myself growing from within. I was growing with a new understanding for what had taken place with me on this night. But it would be an understanding that my spirit would carry for me until the time would come when I was prepared well enough to understand it, as well.

The straight descent we had taken was not changing direction. But instead of going down in a straight line, we were forming a great circle. One that was still going toward the mountains that were within the other mountains.

And now, there was no longer the rainbow before us, for it had seen its time was over and had left and returned to the sky nation to await its rebirth over these lands once again.

Now there was only eagle, who was leading, and

bear and buffalo who were on both of my sides. And together, we were still forming the circling movements as we continued with our descent into the place the spirit chanting had been coming from.

Looking at eagle ahead of me, I could see that the circle he had been forming during this descent was becoming smaller. It was not as wide as before, but our rate of descent had not decreased any.

Then, looking below me, I could see a clearing. It was filled with a great beam of sunlight that was radiating over a small portion of the cleared part of the valley we were going into.

As I looked around and into the other directions, I could see there were many clouds and they were sharing their blessings over these lands with snow. Snow that was coming down in very large portions.

Now as we were coming even closer to the clearing below us, I could see there were people sitting around a fire. They had assumed the same positions as had the small little cloud that had formed around the moon.

There were three sitting in the north, three sitting in the south, three sitting in the west, and two sitting in the east.

Once again, I was puzzled by the fact of there only being two sitting in the east place of what appeared to me as the same circle that I had seen earlier this night.

And as this thought came to the front of my thinking mind, I was lowered into the middle of the circle of medicine that had been formed, yet still remained away from the earth.

As I looked over to my right, this place of the east where there were only two sitting, I saw that eagle, bear, and buffalo had taken a place of sitting just

behind them and seemed to be waiting for me to begin
what had been prepared for me to do.

Looking into myself, I heard the calling voice of
my spirit come to me. It was sharing with me that I
was to go to each of these people and look onto their
faces and into their eyes. As I would do this, I would
complete another circle of understanding...one that
would allow them to begin this sharing with me that
I had been in need of.

Somehow, I began to float around all of those who
had come to sit in their places by the fire. And as I
would look onto each of their faces, I could see that
there was age on them that could not be counted...but
as I looked into their eyes, I could feel the youth of life
that would always be young.

Then, as I continued to observe them, I noticed
that their circle consisted of six women and five men.
And even though all of them were of many ages...ages
that had been long ago, I held the knowing that there
was a life flowing through them just as the waters of
the streams flow through the mountains. One that
would not ever come to an end, and one that would
continue to be filled with the blessings of life that we
would all know as good.

I noticed that while each of them was holding a
sacred place as they sat within this great medicine
wheel of life, they did not have any of the colors of the
directions on them. There was no color over any of
them other than white. This came to me as a great
surprise at first, but later it did make sense.

For I remembered while there were the separate
colors of the four directions being held by the rising
flames, as well as eagle, buffalo, bear, and myself, that
while we would hold onto them, there would not be

any forward movement. And until we allow our colors to blend with the others and become the white that is the presence of all colors, we do not advance.

Now, this came to me in a way that I could understand why these old ones would only wear the color white. For they had, in truth, gone beyond the great separation that holds us as being different from all other life that is around us. They had come to the place of being one with the one and for this knowing, I held it to be good.

"It is good that you can see this, Speaking Wind," came the voice from the elder in the north.

"The time has come for you to join us. Please do."

As these speaking words came to me, I felt myself lowering to a place that was no longer in the air above this circle of the Old Ones. This allowed me to set both of my feet in the middle of this great medicine wheel of theirs and rest on the same ground they were on.

It was then that I knew. It was when my feet first touched the earth that I was filled with the knowing and understanding that I had arrived at the place I had been seeking. This place that has been sung about for so many generations by our people.

I had arrived in the domain of the Ancient Ones. The Ancient Ones who have always been with us to provide us with their light of direction, wisdom, and truth.

And now that I was among them, I was filled with a great feeling of relief. A feeling that was being shared with them by the water that was beginning to run out of both of my eyes as I stood before them.

Finally I had arrived...and now I would be shown.

CHAPTER THREE

THE MESSAGE FROM THE ANCIENT ONES

THE MESSENGER

Looking over to the place where the elder of the north was sitting, I held a great question in the front of my thinking mind. One that needed to be answered for me before I would have any room for more. I needed answers before there could be any more room for me to accept those things that were about to be offered.

However, as I looked over the faces of those elders who were with me, the Ancient Ones of our ancestors, I could not find the proper path to address such a question. Nor could I find the speaking words to put my thoughts together.

Just at the place where I thought I would explode, the elder in the north made my task a little easier and I could feel him as he prompted me from deep in a place within me. This was the same place where Grandfather and Two Bears would often travel to see whether I had been able to keep up with their speaking words.

"What is this question that you would like to have answered, Speaking Wind? We can tell that it is giving to you a great weight. One that must be lifted from you before we can begin."

Looking at the Ancient One in the north position, I tried to fill my lungs with as much air as I could. Then exhaling, I attempted to place as much of a tone of respect in my speaking words as was possible for me to do.

"It is a question that has given to me a great weight, Old One. And it has come to me from an observation of each of these events that have brought me to you and this place we are sharing together.

"From all of the events that have come to me, Old Ones, I have held the knowing of what they were, in truth, representing. They were a sign of the medicine wheel of life."

"From this place, your observations are good, Speaking Wind," came the reply from the Ancient One in the north.

"Tell us now, is this your question? If it is, then I must say that it is a very poor one indeed."

"No...no. This is not the question, Old One. It is only the beginning of it," I said in return.

"My question is why has there always been one position left out and why has it continually been the one that was in the east?

"This then is my question and I ask it with the utmost of respect to all of you."

Finishing my speaking words, there was a silence that fell over this land of the Ancient Ones. One that would have allowed me to sit on it because of its thickness.

Then, and from places that were all around me, I could feel the warmth of these Ancient Ones smiling at me. This was filling me with a great hope...one that shared with me that this question of mind had been accepted by them and would soon be answered.

"In truth you do not know of this reason, Speaking Wind. For we can see it in the colors you are wearing.

"And because you are right when you have assessed this question as one of importance, we will share with you the reason. This reason for the one space that was always in the east to have been missing.

"This reason is very simple, little one," the old one from the east continued.

Turning my head to a place where I could see him, I could see he held a great smile over his face. And from what I was feeling from it, I knew this had been done for my benefit.

"This space that you have seen unfilled has been presented to you in this way because it has been waiting for your return to it.

"The empty space is yours, Speaking Wind. It is reserved for the messenger of those things we are about to share with you."

I could feel the surprise come over me as these speaking words reached their target. And as this was being allowed to filter within me, I could see there were smiles of approval coming to me from all of the Old Ones who had been sitting around this council fire that had been built on this land.

"Does this surprise you, Speaking Wind?" came the voice of the elder that was sitting in the south.

"Yes, Old One...yes, it does," was my reply.

"And can you share this reason for your surprise, little one?"

"Well...," I began, still searching for the proper set of speaking words to share with this council.

"Well...it is because I have not ever come to perceive myself as being anything but normal. Yes...yes this is the reason I have been looking for."

Suddenly there was a feeling of something that was big and hot, and it was filling all of the air and lands that were around me.

Looking over to the place where eagle, bear, and buffalo had been sitting, I could see that this feeling was making them uncomfortable and they were trying to shift their weight on their sitting position. They shifted their weight in a way of countering these things that they, too, were feeling.

"Speaking Wind!" came the commanding voice of the elder of the north.

"There is one thing that must be clear to you and all others who are like you. And that is a truth that has been forgotten for a very long time.

"This truth, and it would do you well to keep it in the front of your thinking mind for the rest of your seasons, is this.

"There is not now, nor has there ever been anyone who is normal. If you would only open your eyes to see this, you would be well ahead of many of the other two-legs that are searching in your domain.

"To even think of yourself as someone who is normal is to have sold yourself and all that is within you to one who wants to control you.

"This is a truth that even now will bring a great amount of pain to those who would follow it. For it brings a great deal of sorrow to us who sit by this council fire and observe all who come to enter the domain of the Earth Mother's.

"When we will see one who will have considered themselves as being normal, as you have said, then

=⊕=

we see one who has no longer the will or strength to follow their own life path. We see one who has willingly allowed themselves to be controlled by others of their own kind. And for this, we know there will not be any learning that will come to them, and there will not be any advancement of their spirit.

"And for all of this, the seasons they have been given to travel their life path with the Earth Mother, those seasons will have been wasted and so will the time they have used up selfishly for themselves.

"You see Speaking Wind, for each one who has been allowed entry into this domain that your people call the Earth Mother, there are millions who have been denied this blessing. For to have been allowed entry into her domain is a great blessing in itself and one that has been given to them out of her love.

"So when we will see or hear one who would call themselves normal, we see one who has been wasting their time on their life path. And we will begin to think of all those others who wanted their space and it makes us sad.

"The spirit who is within you will hear our tears, and spirit will come to you in a way that will most likely not be enjoyable for you to encounter. For spirit within will tell you of your mistake either by making you stub your toe, cause you to lose something that you value very highly, or bring to you the remembering of an emotion that will not be pleasant from your past.

"But spirit is doing this not so much out of what it is feeling from us, but out of the memory of why you have been allowed entry into this domain to begin with. And this reason was not for you to come to want to be accepted by others so much that you would allow yourself to be controlled by them. But the reason is to learn...and this learning cannot come to you unless you travel your own path....this path that is only for you to do...and no other.

"Do you hold an understanding now of what it is we are willing to share with you, Speaking Wind?" the elder in the north asked.

"Yes Old One, I hold this understanding now," was my response.

"Then please share this with us once again, and in your own speaking words, little one," came the voice from the elder in the west.

"It is important for you to hold this understanding well within you. For as the messenger, there will be many great tests that will come to you. And if you will not have this beginning lesson in a place of under-standing, then you will continue to hold yourself back from doing those things that need to be done.

"When we see that this understanding has come to live with you little one, then we will invite you to come sit in your place next to me," came the voice of the elder in the east.

"...But not before."

As their speaking words had finished, I could feel spirit within me growing in strength and in wisdom. And as it was doing so, I could feel the understanding that had been given to me begin to take on a face of its own. One that I would now be able to share with the Ancient Ones.

"It is this process of being in the place called normal that we find our most comfortable place of being. And this place of comfort will be seen by us as one that will not allow those things that we fear come to face us. Those things that we do not understand will be cradled in this face of fear.

"By trying to find this place of being normal, we will not have to deal with so many of the events of uncertainty that will come to us. And by trying to be normal among the others, we will have the believing that all things that will come to us will be alright. For it will no longer be our own interpretation of our life that we seek, but it will be the interpretation of the ones who are over us that we will seek out and try to gain acceptance for.

"I can see now that the more we will try to become normal—this term that is used to make us be as what others would wish for us to be—by using and trying to be this thing that we are not, only takes us further away from our path. This path that we have to travel that can only be found by our own working through those events and lessons that will come to us.

"And it is only when we will be willing to do our own work for those things that we will need in this life path that we will discover who and what we are in truth.

"So it is, as I have seen it, that when we will say that we are normal, we will not be ourselves, but we will have become one who the others would wish for us to be. And as long as we will try to stay normal, we will not be in touch with ourselves.

"This then is the understanding that I have held from what all of you have been willing to share with me.

"Have I found a place to begin?"

From all of the Ancient Ones, as well as those who had come with me to this place, there was a silence that covered us once again. It was a silence of acceptance for the understanding I had offered to them.

And now...now that this silence was coming to a close, I could see the looks on all of their faces come to me. The looks that had been there upon first arriving with them had returned, and for this...I knew it to be good.

"It is good, Speaking Wind. This is good to see from you. For you have just now begun your long journey back to us. Back to the place you belong," came the speaking words from the elder in the north.

"Come, my brother...," the elder in the east said. "Come and take your place...it is here, next to me."

Looking over at all of the faces of these Ancient Ones, I could see there was a look that made me feel very good inside. This feeling I had often received from Grandfather and Two Bears when I had learned a great lesson from something that had been presented to me.

Walking over to the place that had been empty, this place that was in the east position of the medicine wheel of life, I could see those same looks were coming to me from the ones who had brought me to this land, this time, this place. I could feel a great warmth from eagle, bear, and buffalo that was filling into my within place. It was a feeling that shared with me that all was as it should be and it, too, was good.

THE MESSAGE

Taking my place in the east position of the medicine wheel, I could hear the sounding of the spirit wind as he was passing through the tall trees that were all around us. Passing through the standing people and their nation.

As I was listening to him, he was showing me a direction, and this direction was from the east.

"It is good that you have learned to listen to your totem, Speaking Wind," the elder in the north said.

"This will assist you greatly in those times that are ahead of you...and hear me when I say to you that they are coming."

"What times are these, Old One?" I asked, sitting as still in my new place as I could.

"The times that we are about to share with you, little one," the elder in the south stated.

"Very soon now it will be the 'Season Of The Long Shadow' over the Earth Mother. And this is the same as you will see when the ending of one day will come over the domain you have known and traveled through for so many seasons.

"When this 'Season Of The Long Shadow' will come into its life path for the Earth Mother, you will be awakened from what will have come over you as the sleep of preparing, Speaking Wind.

"This sleep of preparing will be much different for you than will have been the sleep of illusion. It will be different for you in this way.

"While you were sleeping in the illusion, there was nothing that was visible at all...not for what it was in truth. But while you are placed into the sleep of preparing, there will continue to come to you the face of truth in all things. For you will be allowed to see those things for what they are...but you will not yet have the understanding for what they will mean.

"And it will be while you are sleeping in this preparation that many of these things we are willing to share with you now will be understood. This will

be the time when you will find the needed understanding for what we are offering so you will be able
to share this message with many who will then come
to the place of awakening from their own sleep of
illusion. And when they come to this place, Speaking
Wind, they will have been prepared to listen to what
it is we have given to you to share with them.

"They will understand our speaking words of
truth through you and because they will understand
them, they will know what they must do for themselves.

"When the 'Season Of The Long Shadow' begin,
Speaking Wind, you will be sitting in a place that will
only have you in it. And we will come to you in a way
that you will not be able to mistake.

"You will know us...and we will say to you, 'Speaking Wind, it is time.'

"When you will hear this...you will know that it is
time to write down all of those things we will share
with you in this place...and in this time.

"Until this will come to you little one, rest. For
when it comes time for you to awake, there will be
need for great accomplishments for you to do. Not
only for the ones who are with you on the land you
travel, but for all of the two-legs as well as the children of the Earth Mother in all lands, and in all places.

"For when we will come to you at that time Speaking Wind, you will know that these times we speak of
are close and there is much to do.

"You will know that already the 'Season Of The
Long Shadow' has begun and your time of becoming
the messenger is at hand.

"Have no fear little one, for the preparing you will
have done at that time will be sufficient for you to see

=⊕=

that those things that are soon to be are needed. And, we will be with you to protect and guide not only you, but those who would wish to prepare themselves as well. This will be the time they will come to you. It will not be necessary for you to always go to them," completed the elder in the south.

"Speaking Wind," the elder in the north began once again.

"We are all tied to the Earth Mother and because we are tied to her, then it is only right to say that where she will go...we must also go."

"But we have always been with her, Old One. Do you mean that she is going some place where we have not been before?" I asked, noting a slight trembling in the tone of my voice.

"Yes, Speaking Wind...she is going to a place where not many will be able to follow. Not those who have not prepared themselves adequately, that is," the elder in the north answered.

"This is the message that we bring to you, little one," the elder from the west picked up from the north elder's speaking words.

"This message that we are willing to share with you must not be changed. For to do so would bring great harm to all who travel on the two-legs.

"But I would not change any of those things you would be willing to share with me, Old Ones. For this I am certain."

"We hold this knowing to be true, Speaking Wind," the elder from the east continued.

"However, if you will look at all those who have gone before you...the ones who have brought many of our messages to the people, you will not find the face of truth left in many of them. What you will find will be the empty words that have been used to carry them...and that has been all that has remained.

"But it is not from the messenger that we sent to carry them. For the messengers that we have sent to this domain of the great illusion have done their tasks well...and for that, Great Mystery has always been pleased with them.

"It has been the ones who have not been willing to stand and look at their own truth that is within them who have done these things. For it has been they who have robbed the face of truth from those things we have sent to the people so they could see all things for what they are and not to be fooled by the illusion that surrounds all of them in your domain.

"It has always been so, Speaking Wind, that the ones who will not want to be faced with their own truth will not want any others to see it either. And they will be driven so much from their fear and greed that they will distort all faces of truth with their own faces of fear.

"And it is this fear that remains for the others to see. This fear that, if they will allow it, will rob them of themselves and the path they travel just so the ones who have robbed truth from them can remain in their power places. Remain in their power places and live with this illusion that they hold any power at all over so many.

"But in the times that are soon to arrive in this domain of the illusion, this will no longer be possible. For those times that are coming will bring with them a great devastation to all...and it will only be the ones who will learn to see that will remain.

"The message we are bringing to you, Speaking Wind, this message that you will bring to many who travel on the two-legs is this," the elder in the north stated.

"From all that has been known of before, from all that has been believed in...those things that have always been with you—they will soon be removed by being destroyed. And they will not return again for their time in your domain is over.

"There will be great drought in lands where there has always been plenty of water waiting for you to drink. And in those places where water will cross the face of the Earth Mother...this water will be poisoned and will take the life of any who would attempt to take it within them.

"The times that are coming to your domain will be filled with great misery, Speaking Wind, and you will see both young and old come before you with their tongues swollen so much that there will no longer be any room for the air to pass into their lungs.

"For them, to drink of the poison waters, this would bring a great blessing to them...even though it would surely end their life path.

"There will be a great many parts of the earth that will shake and tremble, Speaking Wind," the elder in the west continued.

"Parts of the face of the Earth Mother will change so much that there will not be any who will recognize them from what they once were. And as they will shake, there will be many holes that will open and out of these holes will come poisons that will pass over all of the lands.

"These will be the poisons that the two-legs have buried long before, and there will be other poisons. Poisons that have not yet been known to any who travel within the domain of the Earth Mother's now.

And they, too, will cross over this land that you have come to know. And every place they will touch, there will be great numbers who will die.

"There will be poisons that will be carried on the back of the spirit wind. And those who will have themselves touched by them, there will be a great eating of their flesh and it will not stop until they have been completely consumed.

"It will be in these times when one will look as far as their eyes can see and all there will be before them will be the lost, the dying, and the dead. For during these times, there is nothing else that is to be seen.

"And all over the face of the Earth Mother, there will be not only the two-legs, but those of the children of the Earth Mother's who have not prepared themselves, as well. For there will be none who will survive if they will not have prepared themselves, Speaking Wind.

"During these times, there will be those who would try to escape in places that are far under the face of the Earth Mother, but this will not work. For their time, too, will have been marked...and it will have been marked by a terrible disaster that will come to them as well.

"For there will not be any place that will be without the cleansing that is about to come to this domain, Speaking Wind...no place that will be hidden from what is coming.

"The ones who will have thought they have found safety beneath the earth, they will come to know this has also been an illusion to them. The same kind of illusion that they have been living with for all of their seasons of their life path," continued the elder from the south.

"For soon after they will have found their safe places under the earth, there will be a great awakening from the underworld. One that will call to life the ones who have been asleep for many generations. And as they will come to life, there will be great mountains of smoke and burning rock that they will continue to pour in all places that are.

"And this burning rock and poison smoke that will come from them will also find the ones who have traveled under the earth for their safety. And for them, there will be the great burning of their lives and none will ever be allowed to return to the top again.

"For them...it will also be over.

"The two-legs used to know how to live from the earth, but there are no longer many of them who have held onto this knowledge, Speaking Wind," came the voice from the elder in the north.

"During the time when the earth begins to shake violently, there will no longer be the foods they had once obtained in their great stores. For the roads will have been destroyed by this shaking and the fuels that have supplied them with their heat will no longer be available to them, for this will have been taken deep into the Earth Mother for another purpose. One that will be shared with you soon.

"But the ones who will continue to prepare themselves at this time, they will need to remember how to live from the earth. And they will have to learn to leave those places where there are many two-legs, for it will be during this time when one will be killed for having a piece of fruit or a bite of bread. They will not be safe in those places where they once thought their numbers would bring to them safety. They will not be safe there because once these earth changes begin, all of those things they have held the believing in...those things like the laws they have made for themselves to follow will no longer be enforceable, for there will be none left to enforce them.

"All who would remain in this illusion, Speaking Wind, they will turn very quickly into the most base of creatures. And it is only the most base of creatures that will turn on their own kind for food to eat. And this is to be so.

"There will be many who would try to gain their food from the great seas, but when they will arrive at them...they will find all they had discarded of their own wastes in her will have been returned.

"For even the once abundant life that had been with the mighty waters of the Earth Mother will have been killed. But it will have died long before these great changes will have come to a completion. And the most of this will have come from the efforts of the two-legs.

"Those things that they once thought would not matter...those things such as dumping all of their waste they no longer wanted to see or deal with into the great waters of life will come back on them.

"And when they will arrive at these great waters looking for forgiveness from them and the once abundant life that had been within them, all they will find will be those things they caused to poison the life being returned to them.

"There will only be death that will come to them from these waters, Speaking Wind. The same death they dumped into the waters for many generations will now have come back to them.

"For those who still refuse to prepare themselves, they will look back on the lands they once lived on and only see destruction. They will look out on the waters that once gave them life and only see death. They will look on themselves and only see the end...and it will be so for they will no longer continue.

"Then when the underworld has come forth with all of their poison smoke and burning rock, there will come the need for all of the fuel that had been taken under the earth, Speaking Wind," the elder in the east continued.

"For as soon as the burning rock has almost covered much of the earth, there will come pouring out over the entire face of her the fuel that had been held within her for such a long time. And when this fuel comes to the surface, it will find the burning rocks of the underworld and they will meet in a fiery inferno.

"When they will meet and begin their burning, there will be such a great heat that will be felt over the entire face of the Earth Mother, that all that had been left...will die. Then there will be nothing left of what had been. All will be destroyed...that is, from the life that had not been prepared.

"Then when the entire face and beneath of the Earth Mother is on fire, there will come another great sign from the star nation. The star nation will have seen that all of the cleansing of the Earth Mother has taken place and will begin to do their part.

"For they will send a great star body from their and will allow it land deep into the great waters that will be with the Earth Mother .

"When it will land, there will be a great wave of water that will engulf all of the Earth Mother. And as it does this, all that had been burning will be put out and there will be a great cloud of mist rise in all places.

"As this cloud of the great mist will rise, there will

be a great light that will begin to shine through it. And this light will be the signal that the time has come for the beginning of the fifth world to be.

"This will be the sign for those who have been patiently waiting for it to return. To now return to this new world that will be the Earth Mother's and it will be of light and peace. For there will not be anything else that will be allowed to enter from that time on."

Then the elder finished her speaking words and I could feel many drops of water pouring out of both of my eyes.

Looking over to them, I said,

"Have we done so much bad that this is to be our punishment?"

"It is not a punishment, Speaking Wind. This is not a punishment for any of those things that have or have not been done," the voice of the elder of the north continued.

"This is only a cleansing of the Earth Mother and all that will not be cleaned will be done away with. This is necessary for her to enter her new world, little one, and all that has not prepared itself to travel with her...well, it must be torn away.

"This is what has happened, Speaking Wind...this is what will be for it has been told from the beginning. Only the two-legs have stripped out the truth from those many other messages that have been given to them. Stripped out the truth and replaced it with their fear. And this is why not many remember that what is about to come to them has been told to them before."

"When will anyone know that they have come to prepare themselves adequately, Old Ones? Will there be a sign for us to follow?"

"Yes, Speaking Wind," came the voice of the elder from the east.

"There will be many signs but one that will not go unnoticed will be when there will be two people walking next to each other. Walking next to each other and each seeming to have the same kinds of thinking thoughts from what others would be able to see from them.

"Then one of them will disappear from sight and the other one will remain walking.

"This will be one of the signs that will be seen by many during the middle times of the 'Season Of The Long Shadow.' And this sign will not be able to be hidden from anyone. For all will see this and know it to be the face of truth for those things that you will bring to them...from us."

"And when will this take place, Old Ones? Can you share this with me?" I asked, holding my face of respect.

"It will come when it will be time for it to be, Speaking Wind. But it will not be for awhile...until after you have begun to perform your work with them.

"These things have always taken place in this domain that is the Earth Mother's, Speaking Wind. The only difference is when the others have heard of such things, the ones who would control others rather than understand themselves have always managed to get those people who have been around them to disregard such things, calling them unreal and un-true," the elder from the east continued.

"For there have been many messages and many great signs that have been sent into this domain that is the Earth Mother's for all time. But so many of these messages have gone unheeded because they did not follow the wants of those who were in control.

"And now there are not many of the ones who remember what has been. Not many of them because of all the efforts that have been made to get others to forget them. To ignore those things they brought back from this place we are in with you now.

"It is very important that our message remain unchanged this time, Speaking Wind. For this is the ending of a long journey that had begun long ago by all of the two-legs," the elder from the north began.

"And this is because of the ending of this fourth world?" I asked.

"Yes, Speaking Wind...this is the reason for this. And because this is the ending of the last of the worlds that have been given to cleanse the four races, there will not be any more time given to do such things. It is time to move on now, and this is what is taking place.

"Then why were there four worlds given to do this thing, Old One? I do not hold an understanding for this."

"The four worlds came about due to the ego of the two-legs, Speaking Wind," the elder in the north continued as he held a brief look of sadness over his face..

"In the beginning, before there were any worlds as we have come to know of, there was only the being within the one. For there were no separations that were known by any during this time, and all was in balance.

"However, as the two-legs saw this, they became upset and wanted to have themselves set apart from all of this. They wanted to be seen as being different in their ways and life paths.

"This resulted in their all getting together and holding a great council among themselves. It was during this council of theirs that they decided that in order for them to be set apart and become different from all other living life in the Earth Mother's domain, they would learn to speak another language. One that would be so different from what had been known that there would be no one who would be able to understand them. No one but themselves.

"And for this, they had come to believe that they could hold many great secrets away from all of the other life that had until now been able to share with them in all things.

"So it was decided that this would be the course they would follow. But it was not until they realized that this new language they had come to learn did not keep their secrets from being known from all of the other children of the Earth Mother. It only allowed them to find that there was a great separation between those children who they had once been able to speak with and share things freely and the two-legs.

"What had once been shared with them so freely had now been taken away. And it had been taken away from them because they no longer held the knowing and understanding of how they once spoke. There was only the new way of speaking that was with them.

"When they looked to see what it was that had come to them from following this course of their actions, this course of actions that had given to them their new way of speaking, all of them felt left out. All of them felt the great void that had come to them by being separated from all life that was around them.

"And when this had been felt by all of the two-legs, there was a great request to the Earth Mother and Great Spirit to return. To be allowed to return to the place where they once had been...this place that had allowed them to be one within the oneness of all life and to share and be shared with.

"There was a great cry that had come to the Earth Mother and Great Spirit from all of the two-legs, and a decision had been reached.

"It was a decision that would create the four worlds that we are about to finish passing through now, Speaking Wind.

"All of the two-legs were told they would be allowed to regain what had once been held by them, but only after passing through many seasons of cleansing for their own races. And after that, there would come to all a great cleansing and only those who would be willing to prepare themselves in the proper way would be allowed to come back to those places they had once been.

"The two-legs, hearing of this, all agreed to the terms that had been given. And this began the first of the four worlds.

"It has been during the four worlds that have come to this domain that each of the four races have been given their opportunity of cleansing themselves and returning to the place they had once been.

"And this cleansing that we have now come to call 'the preparing' was the path that was shown that would allow those who would be willing to find their way back. To find their way back to the place they had once come to call their home.

"During each of the four worlds, Speaking Wind,

each race was given complete freedom and total domain over all those things that would be seen by them.
This was done to allow them to have their own freedom of choice. To choose which path they would
wish to travel.

"To travel on the path that would lead to the left,
this path that is ruled by the body and fed by the
emotion...or to follow the path that leads to the right,
this path that is led by the spirit and fed by the spirit.

"Once each race had been given their time, the
ones who had come to understand and follow the
wisdom of the path of the spirit would then stand
away and allow for the passing of the next race...and
the next world.

"And all of the wisdom and understanding that
had been gained by them would be removed from the
next world so the next race would be given the same
starting place on their own. This same starting place
would come to each of the four races.

"This fourth world has been the one which has
allowed the last of the four races the opportunity of
cleansing itself, and this time that has been given has
been for the white race.

"It has been during this time when all of the
understanding and wisdom that has been with our
people was taken away. And there were many of
them who would look at what had been allowed to
take place and did not understand it.

"For we would hear them as their prayers would
rise to us from the smoke of their council fires. And
we would be of a heavy heart when we would hear
from them that they did not understand why all of
what had once been shared with them had been taken
away.

=⊕=

"But Speaking Wind, I will tell you this in truth, that it was not only our own people, but it was the people from all of the other three races who had come to this end...this end as they saw it. But in truth, it was not an end, it was only a waiting place for them.

"A waiting place so that this last race could have those same opportunities that the rest of the races had, and with the same freedom to do what they would wish to do for the time that had been given them.

"Soon now, Speaking Wind, all of this will come to its end. And those who have not taken the pathway of preparing themselves...will be left behind. For unless they have prepared in the proper way of seeing themselves for who and what they are, there will not be any place for them in the next place the Earth Mother will be entering. This place we have come to call the fifth world of peace and light."

"Old Ones," I said, keeping as much sincerity in the tone of my voice as I could, "what then may enter there?"

"We can only share with you that there have been many examples of this having happened before, Speaking Wind," came the speaking words from the elder in the east.

"There have been among you in the recent times, the old ones you have called the Anasazi. And they had passed into the fifth world many times and have left their records among your own people as well as on the walls of the caves on your lands with their spirit paintings.

"There are still these records for you to see, and others who would have their eyes opened for them.

"But as to what will be allowed entry into this fifth

world, I can only share with you that what has already been allowed entry has varied from the individual, to an entire village. So it will all depend on what is understood as being needed by spirit.

"If you hold an understanding of those things that we have been willing to share with you, Speaking Wind, those things that are soon to come to all who are in this domain of the Earth Mother's, then we would like to give you the seven steps of preparing. Those things that will need to be remembered by those who would wish to gain entry into this next world of light and peace with the Earth Mother."

"Are you ready to hear of such things, little one?" the elder in the north asked.

"Yes, Old Ones, I am ready for this," came my determined response.

"This is good, Speaking Wind. We will now begin," came the collective speaking words from all of the Ancient Ones who were with me on this place.

"For only the ones who have found and are willing to travel their own path of the spirit will find their way into the fifth world, little one. And what we are now willing to share with you will be the seven steps that will allow them to see and know themselves for who and what they are...and to see the path they have each come into this domain to travel."

=✳=

CHAPTER FOUR

THE SEVEN STEPS TO FINDING YOUR PATH

- STEP ONE -

From The Elder In The South

FINDING THE PART OF YOU THAT LIVES IN ALL THINGS

"Speaking Wind," came the voice from the elder in the south.

"You must remember to share this message with all those who will come to you. Until they have come to successfully complete the first step, there will be no good that will come to them by trying to go onto the second and so on.

"These steps that we are now willing to share with you are meant so that others will have a path to follow. And this path will bring them to see themselves for who and what they are.

"However, we will caution you and those who would be willing to accept our message that there will be a great change that will come to all. And this change that will come to them will be one of a great surprise.

=⊕=

"Whenever one will begin to see themselves for who and what they are, Speaking Wind, there will be a great awareness that will come to them. And it will be from this first awareness that will cause them to fall into this place we call the awakening.

"The awakening will come to them when they will first learn to go within themselves and search for those same things that they share with all of their brothers and sisters. Those things that will cause them to feel a great love that is within themselves.

"For it is this love that is within them and comes out for no material reason. It is this love that will guide them to their spirit path in the domain of the Earth Mother's.

"When they can stand in front of one of the standing people and feel a part of themselves that is covered with this love of sharing, there will be a recognition of what will be returned to them.

"For this standing person will return this part of their love to them, and they will know that this has begun a part of a great adventure. An adventure that will lead them to know who and what they are and know that this is good.

"Within all of the two-legs, there is a place of the spirit. And it is from this within place that they must reach into very deeply in order to find this love we are speaking to you of.

"For it is this love that has no limitations and no boundaries that has been used to bond all spirits together from the one. And in finding it once again, there will become a beginning bond that will be felt...first from the standing person, then from the others.

"Once any two-leg will find this part of themselves that holds this love that we speak of, this love that is within their own spirit, they will feel as if they have uncovered a great truth. One that will now allow them to feel a part of all living life that is within this domain.

"And as they have this doorway opened up to them, there will be a great awareness that they are, in truth, a part of all things that exist. And as this truth begins to fill them in their empty places, there will be a great joy that will come over them. One that will allow them to feel alive and no longer in a place where they do not know what they are to do.

"Many of the two-legs will attempt to find this love that exists within them, but they will not find it. For there has only been for them a part of their living and seeing that has existed on the outside of their selves. There have not been the necessary acknowledgments of who and what they are from their within.

"You see, Speaking Wind, one of the truths that must come to be...before they will be allowed to experience this love that is within them, is that there are two parts to themselves. And it is these two parts that must be brought into balance before they will be allowed entry into their own place of the spirit. This place of the spirit that is holding their love for them.

"It is holding this love of theirs in a good way though, for if it were to be given to them before they had been prepared, they would not know what to do with it anyway. And it is great, Speaking Wind... greater than anything they have yet found on their path.

"So it is that before this small doorway will be opened for them, they must travel within themselves and find their other half. This other half of themselves that will be just the opposite of who they see themselves as being on the outside.

"For many of the two-legs you will see little one, this will be a very strange experience for them to hold. And one that may prove difficult for them to embrace...but it is truth and they should follow it if they are to come to any place of understanding themselves and this path that is being offered to them.

"If they will have the face of a female on the outside, then there will be their other face of the male that they carry on the inside. And if there is the face of the male on the outside, they must travel within to find their face of female...these are the other sides to all living things and must be brought into balance.

"It is only when one will find the balance from the inside as being the same as the balance from the outside that they will come to know the meaning of the one. And it will only be when they will have become this one of themselves that their spirit will share with them the secret of this great and unconditional love that resides within them.

"And Speaking Wind...this is the love of creation. For it was through this love that Great Mystery created all that you see before you. It was through this love that we were created...and it is through this love that the two-legs will once again learn to create for themselves. To create for themselves in a way that was once held by all of them. This way that they have forgotten to remember but still have the chance of learning once again.

"And for all of this, little one, these two-legs will have begun to see what value they hold for themselves and all that is around them. For they will have begun to emerge from their places of being controlled into ones that will allow them to be."

The elder became silent for a moment and remained in a place of looking deep within me. I held the understanding of what it was, though, for I had become used to this kind of traveling to my within place. The Old One had taken the time of seeing if I had been able to keep up with those things that she was sharing with me.

And satisfied that I had, she continued.

"However, we must share with you a warning, Speaking Wind. One that must also be shared with those who would be willing to find their own path of the spirit.

"When any of the two-legs will take this first step...this first step in the many others that will lead them to know what their own path of the spirit is...they will experience a great loss...but it is only a loss for all of those things they have been carrying around with them. Those things they have been hanging onto but neither understand nor do they hold a weight of truth to them.

"Many of the two-legs hold onto such things out of fear of being alone and away from any who would accept them. So from this kind of thinking, they will have close to them many things. Things that will bring them this false feeling of comfort.

"But as they will experience this first step on their way to discovering their own path, they will find themselves standing in a dark place. A dark place that appears empty to them. And this emptiness will make them feel very bad...so bad because they will first feel that everything they had worked so hard for has been taken away from them. And it will be at this time when you will hear many of them cry and scream, looking for another who they can blame for their feeling this way.

"You must share with them at this time, Speaking Wind, that the one who is to blame is themselves. That it has been themselves who have allowed all of those things that have not been understood by them to fall away. And they have fallen away from them so there will be more room for them to grow. So there will be more room for them to place those things they do understand and those things that do hold truth for them in. And these will be the things that will assist them greatly.

"But while they will wish to hold onto all of those things that are not assisting them—all of those things that they hold onto but do not understand...and all of those things that do not hold truth for them—then there will be as there has always been in their past. There will not be the room for them to grow, and there they will remain. Always the observer and not ever the participant.

"This then is the first of the seven steps to finding the path of ones own and very individual spirit, Speaking Wind. Assist them in coming to understand what it is here that is being offered to them. For there will be many two-legs who will be willing to accept this message...just as there will be many who will not.

"For those who would be willing to listen, you will know this to be good. For those who would not be willing to listen...walk away from them and do not look back."

=⊕=

- STEP TWO -

From The Elder In The West

LET DOUBT AND SELF-PITY
FALL AWAY

"For as long as we have seen the two-legs, Speaking Wind, we have seen how much their doubt and self-pity holds them back. Holds them back from becoming what they have entered this domain of the Earth Mother's to become.

"And for all of these times they have been holding themselves in their own dark places, there has always been one distinct part of them that has repeated itself...time and time again.

"This greatest of their own enemies from within is their doubt and self-pity for themselves. For there are none who travel with the two-legs that have not gone into this little one, and in this grouping...we also include you.

"Think now of what it is that is being shared with you, Speaking Wind. Think of all the times you could have come to do something great with your life path...then think of how you allowed yourself to get caught up in this thing called self-pity...and for this sharing, we will include doubt in this same wording.

"For there is nothing sadder to see than one who has been given many talents and abilities not use them. Not use them because they have allowed themselves to feel so sorry for themselves.

"And the truth of this is that there is always the same amount of things to feel sorry about as there are things to feel grateful for. But the two-legs do not

=⊕=

seem to understand this. They content themselves in this feeling sorry for those things they see in others but do not hold for themselves.

"How strange this is, little one, to see this taking place among so many. How sad it is to see them going no where and doing no thing for themselves...nothing other than this feeling of self-pity that is like one of the false spirits that is always allowing you see those things you want to, but not ever showing to you those things that are.

"It is this not seeing the balance in all things that brings the two-legs into this place of self-pity, little one.

"Think for a moment if you will. When one of your kind feel sorry for themselves, what will be the major ingredient in their doing so?

"It will always come from seeing another do something that is very good in their own eyes. From seeing another who has been able to do the work required to perform a great deed that they have seen.

"And since they are not willing to make these efforts, these efforts that would have allowed them to also do this great deed, they will take the easiest way out. They will tell themselves that they could not ever do anything that is so good. That they are not good enough to do something like that. After all...they are only another person who hold nothing special about themselves.

"This then has been the most common of paths the two-legs have found that leads them to this self-pity. And from their feeling this way long enough, they will find themselves trying to control others into thinking that they, too, are not capable of doing great things for themselves. They will be the ones who will bend the other's ears in repeating this enough times for them to hear, that soon...they will have convinced them.

"And from all that they will have convinced, they will begin to spread this self-pity around until it is far reaching.

"However, there is something that they have not seen here. Something that has come to them before from one of our messengers...but another thing that has been stripped of its truth by the two-legs.

"When they will see something great in another, they are not only seeing this in the one they are looking at, but they are capable of seeing this because this same potential resides within them.

"They are capable of seeing this in another because these same talents and abilities reside within their own spirit. If this was not so, then they would neither see this nor could they appreciate this in another.

"And if they can see this great thing that has been done by another, and they can come to appreciate it, then all they will have to do is to go within to find their own path to doing these kinds of things.

"For unless you possess those same abilities, Speaking Wind, you will not ever come to see them from any one else.

"And this is the balance we are speaking of, little one. This balance that will allow them to understand this great truth.

"When your sleep of preparing has come to its end and you are awakened by us, then it would be well to share with the ones who will have a need to allow their self-pity to drop away to learn of this path we will now share with you."

Once again, this elder became silent. And once again I could see that what he was doing was to look within me to find where I had been able to follow and where there might have been the small clouds that were keeping me from seeing with the clarity of understanding.

For I was having a little trouble in seeing, as well, as I thought I should have been, and I knew when the Old One was finished with traveling within me, that they, too, would hold this knowing. That they would also have this knowing and would allow another comparison to be made. One that would assist me in letting this small cloud go.

"Self-pity comes to all who are not focused, Speaking Wind. And when one is not focused, there is not an easy path for them to follow. Not an easy path that would allow them to gain this focus for themselves without assistance from their own spirit within.

"So when you come across the many two-legs who are having this trouble, give to them this exercise. If they will follow it, there will be many things that will become clear for them once again. Those things they will need in order to find their focus within once again.

"Once this has been done, then their self-doubts and self-pity will fall away from them just as the water falls off from your back.

"Tell them to take two pieces of paper and place one on their left and the other on their right. Then on the paper that is on their left, have them list all of those things that they are not grateful for, while on the paper that is on the right, have them list all of those things that they are grateful for having with them.

"Next, have them write the date on both of these

=⊕=

pieces of paper and place them in an envelope. Once this has been done, put it away and during this whole process do not allow them to have another look at what they have been writing. For this is their work and theirs alone. If another would hold an interest in seeing this thing they are doing, then let them do it for themselves. For what is done for the individual, is meant only for them. And another would not have the ability of interpreting it anyway.

"Have them wait one week, as they will think on all of those things they have done. Then with the beginning of each new week, have them repeat this whole process once again, but without ever going back to look at what they had written before.

"When this process has been worked with for eleven weeks, tell them to go to a quiet place. One where they can be alone and carry with them all of those envelopes.

"Then, and as they are sitting in a still and quiet place, have them open up each of the envelopes and place their pieces of papers in their respective places.

"For all of the ones they had listed as being those things they had not been grateful for, place them on their left and in the order of the date they had written them. And for the ones they had listed all of those things they were grateful for, have them place them on their right and in the same order.

"In this way, they will be able to see the progress they have made over this eleven week period. And what they will see is that the list that is on the left has decreased over the time, and the one that is on the right...it has grown in size.

"Then they will be very surprised to see they have in truth, come to a place of seeing all of those things

=⊕=

that have been necessary for them to see. Those things that will bring to them a good face, and one that will share with them the many great gifts that have already been shared with them.

"And when they see this, they will be ready to begin the second part of this focusing on themselves. And they will grow equally from this as well.

"Once they have gotten over the newness of this new-found knowledge that has been with them all the time, have them do the same process once again. And once again, remind them that this is only to be seen by themselves. For work that is needed by the one, must be done by the one. And only when it has been understood, shall it be shared with another.

"Have them take the same two pieces of paper and place one on the right and one on the left. For the piece of paper that is on their right, have them list all of those things they need. While on the piece of paper that is on their left, have them list all of those things they want.

"Remember this, Speaking Wind, while you may want the world...you only need a place to live. And this will be the balance used in determining the separation of what is a want and what is a need.

"Have them do this same process once a week and then after the eleventh week, have them return to that same quiet place and look at their progress. And they will have once again discovered a great growth within themselves. One that will allow them to see all of those things that are in front of them for what they are in truth.

"They will not only have found that the list of wants has decreased, and the list of needs has decreased as well, but during this whole process, they will come to understand many of those things that had once been held by them from a place of confusion. A place that was not allowing them to make good decisions for many things.

"And little one, once a two-leg discovers they can, in truth, make their own good decisions, they will not have any more time to carry on with self-doubt or self-pity. Then they will have come to a place of successfully completing this second step and will be allowed to enter the third."

- STEP THREE -

From The Elder In The North

PLACE YOURSELF FIRST AND BEFORE ALL THINGS AND OTHERS

"Remember how we have shared with you that most of the truths that have been sent to the two-legs have been stripped away, Speaking Wind?" the elder in the North began.

"Well, this then is another of them. And it is perhaps one of the greatest truths that has been made available to the two-legs.

"In recent times for the two-legs, there have been great efforts among the white path (the white race) to teach one prominent teaching. And it has been a teaching that has been misconstrued and the truths that had once been with it were stripped away so they could benefit those who would wish to control and dominate many others.

"This teaching that has been spread around many of your own kind is this...

"To Place Another Before You Is The Noble Thing To Do...To Place Another Before You And All Of Your Needs Is The Right Thing To Do...To Place Yourself Behind Another Is The Godly Thing To Do...

"Do these sound familiar to you, Speaking Wind? We are sure that you have heard of these teachings before, just as many of the two-legs have.

"And if you will take the time to look at the results this kind of thinking has done for them, you will see that there has been absolutely no growth at the individual level. But all that has taken place has been that the individual has been lost to the needs of the others. Their own needs and their own self has been forgotten and left in the dust that lies behind them and this path they travel with their group.

"I will share this with you, little one. I will share with you that whenever you will see many gathered in one place that there will either be a group of those who think alike, or there will be a group of individuals...the ones who we can call 'the people,' each with their own path to travel and each with their own eyes to see with.

"When you will have those who consider themselves to be a part of a group, there will have been exercised over them a control. A control that they have bought into by allowing themselves to be controlled. And by allowing themselves to be controlled by this group, it means that they do not feel the need to think and do for themselves any longer.

"In their believing, all they have to do is to follow this group. This group that is now thinking for them...this group that is doing for them. Doing all of those things they should have been doing for them-selves.

"And from the ones who have followed this group of theirs, they have been led to believe that this teaching of placing yourself behind another or others as being the best thing they can do, is correct for them. For without this kind of teaching, there would in truth be no group. There would be no group because there would no longer be a path to control with.

"Now when you will see a group of individuals, there you will see a group of people. These people have come to understand that there are many paths, and they must learn to see the one they have entered the Earth Mother's domain to travel. And when you will see the people, Speaking Wind, you will see those who will not be controlled because they have found their own freedom. And it is a freedom that cannot be taken away from them because they know it too well.

"Now let us go back to the false teaching of placing another before you as being something that is good to do. This teaching has allowed many of these groups to grow and hold many within them.

"This has been the cause for so many to hate and see a separation from another and has given them an inroad to using the power of this group they belong to as one that will do their own bidding. This bidding that is not ever used for the good of the spirit, but one that is used only to satisfy the wants of the body.

"Whenever you will place another or something in front of you, you are giving to it a place of more importance than you. And when you will see this with the eyes that you have been blessed with, you will hold the understanding that this is not a good thing to do.

"You must keep in the front of your thinking mind, Speaking Wind, as well as all those who will enter your path when the time will come for you to become the messenger, that there is but one reason any will be allowed entry into this domain that is the Earth Mother's. And that reason is to learn from all of the events that have been given to them so they will be able to advance their own spirit to the next higher place of understanding.

"And none of this will take place until they will learn that only they can do their own work. That only they will be able to see what it is that is being offered to them to learn from. And that only they will have to fight in their own battles when they will come to them.

"However, it will be only the lazy spirits who will not want to do their own work in this domain. And it will be they who will wish to travel with this false teaching and place the others in front of them. To place the others in front of them so they may use the power, as they see it, of the group to do their own bidding.

"But when you will come across one of the people, they will see and feel the weight of truth that will come from these speaking words we have been willing to share with you. That to place yourself in front of all things and all others is the only path one may learn from.

"And they will not perceive this as being something that is greedy and making them take all for themselves. But they will understand that when they will place themselves first in all things and before all others, then they will have taken on their own responsibility for all things they will do...and for all things that will be offered to them.

"For from this place of their learning, they will come to understand that all of those things that has come to them have done so because there is a great lesson for them to learn. A lesson that will allow them to increase their own levels of understanding, not only for themselves, but for all things that are around them to a higher level. One that will allow them to see more of what is...and not so much of what others would want them to see.

"Here is the truth of what happens when you will place another in front of you, Speaking Wind.

"When you place another in front of you, you are doing this so they may catch all of the troubles that would have come to you. And in a way, you will be paying them for doing this by placing them in front of all of your wants and desires.

"But when you do this, you will feel they owe you. That is because you have done things for them instead of yourself. You believe they owe you for these services that you have paid to them. And in time, you will come to see them as someone who owes you.

"Now, as it is with all things, there will come a time when this other person will not be in the place you will need for them to be in, or they will not do what you would want them to do. And this is when the many troubles begin.

"For when there will be an event that will come to you, an event that you will want this other person to get in the way of so that it will not reach you, there will be a time when they will either not be there for you, or they will be too busy to make their efforts on your behalf. This will cause you to feel a great pain. This pain that will come to you from this event that missed them and hit you.

"And because you have had to deal with something you did not want to have anything to do with
because this other person was not there, then you will
become angry with them and take them away from
this place that was in front of you. You will do away
with them because you will come to believe that it was
they who gave you this hurt and it was they who let
you down.

"However, the truth is that if you had been willing
to place yourself in front of all others and all things,
this would not have happened. You would have then
been willing to do all of your own work and taken on
all of your own responsibilities and there would not
have been a need to not want this other to be with you.

"You would not have lost what could have become a friend to you. But since you had not been
willing to do this and did place this other in front of
your own needs, then you have just lost one who
might have become a good friend to you. And this
person will not be forgiven completely for what you
believe they have done to you.

"Now, as this will continue to take place more and
more for the ones who have continually placed another in front of their own needs, they will soon be in
a place where they will not believe they can ever trust
in another. That those others who are with them will
eventually always let them down.

"And it is from this kind of thinking that they will
always hold themselves back from giving to another.
They will always keep a great part of themselves
away from those who they would wish to come close
to.

"Because they will always hold back this part of

themselves that they believe could be hurt again, they will not ever come to find another who will be close to them. And this will lead them to feel a great frustration for all things. And it is this frustration that allows them to feel their small bit of satisfaction when they can use this power of the group they are a part of for their own wants. And this they will come to believe is all they can ever expect or hope to find in their earth walk that will bring to them happiness of any kind.

"So it is, Speaking Wind, that when one will try to place another in front of their own needs, they will always be destined to be let down. But when one will place themselves in front of all others and all things, then they will take the entire responsibility for all that will come to them...for all of those things they will do.

"And from placing themselves in front of all things and all others, they will be seen as one who has found a peace within themselves, and that they have done this in a way that is separate from the group. Then those who would see them, will see this as either good or out of the eyes of jealousy.

"If they will see this as good, they will begin to look within themselves for those same qualities and will soon be traveling their own path among many other people. However, if they will see this on you through their own eyes of jealousy, they will begin to attack you. And when this happens, you will look at them and know the path they travel cannot follow you. And you will continue to travel away from them.

"Now, Speaking Wind, you must keep this in the front of your thinking mind and must share this with all those who will be coming to you for this message we have shared.

"Whenever you will do anything in this domain

that is the Earth Mother's, you will only have dominion over one place. And this place is the realm of your
own spirit.

"So whenever you explain this path of placing
yourself in front of all others and all things to those
who are in need, you must remind them that this only
applies to the needs of the spirit. Only to this need
and not to anything else.

"This will clear for them what we are speaking of.
That we do not speak of greed or being selfish with
those things that satisfy the body. For all of those
things will have to be left behind them when their
time comes to cross the great spirit waters.

"We are only speaking of those things that will be
taken with you when your time in the domain of the
Earth Mother's is over. And only for those things.

"All of the other things that are with the two-legs
that will not be taken with them are not theirs to begin
with...they are only being used but not owned. And
to place these teachings we are sharing with you in
that light would be to take a great injustice on what
we are willing to share with you. And by doing this
Speaking Wind, you too would be doing what those
who have gone before you have done with our many
messages. You would be stripping away the truth for
your own needs.

"So it is, little one, that to place another before you
is one of the most dangerous things to do. It is one of
the most dangerous things to do because it does not
allow you to learn from your own lessons.

"When those who will be in need of this third step
to their own path hear these speaking words you have
been given to share with them, they will see that being
themselves is what is needed by them. And there is

nothing for them to gain or learn from by being the one another or others would tell them to be.

"When they will have successfully completed this step, Speaking Wind, they will be given free access into the next one. And they will feel themselves getting closer to discovering the path they have to travel."

- STEP FOUR -

From The Elder In The East

LOOK AT THE BAD EMOTIONS FOR WHAT THEY HAVE TO TEACH YOU

"Many of the two-legs have come to see those things their earth walk would bring to them as being bad and giving to them feelings that they do not consider to be good," the elder in the East began.

"However they have lost the eyes to see with when they will come to this place, Speaking Wind. They have forgotten much of the truth their own spirit carries with it.

"They will see events come to them, events that consist of people, places, things, and feelings that will come to them from all that will cross their path. When they will see them as something to turn away from, they are very far from the truth. Far from this truth that is of their own spirit.

"There is not anything that will ever come to them that will not have their best interest at hand. And to turn one's back on a gift is a great insult. One that can cause imbalance in the way they will come to see themselves and all things that are around them.

"I would have you remind them, Speaking Wind, of a great event that they themselves requested. An event that had been requested from their own spirit to the Earth Mother before they had been allowed entry into the domain that is hers.

"Before any are allowed entry to the domain of the Earth Mother's, before any will be allowed to draw their first breath for their earth walk, they must sit in council with the Earth Mother. And as their spirit who is, in truth, them, sits in this council with the Earth Mother, they both come to see all of those things spirit needs. All of those experiences in the way of events that are necessary for spirit to advance itself to the next higher place.

"And as this is done, spirit holds itself open to the Earth Mother and they both share all that has been learned by spirit and what is still needed by spirit to advance itself. To advance itself sufficiently so that when the time comes for all to rejoin with Great Spirit, they will be able to do so with a good face and a good heart. For they can tell Great Spirit that they have prepared themselves in the way that was needed.

"During this council that is held with Earth Mother, all of those events and experiences and people who will come to you will be determined. And their places and times of their encounters will also be planned by spirit and Earth Mother as they will see the number of seasons that will be given in order to accomplish these things that are needed to grow from.

"Once this has been accomplished, spirit will be given a traveling vessel...this traveling vessel that the two-legs have called the body. And then it will be allowed to enter to begin its great adventure with her. But this adventure can only be realized by finding the path they have entered to travel. And before they can see this, there will be many lessons of preparing that will confront them. Lessons if learned from, will lead them to the place of their own path. This path where spirit holds all of the talents and attributes they will need.

"So it is when one will turn away from an event or experience that will be presented to them, they will be turning away from themselves and all those things they need in order to prepare themselves for the finding. For this finding of their own path to travel.

"When one will first turn away from one of these events or experiences, Speaking Wind, they hold the believing that if they will not think on them that they will go away. But in truth, this does not happen.

"For those same lessons that you and the Earth Mother had designed for you to learn from, they will follow you no matter where you will go or how much time has been allowed to pass from you. For there will be a time and a place where they will find you once again and will be back. And they will be back with another teacher to assist. It will be a teacher that is not easily turned away from.

"This teacher's name is emotion and it is emotion that continues to make those same lessons that you had once come to turn away from become stronger and stronger. They will become stronger until you will not have the strength to do anything but look at them.

"However, as it is with lesson, emotion must now be dealt with. In order to do this, one must see that emotion is a reminder of lessons not learned. To satisfy emotion, you must be ready to look at the lesson with a willing heart.

"You see, little one, for each time one will turn away from the lesson that has come to them—this lesson that has come to them in the way of an event or experience that they themselves have designed—there will be another layer of emotion that will be applied before it. And when it will come to you each time, there will first be encountered this emotion that lies in front of it.

"Now, before you will be allowed to see the face of this lesson for what it is, you will first have to contend with the emotion that is carried in the front of it. This emotion that will only get stronger for each of the times you will have turned away from it.

"The two-legs must realize that lesson cannot be escaped from. For it is as much a part of them and their existence as is their own spirit. And that whenever they turn away from lesson, they are turning away from themselves and the reason they have entered this domain in the first place.

"Because this reason is so important, little one, spirit allows lesson and emotion to confront you. To confront you so that in time, you will be in a place where you will have no other choice but to learn from those things you need.

"Remember that for each time you will look away from lesson, emotion will gain another layer to it. One that will be one more step that will need to be worked through in order to see lesson. This lesson that once held none of the emotion to it.

"Now, when one will come to the place of seeing that there will be a great gain in looking at lesson, they will find that there is a distance between them and where lesson is. And this distance will be filled with emotion.

"When emotion has become so strong that one will feel it cannot be worked through because of all of those feelings that are coming to them, and those feelings are making them feel very bad, there is another path they can travel. A path that will allow them to understand the emotions that are in front of lesson in a much better way.

"When one will come to see and feel the emotion that is being presented to them, it comes to them as a reminder. It is reminding them of a time and a place when they had first turned away from a lesson that had been presented to them.

"Now, when one will look at the emotions that are coming to them, the good, the bad and the bizarre, they will be in a place of learning something that is very good for them. They will come to understand that this emotion is another of their teachers. And one that is reminding them that they cannot run or turn away from those things that are needed by them to learn from.

"When this finally comes to them, Speaking Wind, have them take this emotion for what it is showing itself to them as being, and make a face out of it. That is to form what they are feeling from this emotion so they might recognize it from a place and a time in their past.

"Once they have formed this face to the emotion, then have them review all of their past seasons of their earth walk. To review all of those things that had taken place on it until they will reach the first time they will have seen this same emotion that they are seeing now. And when they have reached this place, they will find the lesson that they had first turned away from.

"And it will be in this place where there will not be as many layers of emotion for them to get through before they can see this face of lesson. This same face of lesson that has been trying to show itself to them for a long time.

"Once they will find this place, and work through the minimal amount of emotion, they will see what it is they had first turned away from. And chances are that they will have first turned away from this lesson either because of or for someone else.

"They will have found the reason they were not willing to look at this lesson that had been coming to them was that there were others in their life who were telling them that this was of no value to them. Others who were enforcing a control over them...a control they had bought into.

"When they will have worked through this smallest layer of emotion this is between them and lesson, they will come to face what this lesson is. And they will come to know it and later to understand it and how it has come to them so that it may assist them.

"Once this has been accomplished, they will find when they return to their present time and place that there will no longer be any of those feelings they once held before them. That all of those things that had been bothering them before are now not with them and their clarity of seeing has been returned.

"When this will take place for any of the two-legs, they will learn of the value of why it is not important to always be looking at others or how they will be seen by them. For they will have found the understanding that will share with them that the most important one is themselves. And to look at any other is to take away from their own path and the advancement of their own spirit.

"Remember, Speaking Wind, that there will not ever be two paths that will be the same. And this is the reason that we share with you that there will not ever be another who can know what you must learn...for this can only be done by you, and you alone.

"For any who will not be willing to do their own work to find this path of their spirit...they will be left behind. They will be left behind for there will no longer be the time left that will allow any to wait for them to learn what they should have learned long ago.

"When they come to successfully complete this fourth step, they will be allowed to travel into the next one."

- STEP FIVE -

From The Elder In The South

ALLOW ALL THINGS TO BE

"The two-legs have forgotten what it is to share with another and even themselves," came the speaking words from the elder in the South.

"They are so concerned with the way things are...that is if they are the way they would want for them to be, that they have forgotten a great truth. One that has allowed them to lose sight of where they would wish to be.

"The two-legs have forgotten how to allow all things to be. And in its place, they have come to try to change them.

"When they learn to accept all things for what they are and not as they would wish for them to be, then they will have found a great truth for themselves. One that will allow them to hold their own understanding for all things as they are. And this will open for them a great doorway that will allow them to share with another.

"Unless there is a willingness to allow all things to be, Speaking Wind, there will only be a giving and taking by all who will not see this. And the giving will always be done by the same ones, and the taking will always be done by the same ones. These two things will not be shared between any.

"We shared with you from the last step that there are only individuals who travel in this earth walk you have been given to share. That only when the individual is allowed to be the individual will there be advancement through understanding. And when the individual ceases to exist, they become the controlled property of whatever group they will find themselves traveling with.

"It is by allowing all things to be that one is willing to allow another to travel their own life path with the freedom they seek. And to allow one to travel their own life path, and you to travel yours, is a great sharing that can come between two individuals, but not ever from any member of a group.

"You see, Speaking Wind, there are so many infinite combinations for all life paths, that there is not any who share your earth walk with you who will ever possess the wisdom that is great enough to see all the possibilities. And to think that one would try to control any part of them is to say that they have the wisdom that is far greater than spirits. This is not a truth and to think in this way only keeps one from seeing themselves for who and what they are.

"It is by allowing all things to be that they will eventually find their own path to be filled with freedom. But it is when the two-legs will try to change all things that will come to them, that they will not find their way through any of those lessons they need to learn from.

"Allow all things to be, Speaking Wind, and by doing this you will find the freedom that will teach you how to share freedom with another. And by sharing freedom with another, this freedom that must first be learned by your willingness of allowing all things to be, you will find great blessings come to you and all those who would be near you, as well.

"When one has successfully completed this fifth step, they will be allowed to continue onto the next one.

- STEP SIX -

From The Elder In The West

TO UNDERSTAND...NOT TO CONTROL

"To understand all things that will come to you, Speaking Wind, is to grow...to attempt to control any of them is to stop all growth," came the speaking words from the elder in the West.

"The two-legs who have not yet found their path to travel have come to believe that nothing can be unless they cause it to be so. And once again, this has allowed so many of them to remain lost. To continue to be lost while they are searching for those things they cannot find.

"It is when one will think of themselves as being the catalyst for all things that are around them that they will try to control them. And they will try to control them in an effort of keeping up with them and not letting them get bigger than they can handle.

"But the truth to this is that there is no thing that is ever presented to another that they are not ready for. There will not ever be anything that will confront them that they do not already have the talents and preparation to work with.

"However, before they can have their own eyes and ears opened for them, they will not see this. You see Speaking Wind, all of these steps that we have shared with you to now have been ones that are very necessary before one can see what we are now willing to share with you.

"If those who will come to you cannot see the step you are sharing with them, then have them go back to review all of them once again. For there has been something they have missed.

"Now when they have their eyes and ears opened for them, they will see that there is no controlling that is necessary of any event or any experience that will come to them. For all of this work has already been done, and to try to redo this work would only be to waste their own time. This time that should be spent in learning and understanding themselves for the path they have chosen to follow.

"The two-legs must come to understand that they will not ever change any of the lessons that will come to them, nor will they ever deter any from their original destination.

"When they come to understand themselves, they will see how perfectly a part all these things have played in their own growth. Only when they will see the perfection of all they have already done will they understand that all they will do has been done in such a perfect way. And all efforts of controlling are only an illusion.

"When they will allow all things to be, they will see that it is better to understand than it is to control. For it will be through this understanding that they will see the wonderful balance that lies within themselves and all things that are around them.

"It will only be through understanding that they will come to know and see themselves for who and what they are, and when they will do this, there will be no thing that will ever come to them that will be too large for them to work through. There will not ever be a lesson that will come to them that they will not be willing to learn from. And there will not ever be a time when they will think that it is they who are doing all of these things. For they will have the understanding that all that is, has been, and all that will be...is with them now.

"When they see that understanding has greater value than controlling, they will be very pleased with what they will see. For they will look back on all of those things that they have ever come to do and will see how well they have prepared themselves for who and what they are now.

"Even if they have not yet completely awakened

from their own sleep of illusion, they will come to understand that they would not be in a place where they could see even this, had they not done all that they had done. And when this takes place, they will see that it was all done at the right time and the right place for them to be where they are now.

"And for all of this, they will become very grateful to spirit who is with them always.

"Once this level of understanding has come to them, and the need to control has left them, they will see that all they are doing now is done from a perfection of balance. And all that is needed by them is to understand that. To understand that all of those things they do are done in the right way, the right time, and for the right reason if they will only come to understand what it is they are doing.

"For there is nothing that is ever done out of accident, Speaking Wind. And when the two-legs will come to let understanding take the lead in their earth walk, they will see this, also. And they will see how well-balanced all that is within their domain is...and it does not need any controlling by them or anyone else at all.

"Remember that for every moment you will spend in understanding, you will have spent another moment in growing. And for every moment you will spend in trying to control, that will be another moment you will spend in fighting only with yourself...and there will be a stopping to all growth.

"When the two-legs who have come to you have successfully completed this sixth step, they will be allowed to go into the next one."

- STEP SEVEN -

From The Elder In The North

THE CHILD GROWS...THE ADULT ONLY GROWS OLD

"When the two-legs come to understand that there is *no judging* and there is *no hell*, then they will have come to a place of having successfully completed this seventh step. And when this seventh step is completed, they will see their entryway into their eighth place...this place where they will see the face of themselves and their spirit. And they will be shown the path they have been given to travel.

"You will have many opportunities of sharing with many of the two-legs, Speaking Wind, and one of the first things that will come to you, when this time of your awakening is right, is that you will find many of them trapped not only in their sleep of illusion but also trapped inside of a role they have all bought into. And that is the role of the adult.

"Even though they will wish to return to their times of being the child, and many of them will tell you they know their child part within them—when you will look into their eyes and feel the meaning of their words they share with you—you will come to know that they are very far away from where they tell you they are. That they are only playing another game with you...and with themselves.

"For those who would do this, it is better to walk away from them and leave them alone. For they will be the ones who will wish to have another do their work for them. They will be the ones who will try and stop your own progress on this path you have been given to travel.

"Do not waste time with those who would not be willing to help themselves, little one. For there are far too many who would be willing to listen to these things we have shared with you so that you may share with them.

"You must keep in the front of your thinking mind that your purpose of this path that has been given to you is not to tend to any other's needs...it is only to show to those who would be willing to see what is possible. And this will come to them when they will see that you are willing to share with them truth. This same truth that we have been willing to share with you.

"Look at all of the two-legs in the domain you travel in, Speaking Wind. Look at this process they all have gone through.

"When they are the small child, they cannot wait to grow up and become the adult. This adult that they see as not having to do anything. For there will not be another who will tell them when it is time to go to bed, there will not be another who will tell them when to take a bath or when and what to eat. And so on.

"Then when they finally arrive at the place of being the adult they have wanted all this time, they find that there is not the freedom they once envisioned. For there are far many more controls over them once they are no longer this child and they do not like it.

"There are controls over them that make them do and say things in a certain way. And there are controls over them that cause them to hold a great fear if they will not comply. And for all of this, if they will do and say all of those things they are supposed to, they will be allowed to live a life of an adult.

"There are not many of the two-legs we have seen who enjoy this kind of living, and as a result of not liking it, they will begin to develop many games to play. Games that can sometimes be very harmful to themselves and all who would come near to them.

"However, at no time will there ever be one of them who will be willing just to be themselves, for there are not many who even know who they are from within. And this causes them to feel cheated. So cheated that they will stop all others who seem to be finding their own way. And they will stop them in such a way that they will instill a great fear into them. A fear that will stop further advances of themselves or fears that will make them not want to ever try to find themselves again.

"And for those few who have succeeded in finding their own way back to their innocence of the child from within, they are met with such force for what they have done by those who have not been able to do the same thing, that there is always a great violence and fight that takes place.

"Look at your own people, Speaking Wind. When the whites first came to your lands, what they saw frightened them greatly. Frightened them so much that they felt if there was not a complete annihilation of all of your people, that surely their own world would be in jeopardy.

"You see, little one, the real issue that had come to exist between the whites and your people was not one that had anything at all to do with land. But it had to do with the freedom that was being lived by all of the members of your people. And this freedom posed a great threat to the control the whites exerted over themselves. A control that would have been vanquished had they allowed many of their own kind to see what they had seen.

"So it was in an effort of keeping their own way of life safe that they killed so many of the ones they considered to be dangerous to them. So many of the ones who had found what they themselves could not find...freedom of becoming the child once again.

"And this continues to take place through all of the time that has been given to the white race. You will see this if you will open your eyes to it.

"For when one of their own begins to find their own personal freedom in their life path, they are chided and made to feel so much out of place that they are hard-pressed not to return to the place they once were. And if this will not work, they will be given a great fear to carry. One that will cause them to wonder greatly if they are to buy into it.

"It has been through judgement and fear that they have been able to exercise such control over so many, Speaking Wind. And this has been with them for such a long time that it becomes very difficult for them to do anything but judge and use the threat of fear for those whom they do not understand.

"However, little one, if you will share this with them, that fear will only come to those who do not yet possess the understanding for what is before them. That fear is not a true face or a spirit unto itself, and when there is an understanding for this thing they once called fear, then it will no longer be seen or felt by them. Then they will have taken a great step through this seventh step to finding their own path.

=⊕=

"When they will come to understand...not only mirror a believing that there is no judging of any other, but only the judging of themselves, they will have taken the second step through these seven steps to finding their own path to travel.

"When they will have taken these two steps through this seventh step to finding their own path, they will also see how silly it is to even think that there is a hell. For the ones who tell of such a place are surely the most lost of all.

"If one would tell you that you are going to hell, Speaking Wind, they are telling you two things. First they are telling you that their wisdom is greater than that of the creator of all life, and secondly they are telling you that they are using this wisdom to judge you.

"And if you will believe in this, then you will not ever come to know yourself in this life path with the Earth Mother. For if you will believe in their words to you, you will only come to a place of knowing how to please them and not yourself.

"You see, Speaking Wind, the two-legs become the adult by listening to those others. But the child is allowed to return to the child by learning to listen and believe in yourself. And this is the path that will return you to the child and the innocence that is within all of us.

"Remember that you have been allowed entry into this domain to learn. And there will be no learning as long as there is a controlling over you.

"For you will not be in a place of learning until you have allowed yourself to return to the place of the child. And this place will not be available to you until you learn to listen...but most importantly learn to understand yourself and all of the life that is around you.

"When this returning to the child has been successfully completed for those two-legs that will come to you, Speaking Wind, you will see a great change come to them. A change that will not be missed.

"At first those who would follow this path would feel as if they have lost all of those things they have had with them. That all of those things they have worked so hard at achieving have been taken away from them. But this is not so.

"There will be a loss by them, but it will have only come to them from their own actions of dropping those things away that did not hold truth and feeling the empty spaces where they once were. For those things they feel this loss for will only be what had been held over them. Only those things that had been used against them so that they could be controlled by others.

"They will have this feeling...but it will not last for long. It will only last as long as it will take for them to fill up all of those empty spaces with those things of truth that will be shown to them, with those things that are of themselves and those things that will allow them to find the freedom they have been born to. This same freedom that has come to all from the loving creation by Great Spirit.

"Once they have passed through this long night of theirs, they will come back to you and share many great blessings that will have come to them. Blessings that will have come to them in a way that has allowed them to see all things more clearly than they have ever done before. And they will share with you that for each passing day, they will see all with even more clarity. But most importantly, they will begin to see themselves in this same way. They will see all of the wonders that are within them. All of these wonderful things they can now do because they have learned to see them for what they are.

"When this will take place, Speaking Wind, you will feel just as we do when we see another of the two-legs wake up from their sleep of illusion. You will feel the fullness of your heart go out to them and you will see another one has found their own way...and by being allowed to do their own work.

"It will be this completion of the seventh step that you will hold the knowing that another has found their way and that another will assist another in finding theirs."

THE RETURN

Then there was a silence over all who had gathered on this place...on this land. A silence that was broken by the calling of all eleven of the Ancient Ones' voices sounding as one:

"You are now in the place you need to be, Speaking Wind. You are sitting in the place that has been yours from the beginning and soon, you will understand the reason why.

"But for now, you must enter your sleep of preparing and there you must stay until we call on you once again.

"It will not be a long sleep, though, and we will be with you through all of this time.

"As you will enter this sleep of preparing, little

one, remember the message that we have shared with
you. For in truth, its time of arrival is much closer
than you can imagine, and its time is assured; for it
has been written to be so.

"And as you travel through the domain you have
entered, you will be protected from those things you
need protection from. For there will be many with
you and the spirit guides who have come to you for
this meeting...they will continue to live with you and
your spirit until your time is no more."

As I heard these speaking words, I could feel the
presence of eagle, bear, and buffalo come near to me.
They came near enough to me so that I could see each
of their faces.

Once they had seen I had recognized them and all
that they were, they entered me and became one with
my spirit. And as they did this, there was a brief
moment of feeling as if I would explode from their
presence within me. That soon passed and though I
could feel them being a part of me, there was no sense
of discomfort within me at all. There was only a
glowing of presence...their presence that was now a
part of mine.

"As you sleep through the preparing, Speaking
Wind, learn to understand these seven steps that will
allow one to find their path. Listen to them and
remember that to understand is to attain wisdom:

1. *FIND THE PART OF YOU THAT LIVES IN ALL
   THINGS.*

2. *LET SELF-PITY AND SELF-DOUBT FALL AWAY.*

3. *PLACE YOURSELF FIRST AND BEFORE ALL
   THINGS AND ALL OTHERS.*

4. *LOOK AT THE BAD EMOTIONS FOR WHAT THEY HAVE TO TEACH YOU.*

5. *ALLOW ALL THINGS TO BE.*

6. *LEARN TO UNDERSTAND...NOT TO CONTROL.*

7. *THE CHILD GROWS...THE ADULT ONLY GROWS OLD.*

"Remember that choice is freedom, Speaking Wind. Do not allow it to die within you for there will be many who will have great need for this.

"There are many who would be willing to listen to these things we have been willing to share with you and their names are the Rainbow Children who have already arrived. But there are many of them who have not yet been awakened...they are waiting...they are still preparing."

Then as these speaking words were finished, all of the Ancient Ones dropped their heads to look at the place of the fire. To look into the silence that was so abundant here when there were not the speaking words of sharing.

As I looked over in the places that were all around me, I could see that there was a heavy snowfall in all directions. It was in all places that I could see...all but for the one we were sitting in.

Then, there was the sounding of a horse walking to my place of sitting. It was coming from a place that was covered in the thickness of the snow.

Soon there appeared an outline of one of our people riding on the back of a great horse, and the horse and the rider rode as one.

Then as he stood just to the outside of the ring of

the falling snow, I heard his voice come to me:

"It is time to return now, Speaking Wind. I have come to assist you."

Then the rider raised his right hand in an outward motion to me, one that bore the feeling of great peace and warmth. I then felt my eyes close. Opening them, I found myself back inside of the spirit circle I had built from the stone people...and the new day was already over this land that had allowed me entry to the domain of the Ancient Ones.

However, there was still another message that came to me. For just as I was getting used to opening my eyes once again, I heard the calling voice of the one who had assisted me in returning;

"Ask Grandfather how to work the bowl. This will be of a great need for you and those who would follow after you."

Then the voice was gone. As I opened my eyes to this place I had begun my journey, I was surprised to see that there was a heavy falling snow once again. And it was of the same texture as the snow that had been falling near the Ancient Ones.

As I looked over these lands, I could see that there was a newness to the life that I could see. For everywhere I looked, there was more intensity in the colors and my awareness of the life that was within all things...and within me.

Looking over to the place that was on my right, I saw three figures and they were approaching me in a way that told me they knew their direction. And this direction was to the place I was sitting.

As they got closer, I was very pleased to see that it was Grandfather, Two Bears, and my best friend, Cheeway. And I could feel more than see that each of

=※=

them held a good face to wear for me.

When they reached a place where I could see them clearly, they stopped and Grandfather made a hand sign that asked me if I had returned completely now. When he saw me return the sign that I had, they entered this land of the flat stones.

As Two Bears and Cheeway went to the place of the fire, I could see that they were bringing it back to life and had set my clothes near one of the warmer rocks next to it. Grandfather walked up to the east stone of my spirit circle and asked me if I was ready to leave.

I told him that I was and rose to lift the east stone out of its place. Then picking up all of the others, Grandfather, Two Bears, and Cheeway assisted me in returning them to their homes.

With this accomplished, I pulled the tobacco out of my pouch and began to thank all of the grandfathers for allowing me to share so much with them and them with me. Then I walked over to the fire, pulled my clothes over me, and we all sat down.

There was one of the standing people that I wanted to give a special thanks to before we all sat down, though, and I told this to Grandfather and walked off to the place where I had first seen Telah.

I looked for the grandfather of the standing people here and finding him, I placed my entire tobacco pouch next to him. As I did this, I saw from the corner of my eyes a figure standing in the far distance that was being covered with the falling snow. Looking over to this place, I saw that it was Telah and she was holding her right hand in an upward position to me...one that was used in greeting friends. This filled me with a warming of belonging.

=⊕=

"We have not ever been, nor will we ever be far from each other, Speaking Wind," she said to me, still blending into the falling snow.

"It is good that our circles have closed, my sister. I will remain with you as you remain with me," was my return.

I raised my hand back to her to share this same giving of ourselves, and when I did this...she returned back to her nation. Back to await for those who would learn to see and hear to return and to wait for the time when we would all enter the fifth world of peace and light.

Returning to the place of the flat stones, I saw that Grandfather, Two Bears, and Cheeway had found a stone overhang and had built another small warming fire under it. This looked like a wonderful place where we could spend the rest of our earth walk together. But I understood that this was more of my spirit vision speaking to me rather than the voice of my spirit. And I held the knowing that all of us still had a great deal of work that must be done yet.

CHAPTER FIVE

WORKING THE BOWL

Sitting under this stone overhang, I spent the time in reliving my vision to Grandfather, Two Bears, and Cheeway. As they listened to those things that had been shared with me, I could feel an acceptance from all of them.

"Then Standing Tree was right when he shared with us that one among us would learn to see the path soon to be with us," came the speaking words from Two Bears.

"It is good you have been willing to share such things with us, little one."

"Grandfather," I said, sitting close to the warming fire.

"Yes, little one. What is it that I may assist you with?"

"Can you share with me what working the bowl is?" I asked.

"Is this something that you have been told would be needed by you?" Grandfather asked.

"Yes, Grandfather...yes, this has been told to me."

"Then it will be good to share with you this thing. For it has come to us from the old ones themselves and has been used among our wise ones as a way of entering the domain of the spirit through the nations of the standing people.

"First, you will have to find a bowl that will call to you. It does not have to be anything that is special...other than to you. For there will be a calling of this one child to you in a way that will not be mistaken. When you hear it, take this bowl into your hands and become familiar with it.

"Learn all about this child, from the outside first then all the way to the inside. And as you will learn of this child, share with it all of those things that are of you. And this will be done by holding and carrying this bowl for many days.

"It is in this way that there will be a bond that will be established between both of you. And through this bond, there will be a great sharing for what is about to be done.

"When you have both become comfortable with each other, take this bowl and travel to the place where you feel most comfortable. It does not matter if it is in a forest, or the inside of your own house. But find a place where you feel comfort for your spirit.

"Next, find the closest child. This child will be one of the growing ones with leaves on it. As long as there is one of the leaved ones near you, you will be within the family of the standing people. For all of them are related and continually speak to each other.

"Next, sit down in a crossed-legged position next to this child and hold the bowl in both of your hands in your lap.

"Then lower your head toward the bowl with the part that is between your eye brows being centered in the middle portion of the bowl. Allow all of those things that are you to fall into the bowl that will hold them safely for you.

"Think of your personality and let it drop into the bowl. Think of all your problems and let them drop into the bowl. Think of all things that make up you on the outside and inside and let them take on a weight and drop into the bowl. Repeat this process until there is nothing left that is you...except one thing. And that one thing is what you are seeking assistance for.

"This will be the only thing that you will keep with you. And it is what you will be taking with you into the silence to gain insight on.

"Once you have allowed all of these things to drop away from you...all but the one, just breathe and set the bowl to your right side, then return your hands back to your lap.

"Soon you will feel a rocking back and forth come to you. This movement is not from you, but is a sign of acceptance from the Earth Mother. For what you are feeling is the beating of her heart. This is the rhythm she will allow you to enter into the silence with through this small one you are sitting next to.

"Then you will be taken into the silence, and what will take place there will only be for your spirit to know of. But when you return, there will be a higher level of understanding shared with you for this problem you have taken. And you will see the path you need to follow to find your answer.

"When this has been completed, pick up the bowl with your right hand and pour it back into your left hand. All of those things you had set aside from yourself will be returned through this process, all but those for which you have gained understanding of. For once you will begin to understand them, there will no longer be any room for them to return to you.

Not in the way they had once been...and that was to hold fear or uncertainty for you.

"This process can be done for each event that will come to you that you do not hold the understanding for. And as you come to understand more that is within your life path, little one, you will come to see yourself more clearly. More clearly for who and what you are in truth.

"Does this assist you in finding those things that will be of need for you, Speaking Wind?"

"Yes, Grandfather, they do," was my return.

For the rest of the day, we all began to share our pieces of understanding for this vision that had come to me. For this vision that had been shared with me by the Ancient Ones of our people.

As we all continued to share our parts of understanding for this spirit vision, I was looking over their faces, one by one.

Something was telling me from the place of spirit that there would not be much more time left for all of us to continue to share with each other in this way. And this was bring me to a place of understanding. A place that was sharing with me that soon...very soon, I, Speaking Wind, would be the last of our council of four to remain in this domain of the Earth Mother's.

But I was also given another knowing, as well. And it was one that shared with me that all things are as they should be and for this, I only needed to understand...to understand and wait for the sleep of preparing to complete its own path for me. At this time, I would awake to those things I had

=⊕=

entered this domain to do...for the Earth Mother...for her children...and the two-legs.

And I understood...and it was good.